D0591852

Teaching Practice Handbook

Roger Gower

Principal, Bell School, Cambridge

Steve Walters

Principal, Bell School, Bath

HEINEMANN

skills are wo
making TP re
basing it on w

How can parti

At the end of
They don't for
others. Some
'get-up-and-d
thing without
would have no
it is going to be

Does this mear

No. TP is a tim
have for trying
observers. You
well-prepared l
good for anothe
 When anythin
the lessons that

What should be

After TP you sho
– be more aware

– be more aware

– be more sens
 affect their lear

– have some awa

– be in control of

– be able to plan
 which are relev

– be able to prese

– have some basi
 and less controll

– be able to set up

– have some contr

– be able to identif

– think critically an

1.2 Getting the be

Co-operating with o

Other teachers can.

– to creat

– to expo
    differen

Of course

How is prc

Sensitivity
your stude
lesson are
and obser\
what they a

To help)
and outside
them the o
language. T
they found
other.

Other trai
awareness.
nerves and ;

The skills
are obvious,
see someon

A distinct
throughout a
with the clas
the learning ε

The same
different tecl
recur enougl
noticed – a lo
pre-lesson pr
times say 'Th
way of doing i
have to work
means taking
situation is not

How is it decid

Supervisors or
teaching points
gradually withd
and in preparin
    The aim of a ;
like to give out
should ideally ri

Shouldn't TP be

In some ways t

guidance as to what materials to use, others may tell you what you want to know about particular students. They can also give you a good picture of what teaching is actually like.

However, they are likely to be busy and preoccupied with their classes and shouldn't be pestered unnecessarily. They are also likely to have a greater territorial feeling about the place, so:
– clean the board when you finish

– return borrowed tapes and books

– start and finish your lessons on time

– make sure you know how to use the machinery; don't break it!

Remember: if they are teaching the same students as you, they can make a big difference to how those students think of you.

It's also worth remembering that both teachers and students have expectations as to personal appearance. In many institutions a certain informality is acceptable, but lack of cleanliness and tidiness isn't.

Working with a supervisor

In most institutions the supervisor's role is:
– to help with lesson preparation

– to observe critically

– to give helpful feedback.

However, it's vital that you are not over-dependent on your supervisor. Certainly, ask for clarification of any point you are supposed to be teaching – you can't say to a group of confused students that you don't understand what you are supposed to be doing – even ask for your lesson plan to be checked, provided there's enough time for changes to be made, but your attitude is all-important. It shouldn't be *I don't know how to do it* but *I didn't really know how to do it but I thought this might work. What do you think?*. You should always be moving positively towards independence and get close to the real-life situation when you will be working in a school without help.

Don't blame the supervisor if things go wrong; you're the one with responsibility for the class while you are teaching it.

Respond positively to criticisms; give your reasons for doing something; try not to be defensive. Remember: the supervisor is in a better position to see the reactions of the class than you are.

Working with other trainees

Other trainees are an extremely useful resource. They can give ideas and information about language, materials and about students. But they'll be less inclined to give unless *you* are willing to give. Offer help, and spare time to socialize. Remember: TP may be the only opportunity you'll ever have to talk about real students and real classes in any depth with other people.

Offering criticism, too, is helpful but it needs to be done with tact. *Why on earth didn't you show everyone the picture?* is likely to provoke a defensive reaction and will not help future relationships, whereas *I don't think everyone could see it* is likely to lead to a more fruitful exchange. Remember: being aware of the effect language can have and being able to offer non-deterring criticism are part of your job as a teacher.

'Peer teaching' involves one of you teaching the others who are either pretending to be students or just being themselves. It is particularly useful for the isolation and practice of classroom techniques and many exercises are suggested in this book. It's often worth spending time discussing this approach with your peers. It can be a waste of time if everyone collapses with laughter every time they pretend to be a student. (For further reading see section on Microteaching pp 53–65 in *Teacher Training*, ed. Holden, MEP Publications)

Your own attitude

We can't change our personalities but we can alter the impression we give in a class
- by smiling; that doesn't mean you have to walk around with a fixed grin, but showing a friendly attitude warms the students to *you*.

- by responding to what students say as communication; don't treat every utterance as a model to be corrected or congratulated upon!

- by taking time, by showing an interest in both the learning *and* the personal problems of the students.

Preparation

Preparation doesn't mean scripting the lesson – that can't be done and shouldn't be attempted except possibly as an exercise to help you reduce the amount you talk during a lesson. It means working out *what* you want to do, *why* you want to do it and *how* you're going to do it. It means thinking through the stages of the lesson, trying to link them, working out what the point of each stage is and jotting down enough notes to help you remember what you thought of.

Overpreparation
This usually means
- getting stuck in your plan and not responding flexibly to the class

- getting obsessed by your own ideas and techniques

- insensitivity to the students, what they're doing and not doing.

Underpreparation
This means
- long silences while you decide what to do next (demoralizing for you *and* the students!)

- unclear aims and poor presentation

- underexploited activities.

If the material you have prepared turns out to be unsuitable, then don't be frightened to abandon it if you can think of something better. Be sure, though, that you're actually teaching something and not just filling in the time.

Keep lesson plans simple (see Unit 4.1). They need to be something you can work from in the classroom, to remind you of the stages of the lesson. Cut out prose descriptions, number sections clearly and underline language models. Use coloured pens to draw boxes and circles around important elements.

The class itself

If the students are happy and learning – the two don't always go together – then you can be reasonably sure your classes are going well. Good preparation should ensure good learning so try and free yourself of anxieties and enjoy their company as a group. Always try and put yourself in their position, remembering their very often clear needs, their time limitations and their different approaches to learning. Find out about them. Get to know them. Make good use of breaks. Show that you're enjoying teaching them as you're teaching them.

Remember: if your nose is buried in your lesson plan throughout the lesson, or you fumble with scribbled notes, you are reducing your chances of relating to them or directing their learning effectively.

Feedback

This is normally given soon after you've finished teaching – even if sometimes you can't face reliving it all again! It is usually oral, although many supervisors like to give out a carbon copy of their written notes.

The trainees who improve most quickly are those that recognize their strengths and weaknesses, through the help of the supervisor and other trainees, and respond by asking *What can I do to correct the problem*? From time to time you might like to do a critique of one of your lessons. If you need a checklist, try using the contents page of this book.

It's easy to get demoralized when you don't see any improvement. This is often because:

– the students' needs are rightly being considered first

– you are trying out new ideas, totally unpractised

– you are not able to demonstrate what you *can* do

– you don't get the chance to have another go at something you messed up.

But your supervisors are aware of these sorts of problems and will provide support. They're aware of how little you have actually taught! The fact that you survive without passing out or running out of the classroom in terror should be a source of constant congratulation! After each lesson, it's worth noting the skills you have used and referring back to previous criticisms. It's often surprising how much you are doing for the first time. In fact, if you've shown yourself to be good at some particular strategy it's often worth *avoiding* it on TP, to give yourself practice over a wide range of skills. Don't worry about always showing your good sides. Think of TP as PRACTICE.

TP files

It is well worth keeping a TP file, even on courses where the tutor doesn't require one to be handed in at the end. It should include lesson plans, reflections on your own teaching, copies of supervisor's comments, examples of materials and visual aids used, students' written work and sources of ideas when you are actually teaching.

TP diaries

You might also find it valuable to keep a personal diary of TP in which you reflect on your successes and failures. Having to articulate an experience helps not only to get it in perspective but to develop better self-awareness generally as a teacher. As it is essentially of private value you may or may not decide to show it to others.

2 The Teacher

Introduction

Contrary to popular belief, it is not true that you have to be an extrovert to be a good language teacher. Some good teachers are very low-key in the classroom, while other teachers, both lively and amusing, survive only as entertainers. Although some teachers develop a special classroom manner, in the main your style of teaching will depend on the sort of person you are.

However, while personality is impossible to prescribe, for a class to learn effectively you must know how to be firm and directive when necessary as well as unobtrusive when the students need to be left alone. In other words, you need to subtly alter your role according to the activity without going to the extremes of dominating a class or leaving it without anything to do.

In this chapter, the aim is to discuss this and other general aspects of manner.

2.1 Eye contact

We all know how difficult it is to talk to someone who never looks at us or someone who looks us in the eye *all* the time. Similarly we know how important eye contact is in signalling such messages as *I want to speak to you* or *I'm addressing this remark to you*. Now turn to the classroom. Observe, for example, how, when and why your tutor makes eye contact with you and your colleagues. The main uses of eye contact in the language classroom are:
– to help establish rapport. A teacher who never looks students in the eye seems to lack confidence and gives the students a sense of insecurity. On the other hand, having a fixed glare doesn't help either!

– to indicate to a student that you want to talk to him or you want him to do something. (Don't overdo it, though, he might feel persecuted!)

– to hold the attention of students not being addressed and encouraging them to listen to those doing the talking. (Be careful, though. Looking at one student too long will make the others feel excluded.)

– to take the place of naming students, for example when conducting a fast drill.

– to show a student who is talking that the teacher is taking notice.

More importantly, though, a teacher needs to look at the students to notice their reactions. Do they understand? Are they enjoying the lesson? Are they tired? Are they bored? Would it be a good idea to change the direction of the lesson? Does anyone want to contribute or ask questions?

How will eye contact vary at different stages of a lesson?

1 Presentation of new language
Use eye contact:
– to check that everyone is concentrating. When presenting new language, particularly at elementary levels, the teacher is often very much 'up front', directing, eliciting, giving models and conducting.

— to maintain attention. This means a constant moving of the eyes so that no student is left out. Since you need to keep the class together, be careful not to neglect the students closest to you.

— to keep in touch with other students when you are dealing with an individual, perhaps correcting him. Your eyes can say to them: *You're involved in this too.*

— to encourage contributions when you are trying to elicit ideas or specific language from the students. Frequently, you only know students have something to say by looking at them.

— to check that the students understand. Puzzled expressions quickly tell you you need to try again!

2 Controlled practice
Use eye contact:
— to indicate who is to speak. Using names can slow a drill down and pointing might be offensive.

— together with a gesture such as a shake of the head, to indicate that something's incorrect.

— to ensure that the students have understood what they're supposed to do and know what is going on.

3 Pair or group work
During any activity that doesn't demand teacher-centred control, avoid eye contact, unless you are specifically asked for help or choose to join in. As soon as you establish eye contact, or the students establish eye contact with you, you are brought into the activity, thus making it teacher-centred. However, you can use eye contact:
— to signal to a pair or group to start, to stop or to hurry up. It can be far less dominating than the voice.

— to indicate, with an accompanying gesture, that groups are on the right or wrong lines.

Is there any point in encouraging the students to look at each other?

Yes. Very much so. Confidence is gained and shyness lost through eye contact. In addition, a student who has difficulty understanding is more likely to understand if his eyes are on the speaker's face than if they are on the ground. So, when students ask each other questions, or help and correct each other, whether in pair work or student to student across the class, they should look at each other. It might be better to get them to move their chairs to make it easier.

Exercises

Ex. 1

AIM
To learn to pace a lesson by looking at individuals in the class.

PROCEDURE
1 Stand at the front of the group so that you can see everybody.

2 Dictate a short passage to the group, judging when to start each phrase by looking at everyone's hands. The aim is not to leave anyone behind.

COMMENT
Get the views of the group at the end, particularly the slowest writer, as to how effective you were.

Ex. 2

AIM
To encourage full eye contact and to practise spreading attenticn randomly round the class.

PROCEDURE
1 Call out the names of members of the group.

2 Make eye contact with each person as their name is called.

COMMENT
1 This exercise needs to be brief and rapid to make the point. It's probably better to make out a random list of names beforehand rather than try to do it off the top of the head. The exercise can be a useful aid to name-learning!

2 If you know the names well and it's a reasonable-sized group, try it without a list. Aim to cover everyone in the group once only in random order. Ask the group if they were all called and where you tended to focus your attention.

3 A later variation might be for the group to be less willing to make eye contact. This should show you that your position as teacher is quite strong and that a student resisting eye-contact can feel quite uncomfortable.

Ex. 3

AIM
To encourage evenly spread but random eye contact and to practise using eye contact in place of students' names.

PROCEDURE
1 Write a simple substitution drill.

2 In random order, drill the group using eye-contact instead of names. Make sure you include everyone.

3 Ask each member how many times he was called on.

COMMENT
1 An exercise with applications outside the problem area of eye contact and one which can usefully be repeated. A simple variation would be to use a facial expression to indicate that a second repetition is required.

2 You might find there are reasons deep-rooted in your personality if you are reluctant to make eye contact. Though it may be difficult, you will need to try and overcome these if you are to have effective control over a class.

Ex. 4

AIM
To provide the basis for a discussion on what eye contact can tell you.

PROCEDURE
1 Find a partner.

2 Give your partner the following card:

> A: Talk to your partner for three minutes about your family. Your partner will take notes.

3 Note down the amount of eye contact your partner makes and what he is saying when he makes it. He should not be aware of your real aim. Make sure you ask some questions and comment on what your partner says. Don't let it be a monologue.

COMMENT

1 If this activity is controlled by a supervisor, the other partner will want the following card:

> B: Your partner is going to talk to you about his family. He thinks you are going to take notes. What you are really interested in is the amount of eye contact your partner makes and what he is saying when he makes it. Make sure you ask some questions and comment on what your partner says. Don't let it be a monologue.

2 The exercise is best done without prior explanation since once eye contact has been mentioned everyone becomes very self-conscious. Therefore it can only really be done once.

3 The kind of things to follow up in discussion are:
   – how far eye contact influences the conversation

   – the role of eye contact in starting or finishing an exchange

   – what happens when questions are asked and answered

   – how what has been discovered affects the classroom.

2.2 Use of gesture and facial expression

Gestures and facial expressions are an integral part of any communication where people listen and speak to each other. They help us get across what we want to say. For example, when we give directions in the street to a stranger, we not only use our voice to give special emphasis to the important points, we often use our hands to make things clear as well.

If we are deprived of what the body can express, for example when we talk on the telephone or listen to the radio, we are forced to use our imaginations and try and extract all the meaning from the inflexions of the voice or the words themselves. With direct contact we often look at the other person's face to gauge what their real feelings or attitudes are.

How does gesture affect what we do in the classroom?

– The English and other English-speakers use gesture differently from, say, the Italians. It is a part of the language and it needs to be understood. Teach it if necessary.

– At the same time, if we are in a country where we don't speak the language, gesture will help us to get the gist of what is going on. Equally, students, particularly elementary students, are dependent on the gestures we use. So use gestures carefully and clearly.

– We should always be aware how difficult it is, even when it stimulates the imagination, for students to listen to audio-tapes.

– Gesture is one way for you to convey the meaning of language.

– You can use gestural signals to manage the class, but they need to be clear and unambiguous if they are to reduce the amount you talk.

1 Conveying meaning

– If a student doesn't understand the word *tall* the appropriate hand gesture to help get the meaning across is easy to make, although frequently mime is less ambiguous. (You *can* indicate the meaning of the word *stagger* by hand gesture but it is probably preferable to stagger!)

– If you are presenting a dialogue, it is well worth adding physical expression to bring it to life.

In the early days it is often better to exaggerate your gestures a little because:
– they need to be a conscious part of your repertoire, deliberately doing what they set out to do

– the students need to understand them. If they are exaggerated they are usually less ambiguous

– many teachers are more frozen than they think they are and move little more than their lips!

Excessive exaggeration, though, can be silly and counter-productive. It mustn't be at the expense of the language you are teaching.

We can also teach the students to understand special gestures, to help us convey meaning or highlight aspects of the form of the language, e.g.:

PAST TIME – hitch-hiking gesture over the shoulder

PRESENT TIME – pointing to the floor by the feet

FUTURE TIME – pointing into the distance in front

INTONATION – indicated by making wave motions with the hand

STRESS – indicated by beating with the hand.

(The students, however, need to learn what these gestures mean and you need to know they understand. Pointing to the floor could mean 'here' and pointing in front of you could mean 'over there'. So teach them and check that the students understand them.)

2 Managing the class

Every language teacher develops a personal set of gestures to get a class to do what he wants with the minimum of fuss and the minimum of language. There are some, however, which are fairly standard, e.g.:

Listen – hand cupped behind the ear

Repeat in chorus – firm sweep of the arm, or similar gesture to get everyone starting together

Repeat individually – beckoning gesture with the whole hand

Get into pairs – arm, hand or finger movement to show you are 'joining' the students

Stop (pair work, group work, noise!) – raise hands or clap

Contract words/join sentences – link index fingers

Give a complete sentence – hands held apart horizontally, as though holding a brick at either end

Say from the beginning – rotate index fingers round each other backwards

Good – thumbs up

Not right – shake head or index finger

Break the sentence down into words/ – use each finger of the hand(s) to repre-
the word into phonemes   sent a word/phoneme

A voiced sound – point to the throat.

Some of these expressions can be conveyed by the face, e.g:

Good – show a pleased expression

Not right – screw up the face

Other useful facial expressions are:

Interesting idea – raise the eyebrows

Not quite right, I think – make a doubtful expression

Repeat individually – nod in the direction of the student and raise the eyebrows.

Is there anything to be avoided?

Yes. Quite a lot:

– Unclear, ambiguous expressions and gestures

– Gestures which are not obvious and which you haven't taught or checked with the class

– Gestures which are rude or obscene to the students. Common ones with some nationalities are: pointing, using the middle finger, showing the sole of the foot or shoe, holding up the index and small finger of the same hand. Remember the English have a two-fingered gesture! If you are unfamiliar with the culture of your students, it's worth discussing different gestures with them to find out what to be wary of. (If you're English and teaching out of England it's absolutely essential: students are less likely to suspend their own expectations than if they are in England. On the other hand, don't worry about them to the extent that every move you make is fraught with terror! If in doubt just stick to the one basic rule; never touch your students on anywhere but the arm – although even that might be taboo in some countries!)

– Irritating habits, such as grinning or blinking too much. They can be very off-putting; even language 'ticks' such as *OK* or *all right*? can annoy students. If you don't believe it when somebody says you are repeatedly stroking your face or pulling your hair, try to watch yourself on video if you can. Failing that try and get other trainees to note down your habits and the number of times you practise them. Getting rid of a habit can paralyse you with self-consciousness but it's worth it in the long run!

Should students be encouraged to imitate the teacher's expressions?

Probably not the ones you use to manage the class unless the students are doing the teaching! Probably not the ones to highlight aspects of the form either, unless you can use them to help you check understanding. But the realistic gestures and facial expressions, certainly. If students are practising a dialogue it'll help them to say it as though they mean it and they'll make it far more memorable.

Exercises

You can probably most usefully practise classroom gestures in front of a mirror! However, the following are useful supplementary exercises. If you are shy, make sure the group is divided into two and the exercises are done simultaneously. This will give you the cover of background noise and activity.

Ex. 1

AIM
To encourage trainees to make more use of gesture in front of an audience.

PROCEDURE
Play *Charades* in teams (one person in a team mimes the name of a book or film and the other team has to guess what it is within a certain time limit). Make sure beforehand the gestures used are the special ones you might use to direct a class (e.g. a sweeping gesture to encourage everyone to contribute; a 'nearly' gesture to show semi-approval of an answer). You might discuss them with the group before doing the exercise.

COMMENT
1 One advantage of this game is that in the playing of it self-consciousness is often forgotten. The drawback is that those trying to guess the name of the film, book etc. are willing and enthusiastic in what they give. A normal class might be less forthcoming and more eliciting gestures would be needed. This could perhaps be covered by instructing the 'audience' not to offer anything unless called upon by a gesture.

2 The most valuable variant of this exercise is to replace the book or film with a sentence which has to be mimed/gestured.

Ex. 2

AIM
To show the value of gesture and facial expression in conveying meaning.

PROCEDURE
A 1 Tell the group a short story without any gesture, movement or facial expression.

2 Repeat the exercise using as much physical expression as possible.

3 Discuss with others in the group the gestures and expressions most helpful in getting across the meaning and mood of the storyteller.

COMMENT
This should help show the extent to which all of us rely on physical expression to convey and interpret meaning.

B 1 Pass a message round the group through a series of mime gestures (rather like a mimed version of *Chinese Whispers*). Make sure members of the group who have not yet received the message do not watch. It might be best to have everyone leave the room and come back in one at a time to receive the message.

   2 Compare the final mime with the original message.

Ex. 3

AIM
To practise the appropriate gestures for getting students to listen to a model, repeat in chorus and repeat individually. (Also see exercises on pp 95–97).

PROCEDURE
1 By gesture alone (e.g. hand behind ear) get some of your colleagues to listen to an utterance (either in a nonsense language or a foreign language).

2 Pause and check through eye contact that everyone has heard.

3 By gesture alone (e.g. a gathering-together two-arm gesture) get everyone to repeat, making sure they all start at the same time.

4 Get the group to repeat individually, quickly and randomly, again by gesture alone (e.g. beckoning with the whole hand). Make sure that everyone gets practice and that those that need it most get most.

Ex. 4

AIM
To help indicate intonation and stress by gesture.

PROCEDURE
1 Read out, or play on tape, some one-word utterances, one at a time.

2 As the words are uttered, indicate stress by a beating gesture and the main pitch movement by a lift or a fall of the hand.

3 When this has been practised sufficiently, make the utterances consist of more than one word. Indicate by appropriate gestures where the main stress comes in the utterances and the pitch changes caused by it.

COMMENT
1 To help the group, read out the utterances and get them to make the gesture instead of you.

2 It is important to use the gestures you feel comfortable with rather than copy someone you have seen. Discuss with the group which are the clearest.

Ex. 5

AIM
To help in an understanding of the extent to which meaning can be conveyed without words.

PROCEDURE

1 Mime to the group one of the following lists of words:

A	B	C	D
walk	bake	shoot	scrub
stroll	fry	suffocate	brush
dash	grill	smother	wipe
jog	boil	drown	sweep

2 Ask them to write down what they think the words are.

3 Get others in the group to mime the other lists.

4 Compare results and consider alternative gestures.

2.3 Position and movement

In the classroom, students quickly become sensitive to where you are placed. It tells them:
– what type of activity it is

– what your role is

– what the students' role is expected to be

– who you are attending to and not attending to

– whether you expect a student to talk to you or not.

Concepts of personal space vary from culture to culture. For example, Arabs when they talk to each other like to get closer than Northern Europeans. In multi-cultural classes, students sometimes cause offence to each other because they get too close.

Activities with the teacher at the front of the class

Some activities (e.g. presentation, controlled practice, giving instructions) often demand that you are directing what is going on. You stand at the front so that:
– you can see what everyone is doing or trying to say

– you can maintain control through gesture and eye contact

– the students can see any visual aids or mimes you may need

– you are mobile enough to help and correct individuals

– the students can focus on you; they need to see your facial expressions and gestures, as well as your mouth, since these all reinforce what is being said. It's *essential* students see your mouth if you are going to ask them to pronounce what you are saying. If you stand at the back of the class or even at the front with your back or side to the class you are depriving them of the best conditions for hearing and understanding.

Be careful, though, not to:
– be totally frozen out there in front

– move around too much, distracting students by constantly pacing the floor

– develop habits like rocking backwards and forwards from one foot to the other.

Find the optimum position: not so close that you are on top of the students, nor so far away that they can't see or hear you; not blocking any essential visuals or writing on the board; not blocking students from communicating with either you or each other.

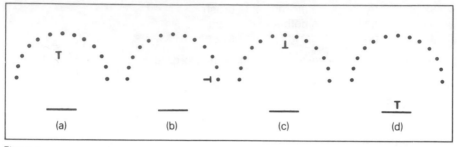

Figure 1

For example, Position (a) (teacher facing students), excludes students at the sides, Position (b) focuses exclusively on a few students and position (c) (teacher with back to students), removes control over part of the class and stops them from seeing the board. However, Position (d) is ideal for a small group seated in a horseshoe shape, unless you are helping an individual or trying to make the board visible.

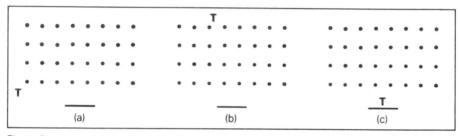

Figure 2

In a large class with the seats arranged in rows, Position (a) weakens your control over the far side of the class, (b) can be rather menacing if you are talking to the class (unless you are reading from the board or showing slides) and, since there can be no eye control or gestural control, ineffective if you are directing language practice, whereas (c) is ideal for most 'up front' teaching.

How can you help an individual student during these activities?
If the layout of the class allows it, move forward. Be careful, though. Unless you retain involvement, say by eye contact, you may well exclude the other students, which is all right only if they've got something else to do. If in doubt stay back and direct another student to help. If you are correcting pronunciation, concentrate on the one student and try and involve the others by getting them to make the sounds as well.

Don't loom over a student or sit on the student's desk, it's intimidating. If it's really individual help you're giving, lean forwards or crouch in front.

How can you write on the board without turning your back on the students?
You can't, and for that reason many teachers now prefer to use an overhead projector (OHP). However, you can involve the students in what you are writing by asking them what comes next, how to spell new words etc., provided you don't

overdo it and slow the lesson down too much. If you have a lot to write up, do it in small chunks and turn round and face the class from time to time, perhaps to ask the students some questions (see pp 160–161).

Pair and group work

For this either:
– sit down, on a chair, outside the communication circuits you have set up, listening
or:
– move round unobtrusively.

The more you impose yourself, the more the students will look to you for help. If you make contributions, crouch next to the group or lean over at a tactful distance. Be brief and move on. If you are asked to give your ideas to a group's discussion, *participate as a student*.

Listening to a tape or reading a text

When students are engaged in such activities they do not need to see you. In fact, moving around may distract. So, *sit down and be quiet*. Don't feel that not showing yourself is not teaching. On the other hand, don't stay frozen to the chair after the activity has finished. Go and help a student if asked – and perhaps stand at the front if you're going to ask questions.

Exercises

Ex. 1

AIM
To find out about personal space and the feelings engendered by foreign gestures and movement.

PROCEDURE
1 Give half the group a slip of paper each with a different instruction regarding an alien habit on it (e.g *stand only five inches from the person you are talking to*; *bow every time you address someone*; *hold the person you are talking to gently on the arm*).

2 Get everyone up and ask them to pretend they are at a wine party. The other half of the group should behave normally.

COMMENT
1 This should go on long enough to allow everyone to experience a couple of non-English habits.

2 It is better if particular gestures can be given to people with experience of that culture, to prevent them from becoming too extreme.

Ex. 2

AIM
To highlight the importance of where you stand in the classroom in relation to the class's activity.
    This exercise can be done during TP, during a real lesson, or using a video tape of a lesson, specially filmed to concentrate on the teacher.

PROCEDURE
1 Make a rough grid plan of a classroom, e.g.:

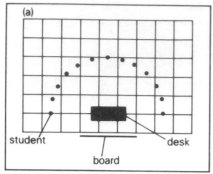

Figure 3   Figure 4

2 Every two or three minutes, or more frequently if the lesson is a short one, make an entry in the appropriate square to show the approximate position of the teacher. The first entry is the number 1, the second 2, and so on. The grid ends up looking something like this:

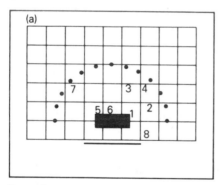
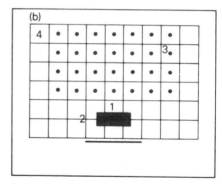

Figure 5   Figure 6

3 Indicate whether the position is appropriate by making a separate list of the numbers and marking them at the same time √ (OK), × (wrong) or ○ (not sure).

COMMENT
1 Like most observation tasks this can become tedious if it goes on too long, so it is probably better to limit it to about twenty minutes.

2 Discussion should focus on how static or how mobile the teacher is and the effect this has on the students.

Ex. 3

AIM
To help modify patterns of movement during a class.

PROCEDURE
1 Write your TP lesson plan leaving a broad margin down the right-hand side of the page.

2 In the margin, mark the approximate teaching position most appropriate to the activity, e.g:

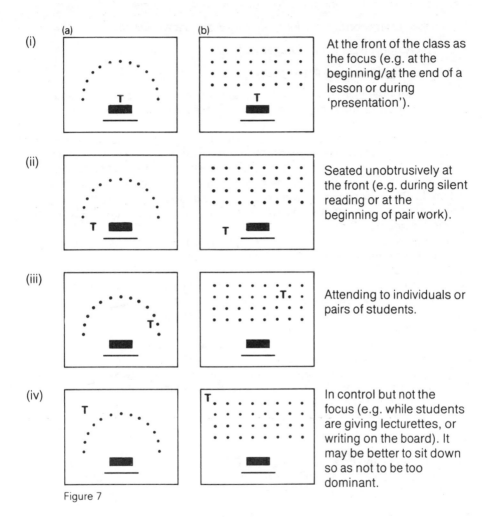

At the front of the class as the focus (e.g. at the beginning/at the end of a lesson or during 'presentation').

Seated unobtrusively at the front (e.g. during silent reading or at the beginning of pair work).

Attending to individuals or pairs of students.

In control but not the focus (e.g. while students are giving lecturettes, or writing on the board). It may be better to sit down so as not to be too dominant.

Figure 7

3 Compare predicted positions with reality, after TP.

COMMENT

1 Don't be unnecessarily exact. Restrict the positions to, say, four or five typical positions and use simple symbols to indicate them.

2 The technique of using a right-hand margin as above can also be employed to concentrate on such areas as gesture, the relative amounts you and the students are expected to talk in the class, and types of activity. Symbols are much more striking and easily read than words.

2.4 Attention spread

The ideal in most types of classes where the practice of language items is the focus is that all students:
– should be given the opportunity to repeat any new language

– have their errors corrected during controlled language practice

– have individual help and encouragement

– have individualized tasks if necessary

– should feel they have contributed to the class in more or less equal amounts, even though what they contribute will inevitably be different.

Obviously, the larger the class, the more difficult the ideal is to achieve. In a class of forty students you would probably rely more heavily on chorus work and group work than you would in a class of ten. Chorus work ensures that at least everyone repeats new language (although it doesn't ensure that everyone understands it – see pp 98–99). Pair and group work can be used to give everyone practice just as they can give everyone the opportunity to communicate more freely in the classroom (see pp 41ff).

However, a class, no matter how big, is made up of individuals, most of whom want to be listened to or addressed by the teacher directly. Sometimes, in large classes, it might only be possible to give the briefest acknowledgement: a smile, a gesture, a word of encouragement. Even that, though, is worth it. In smaller classes, you should be able to get round to everyone. In either case, use eye contact to draw in all the students when you are directing them together as a class (see pp 7–8).

Any time you give individual students attention, e.g. when you are asking questions, giving help, getting them to repeat, correcting, etc:
– dot about. Don't go round in a line. It's too predictable; students switch off until it's their turn to contribute. It doesn't matter sometimes if the same student is called on twice. It keeps the class on its toes

– involve students who are not being dealt with directly as much as possible (see pp 154ff).

– don't be led by the boisterous students. Quieten them firmly, without discouraging them. Draw out the silent ones. Reassure students anxious to opt out that what you are doing needs their attention

– don't teach exclusively to either the good *or* the weak students. Occasionally, call on the good to help the not-so-good. Give the good students hard questions and tasks and the others easier ones, if possible without either category realizing

– spend longer on students who don't understand or can't do what's expected but, remember, you may somehow have to compensate the others

– remember to stand back and include students at the edge of any seating arrangement. They're easy to forget, particularly those in the front, to the side.

The sixth sense of knowing who's said what when and knowing when you have given enough individual attention without either dissatisfying the individuals concerned or boring the group, only really comes with experience. You should, though, be conscious of the need to develop it.

Pair and group work

As students are working more for themselves or other students in group work, the teacher's attention may not be needed. Indeed, it can be an interference. Group work is often, then, an opportunity to take individuals aside and give them specific remedial help, provided they are not expected to take part fully in any follow-up *class* task. Quiet students can also be helped on these occasions.

During activities that don't involve controlled language practice or depend on the involvement of everyone (e.g. group discussions), it may be better to let students who don't wish to contribute remain silent. Listening and reflection play an important part in the way many students learn a language.

How do you control the noise levels in the class?

One of the inevitable consequences of trying to teach the spoken language through maximizing student talking time is that there will often be more than one person talking in the room at any one time. Using pair work in a class of forty means that there could easily be twenty people talking at once. This is not a serious problem for you and the students. The students are close enough to the person they are talking to to be able to hear easily and you quickly get used to a fairly high noise level. However, the person using the room next door may not be quite so easily convinced, so it may be necessary for you to think of ways of keeping the noise level down at times, e.g:
– by giving each group a different task. If your group work involves a quiet activity as well as a discussion stage, then one group may be talking while the other is reading

– by making sure the students are close enough to each other. This is particularly important for group and pair work. A spread-out group is noisier than a huddle

– by appointing a chairman for groups. The chairman can have several functions, one of which can be to make sure that only one person talks at any one time

– by telling the students to talk quietly. This is an obvious piece of advice but often ignored. The students usually appreciate the problem as much as anyone else and if they are reminded they should do as you say.

With repetition work you might:
– ask the students to whisper – this is particularly useful in choral work. A whispered chorus gives the same sort of practice as one spoken aloud

– break up the chorus. If you only ask a part of the class to chorus at one time it keeps the noise level down

– use the 'round' approach: ask the students to repeat the model three or four times, then indicate that one group or row of students should start, then before they finish, the next group should start, and so on round the class. This can still give a fairly high noise level but it does not have the penetrating quality of a full chorus

– prevent the activity from going on too long. A model sentence chorused a number of times will build to a crescendo, so stop it before it reaches its peak. Group work with a task which expects the students to express themselves will tend to get noisier the longer it goes on. Break it up with fresh instructions and a reminder about the noise level

– tell the students to repeat a model sentence *to themselves*. If they can do it at the pace they want rather than all together, it will be quieter than a full chorus and there is still background noise to hide the efforts of the shyer students

– check with other teachers beforehand. If you anticipate a noisy lesson it is best to check that the class next door is not doing an exam at that time.

Exercises

Ex. 1

AIM
To increase awareness of how much attention is being spread around the class.

PROCEDURE
1 Before TP ask someone observing you to make a chart as in Figure 8, allowing one box per student, e.g:

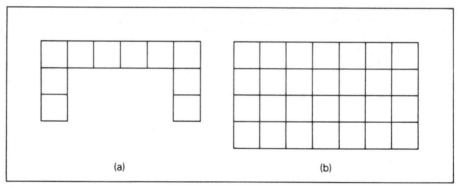

(a)   (b)

Figure 8

2 Ask the person to make a mark in each box when a student is included, preferably during a teacher-directed activity like a drill.

3 After the lesson say where you feel attention was focused and who you thought the weak students and the strong students were.

4 Get the person you asked to show you the chart and discuss the results.

COMMENT
This exercise can highlight the blind spots even experienced teachers have when it comes to distributing attention evenly round the class.

Ex. 2

AIM
To help spread attention randomly between individual students and yet evenly round the class.

PROCEDURE
1 Before TP write out a list of the students' names in random order (*not* the order they sit in).

2 During one predetermined part of the lesson go down the list and make sure everyone is included. If necessary go through it more than once, backwards as well as forwards.

2.5 Using the voice

If your voice does not have sufficient range, variety and projection, you are going to be at a considerable disadvantage in the classroom. Having said that, though, voice quality and the ways individuals use their voices vary enormously from one teacher to another.

How can you use your voice to gain attention?

For example:
− when students are standing around at the beginning of a lesson, talking

− when you want to stop a group activity

− when there's a lot of general noise and you want to regain control.

Rather than standing quietly waiting for students to finish, or clapping your hands or banging on the table, it is often more effective to exaggerate certain features of your voice, dwelling longer than usual on certain syllables and making a joke of it, (e.g. 'All right everyone. Mo*ham*med!') Shouting can convey anger and, in some cultures, disastrous loss of face, so avoid it unless really necessary. A slight increase in volume and higher pitch is often all that's necessary.

Can you help to hold the students' attention with the voice?

Yes. Attention can easily be lost by speaking:
− too quietly

− too monotonously, without varying the pitch of the voice.

When you are 'up front' it's as much <u>how</u> you say something as <u>what</u> you say that keeps your students' attention. Try recording yourself and listening to how wide your voice range is.

What about when you are announcing changes in the stages of a lesson?

It's not necessary to say: *Right! This is a different part of the lesson. New activity coming up.*
    Read, for example, the following transcript of a lesson aloud:
T: *So, what's the 'rule', then?*
S: *After 'would like to', always use the infinitive.*
T: *Good. Everyone clear? Let's have one more example. Tell me about your holiday next year . . . Sami.*
S: *Eh . . . I'd like to . . . mmm . . . I'd like to go to Scotland.*
T: *OK. Good. Now, close your books. Stand up and put all the tables against the wall.*
When you reach *Now, close your books* your voice should increase marginally in volume and rise in pitch considerably to highlight the change of activity.

In what way does the voice vary?

The voice alters fairly naturally, according to the activity, the size of the class, the room, etc. When talking to individuals, pairs or groups, we reduce the volume, lower the pitch and narrow the range. When addressing a large class in a large room the opposite usually takes place, although some teachers can get a class under control by talking <u>more</u> quietly than usual!.

The greater the variation in the voice, usually – providing it's appropriate – the greater the effectiveness. For getting the class's attention and for giving gentle, individual correction the quality of the voice should be very different. To sensitize yourself to your own skills in voice control, try recording yourself reading a dialogue or, if possible, giving a set of instructions to students.

Exercises

Ex. 1

AIM
To help identify the main uses of voice for three major functions within a lesson.

PROCEDURE
1 In groups make a list of the different functions of the voice in a class.

2 Categorize under three main headings, e.g.
   Gaining attention of whole class
   Maintaining attention of whole class while talking
   Talking to individuals so as not to distract group activity

3 During a lesson you observe (possibly on video), for twenty minutes note down under these headings what was being said and what different types of voice are being used.

4 Discuss with peers, focusing on the effectiveness of each.

Ex. 2

AIM
To develop awareness of the role of the voice.

PROCEDURE
1 Record part of a real lesson.

2 Together with someone in your group identify the changes of pitch and volume in the teacher's voice and discuss the reasons for them.

3 If videoed, discuss how the changes relate to gesture and movement.

Ex. 3

AIM
To improve the use of the voice.

PROCEDURE
1 Make a genuine announcement to the group in the classroom or to a crowded common room full of students!

2 Ask someone in the group to assess your performance in getting attention, holding it and getting the message across.

Ex. 4

AIM
To encourage use of the most appropriate voice for the various stages of the lesson.

PROCEDURE

1 Plan a short lesson where you are familiar with the techniques and content involved (e.g. part of a previous TP lesson).

2 At suitable stages in the plan, write a short, simple script in a different colour ink (not necessarily the exact words you will speak).

3 Underline those sections where a voice change is necessary and indicate the type of voice required.

4 Teach the lesson and discuss the results with anyone observing it.

Ex. 5

AIM

To help develop different kinds of voice.

PROCEDURE

1 Identify three different types of voice that you can use fairly easily (e.g. a voice to get attention in a crowded room, a voice for giving a language model or a voice for talking to an individual student whilst the rest of the class is involved in pair work). Get someone to confirm that you have got them right.

2 Write down two or three appropriate phrases for each type of voice.

3 Practise saying them to yourself in the right kind of voice.

2.6 Metalanguage and the amount you talk

Metalanguage is the language you use in the classroom in order to explain things, give instructions, to praise or to correct – in other words, all the language that isn't being 'taught'.

The aim of most language classes is usually to get the students using the language. When you talk too much then the chances are the students aren't being given maximum opportunity to talk. It's also likely that you won't be listening to the students closely enough, thinking too much of what you are going to say next. (Teacher talking time is often referred to as 'TTT' and student talking time as 'STT' – high STT and low TTT is the aim of most language classes).

At the lower levels at least, if you are a native speaker using English, metalanguage needs to be minimal and, in the case of instructions, checked that it has been understood (so that the students do the activity as quickly and efficiently as possible – see pp 36ff).

Students, however, learn a lot from metalanguage because it is genuinely communicative language. That is one reason for trying to avoid using the students' mother tongue if possible. There is nothing artificial about a situation that involves you praising a student or asking another to be quiet. The context is clear and the language used within it serves a real purpose. Metalanguage, then, should be natural and free of teaching jargon.

Do you have to grade metalanguage if it is in the target language?

Yes. Metalanguage, unless it is language the students need to know because they'll hear it frequently, should generally be *below* the level of the language being 'taught'. It needs to be understood immediately by everyone. At higher levels, you can take more risks because the students often identify areas of metalanguage they don't understand and learn from it. At lower levels, though:

– choose words and structures the students already know

– avoid grammatical terminology (like PRESENT PERFECT) unless there's a good reason not to (see pp 65ff).
At all levels:
– avoid 'teacher's language' (like *concept questions, drilling* etc.)

Sometimes to avoid confusion it might be more efficient to use the students' mother tongue if you simply want them to carry out an activity, though in doing so you're denying them the opportunity to learn from metalanguage.

How else do you reduce the amount you talk in the classroom?

Don't be tempted to describe your every intention. Indicating a major change of activity for the students is acceptable (*All right. Now we're going to write a letter together* very usefully signals a change of gear) whereas revealing all your strategies isn't (*Now I'm going to check your comprehension* is information the students don't need to know and sounds heavy and pedantic).

Avoid running commentaries on your lesson, both to yourself and your students (*I didn't present that very well, did I?*). They're very distracting.

Don't feel you must be polite all the time. You may want to say *I wonder if you'd mind repeating this* but a straight imperative such as *Repeat* together with a gesture (see pp 10–12) will be more efficient. Equally, *Quite good* together with an appropriate facial expression is better than *That might have been better*. In general, at elementary levels, avoid the use of grammatical structures, particularly complicated ones, when 'content' words will do. It not only makes you understood more easily, allowing the students to get on with the task in hand, but it also adds to the impression of you being an efficient, directive teacher in charge of your material and the situation.

Although not strictly concerning metalanguage, you can limit what you say by not repeating yourself unless you have to (asking questions twice can be a nervous habit) and by not repeating what the students say. So:
T: *Well, what's Susan doing? Juan?*
J: *She's having lunch.*
T: *Yes, she's having lunch.*
This is often known as 'echoing' the students. Some teachers echo correct responses with correct responses as well as incorrect responses with correct responses (often without realizing the student's response is incorrect). Usually, the effect of this is to increase the TTT (thus giving the impression of a teacher-dominated class), to encourage the students to listen to you instead of each other (thus cutting off a lot of useful interaction) and to weaken your ability to listen to the students and correct effectively. Some teachers 'echo' incorrect responses with exaggerated intonation. This can be a humorous way of drawing attention to the students' mistakes but you need to have confidence and a relaxed relationship with the class if it's not to be insulting.

A final word: convey as much as you can through gesture, facial expression and intonation.

What other things affect the ease with which the students understand you?

– If you are using the target language, *your speed of delivery*. Don't gabble, but don't allow a class to get used to an unnaturally slow delivery (e.g. de-contracted words such as *I am* for *I'm*; or distorted sounds such as /ðɪ/ for /ðə/).

It won't help them understand native speakers since you are, in effect, inventing a language!

– In a multinational class, *your choosing language according to the students' language backgrounds.*

The word *advertisement*, at least in writing and probably in speech, will be understood by French students even before they have learnt it. Not so by Japanese. Neither, however, would understand the abbreviation *ad.* So, if you know your students' language, think what they will easily understand. There are many international words, such as *hotel* and *Coca-Cola*, that nearly all students understand if pronounced the way *they* pronounce them! These can be a great help sometimes when practising a new structure: they give a comfortable feeling of familiarity.

Other suggestions
1 When a student doesn't understand, simplify what you've said e.g:
   T: *What have you got for No. 6, Abdul?*
   A: (Silence)
   T: *No. 6. What did you write, Abdul?*
   A: (Silence)
   T: *No. 6, Abdul.*
2 Give the students time to do what you ask them. Often the students do understand and need a bit of time. If you are nervous and concerned not to let the pace of the lesson flag, it's not always easy to remember to hold yourself back.
3 Find out what your students find easy and difficult to understand and adapt your language to them. If you are teaching a class of doctors, you'll soon discover that their professional knowledge will contribute considerably to their understanding of certain specialized words and phrases.

For further reading in this area see *Teaching English through English* by Jane Willis (Longman) and *Classroom English* by G. Hughes (OUP).

Exercises

Ex. 1

AIM
To help identify different degrees of complexity in language.

PROCEDURE
1 Rank the following instructions in order of how easy they are to understand:
   What's his name?
   Could you tell me what his name is?
   His name, please.
   Ask him what his name is.
   Can you find out his name?
   Ask 'What's your name?'

2 Compare your ranking with someone else's in the group and discuss why one instruction is more difficult than the other.

Ex. 2

AIM
To help simplify the target language for classroom use.

PROCEDURE

A 1 Look at the following questions:
      What do you think this object's called?
      What might he be involved in?
      I wonder if you can remember his destination?
      What happened next?

   2 Write down simpler ways of saying the same thing and compare your questions with someone else's.

B 1 Work with two others in your group. One should be, or pretend to be the native speaker, the other should pretend to have almost no English. If possible record the exercise.

   2 Tell the 'native' speaker how to do something difficult, e.g. to start a car.

   3 Tell the 'elementary' speaker how to do the same thing in simpler language.

   4 Compare the language used for both, possibly referring to the tape.

Ex. 3

AIM

To create an awareness of how what is everyday language to the native speaker can seem difficult to the foreign learner.

PROCEDURE

1 Get hold of a set of instructions for something relatively simple like an everyday electrical appliance.

2 With another member of your group, discuss the likely difficulties that low level students would have.

3 Write the instructions again trying to eliminate the difficulties.

4 Compare your results with others in the group.

5 Try out the instructions on an elementary student.

6 Go through the same procedure with the instructions in a textbook aimed at higher levels.

2.7 Rapport

Many of the things that need to be said under this heading have been referred to on previous pages (e.g. pp 2 and 6) and are implicit in any discussion on how you look at your students, how you address them and where you stand in relation to them. It is, however, such an important factor in determining whether a class is a success or not (even more in the early days when teaching skills are less developed) that it's worth making further points here.

Obviously, students are prepared to 'play the game' more – and so contribute and learn to use the language more – when the atmosphere is relaxed and you and the students all get on well together. While to a large extent the students create their own atmosphere in the classroom, it can nevertheless be encouraged or deterred by your general attitude.

Showing personal interest in the students

Both inside and outside the classroom, find out about their opinions, their attitudes and their day-to-day life when they're not learning English. In multinational classes, find out about their country and culture. Apart from anything else, knowing what interests them and what offends them can help determine topic areas for your classes. Also, being able to refer occasionally to something you know about individual students in the class is, if done with tact, a good way of building up a relationship with the group as a whole. Providing it's not over-indulged in, it's sometimes good to reciprocate and reveal something of yourself, too.

Being interested in their progress

Talking to students informally can also tell you what students think they need to learn, what they think their good points and weak points are. It also gives you the opportunity to judge their language needs for yourself, in normal relaxed circumstances outside the conventions of the classroom. Students can also tell you their difficulties and why they think they're having them. Such information should help you decide what to do in the classroom when you work out what the group as a whole needs.

Asking for comments on the classes

It's well worth asking your students individually and occasionally as a group what they find useful and not so useful about your classes, providing you have enough language in common (it's not so easy with complete beginners if you don't speak their language!) After all, you are only teaching for *them*.

Having the right manner

Most teachers try to balance directive control over a class with a relaxed, helpful manner, but everyone has to find his own style. Teachers who get away with being rude to their students are only effective because the students recognize under-lying sympathy and humour. By the way, it's not a style recommended for the early days of TP!

Responding and reacting to what students say

In class, it's not that easy to respond when you're trying to remember what to do next. One of the problems is that your nerves often prevent you from hearing what the students are saying! Another problem, particularly outside the class, is knowing whether to comment on the *accuracy* of what has been said or whether to respond directly? Compare these two dialogues during a break:

1 T: *Hello, Helmut.*   2 T: *Hello, Helmut.*
   S: *You come to party?*   S: *You come to party?*
   T: *ARE YOU COMING!*   T: *Sure, what time is it?*

In Dialogue 1, Helmut might be confused, thinking he's being asked, rather assertively, if *he's* coming – in fact, his English is being corrected. While there's a time and place for correction (e.g. during a drill) it's often more useful for a student to know to what extent he has succeeded or failed in communicating, at least if that's what he's trying to do. It's also helpful, even during a drill if you sometimes respond to utterances as though they were genuinely being made. It makes all language, even practice-language, more meaningful.

Other affective considerations

Obviously, the larger the class and the fewer number of hours a week you teach it, the more difficult it is to be concerned with how the students feel about each other, or to be able to relate their learning activities to feelings, except in a vague general way. (For what lies behind this remark you might like to refer to *Caring and Sharing in the Foreign Language Classroom* by Gertrude Moskowitz – Newbury House). While such considerations are essential in small classes where the students have many hours studying together, in all classes, no matter how large, you should at least try and develop a co-operative atmosphere, with students taking each other into account as much as possible and learning to share language and ideas. When students learn to learn from each other, the group as a whole benefits. Their dependence on you is reduced and yet their motivation increases. The group develops its own positive dynamic.

Some simple practical hints to help you encourage this spirit are:

– Make sure you know everyone's name and that they know both yours and each other's! At the beginning of a course you might ask them to put their names on the desk for all to see or perhaps wear name-badges, or, in a small class, you might write their names on the board and get everyone to practise putting a face to the name. An amusing name-remembering game goes like this:
  T: My name's John.
  S1: (pointing) *His name's John and my name's Abdulla.*
  S2: (pointing) *His name's John, that's Abdulla and I'm Ingrid.*
  S3: (pointing) *John, Abdulla, Ingrid and I'm Thomas.*
  and so on until you go round the whole class. If you have a class of more than, say, twenty, it's probably better to split it into two halves.

– At the beginning of a course of lessons have an activity to break the ice and get everyone talking to each other, e.g. in a medium size class you might ask the students to get up and find two people with whom they have hobbies in common. They must then interview those students and find out as many personal details as possible. If there's time, each student could report back to the whole class on the other person. In a large class, you could divide the students into groups with each group having to fill out a questionnaire, with general questions on it like: *How many people in your group drive*? Each group could then report back its findings. Even if the students' English is not good enough it's still worth them doing this activity in their mother-tongue, but make sure you explain the reasons for it first!

– Have plenty of group work, both for controlled language practice and for the sharing of ideas (see pp 41–44). Apart from increasing the amount the students contribute to a class, it brings them much closer together.

– Have a lot of activities which the group can enjoy, relating the activity to what suits the group best (e.g. songs, games, mimes, etc. are popular with many classes). All such activities can have specific language purposes.

– Most important, don't dominate a class. Let it develop its own atmosphere and encourage its own positive characteristics. If there are some students working against the interests of the group spend some time talking to them and sorting out their problems. It's worth it in the long run although be careful not to let them command *all* your attention. You might easily provide the wrong sort of encouragement and lose the rest of the group!

3 Classroom Management

Introduction

There is, inevitably, some overlap between this section and the previous section; how you talk and behave are important factors in managing a class. In this section, however, the focus is more on what you have to do to make the *conditions* in the classroom right for various learning activities.

3.1 Seating arrangements

Where the students sit in a classroom can determine:

– their attitude to each other and to you

– your attitude to them

– how they interact

– the types of activity they can perform.

Should you determine who sits next to whom?

Yes, sometimes. It's not always good to have students with the same mother-tongue sitting together – or two boys, or two girls, or two people who are always chatting. So feel you have the authority to move them, politely but firmly. Remember, though, we all get attached to our own territory and moving can be a wrench. While shuffling up a class *for an activity* is acceptable – provided it's done in the right spirit – it can be unsettling if you do it too often and with no apparent reason. If you feel a student is deliberately trying to sit outside the areas in the classroom where most of the activity is taking place, say at the back, it may need good-humoured encouragement to bring him in. Sometimes, students try to set up space between themselves and other students and between themselves and you in order to establish their own superior-seeming relationships, so you will need to be sensitive, yet positive, from the very beginning.

How do you change the arrangement to fit the activity?

On TP, you may be restricted by the types of chairs, tables or desks in the classroom. If you are lucky they will be freestanding but very often they are fixed or too heavy to move. Classroom furniture always affects the learning atmosphere to some extent but the choice will almost certainly be outside your control. Inevitably then, you can only have flexible seating patterns within the constraints of the institution. However, if you *are* one of the lucky ones make sure you take full advantage of it.

1 Activities where you need to direct the class from the front
With moveable desks, tables or seminar chairs in a class of probably no more than sixteen students, a horseshoe arrangement will allow easy, face-to-face contact between the students and between you and the students:

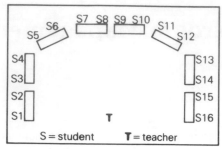

Figure 9

The more horseshoe-shaped it is, the more likely S16 is to be able to talk to S5.

If the class has more than sixteen students you may be forced to arrange the furniture in rows but it helps if the two halves are slightly at an angle:

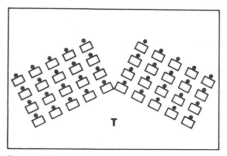

Figure 10

2 Pair work

When two students talk across the classroom under your control, giving other students the opportunity to hear, the activity is known as 'open' pair work. For this there is obviously no need to change the position of the seats. If, however, all the students are working together in pairs, outside your direct control, then they need to be able to look at each other (this activity is known as 'closed' pair work). So either get them to turn their chairs slightly towards each other (Figure 11, which shows pair work is possible even when the desks are fixed in rows) or lift their chairs and work facing someone other than their neighbour (Figure 12), depending on the amount of time the activity is likely to take. For some activities, where it is important that the students do not see what the other student is looking at, it is often best to work back to back.

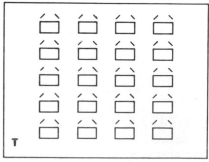

Figure 11

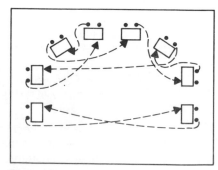

Figure 12

3 Group work

How the seats are arranged depends on the size of the class, the size of the groups, the types of activity and the style of the furniture. For many activities, however, say with four students per group, the ideal is probably either Figure 13, where the students sit round desks, or Figure 14, where the desks are removed:

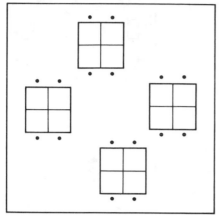

Figure 13

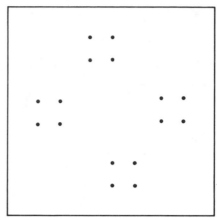

Figure 14

If possible, move furniture to make use of the corners of the room. At all costs avoid:

– all members of a group on one side of a table; they need to face each other

– separating the members of a group too far, making it difficult for them to talk easily.

4 Individual work

If there is a lot of reading or writing involved, it may be worth considering turning students away from each other to give them the freedom to concentrate. The isolation they can usually get in a language laboratory is a clear example of how useful this can be.

Exercises

Ex. 1

AIM

To consider the value of different classroom seating arrangements.

PROCEDURE

1 With others in your group, consider the advantages and disadvantages of the various seating arrangements shown in Figure 15.

2 In particular, consider the following questions:
   (a) How is the relationship between the teacher and students likely to vary in each case? How will it affect the classroom atmosphere?

   (b) Which arrangements are the most conducive to the teacher maintaining effective control over the class?

   (c) In which situation will the teacher dominate most? What will his role be in each case?

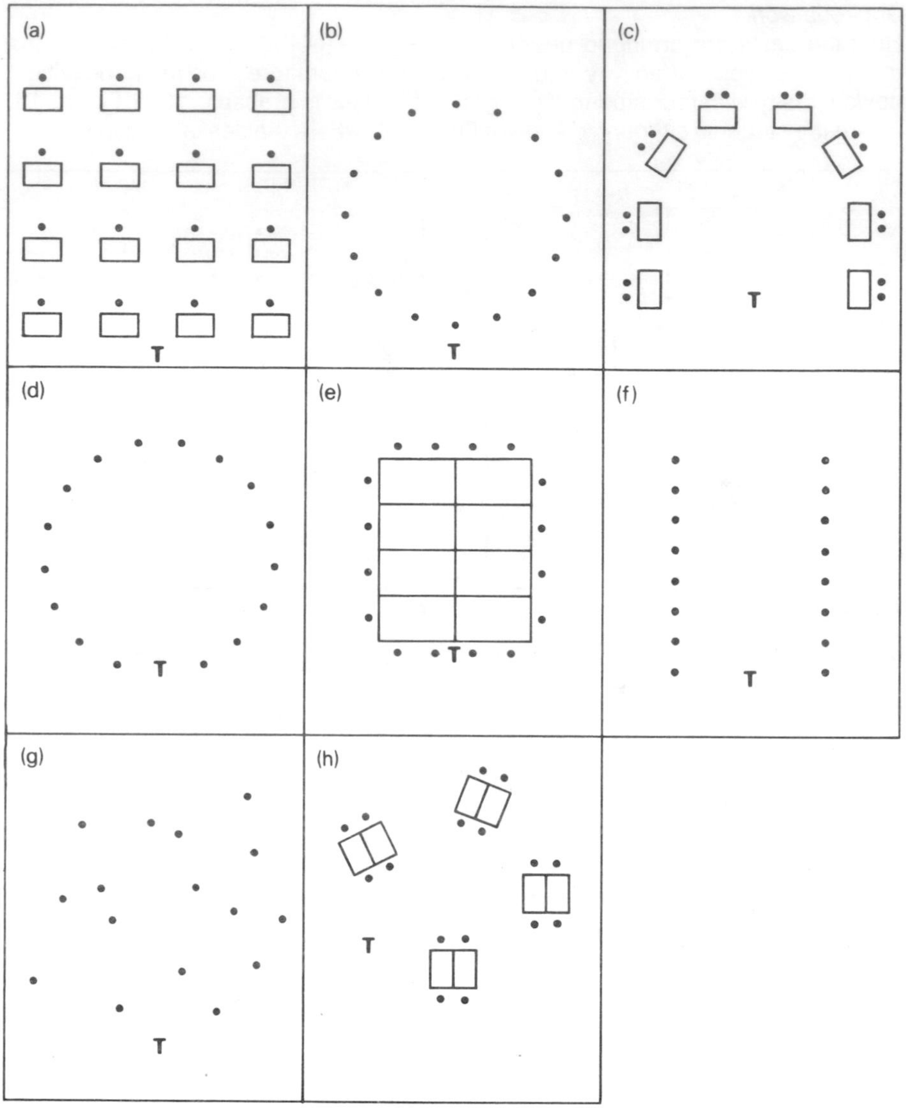

Figure 15

(d) Which arrangement is most suitable for the students to be able to talk to each other?

(e) Which arrangements allow for the students to communicate without interference from the teacher?

(f) How will the size of the group affect the arrangement?

(g) What activities might be suitable for each arrangement?

Ex. 2

AIM

To increase sensitivity towards good and bad seating arrangements.

PROCEDURE

1 Prepare a short talk which involves asking some questions of the group.

2 Mix up the classroom furniture and ask everyone to sit down.

3 Give the talk.

4 After two minutes stop and discuss the seating problems.

5 Ask the group to rearrange the seats as they would like.

6 Continue the talk.

7 Re-evaluate.

8 If possible, set some group work asking the others how it would be best arranged.

Ex. 3

AIM
To help bring out some of the differences seating arrangements can make.

PROCEDURE

1 ˙Work out three or four different possible seating arrangements for a class you know.

2 Discuss these with someone else who knows the class, going into detail about individual students and the activities you can do with them.

3 If possible, try them out with the class, explaining beforehand what you are doing.

4 Ask the class of students to rank the different arrangements on scales of, say, 1–5 (so 1 = easy to talk to partner, 5 = difficult to talk to partner; 1 = easy to see teacher and board, 5 = difficult to see teacher and board). Comfort and ease with which written work can be done are other possible considerations.

COMMENT
As the class is brought into this activity, you should ensure you choose a class whose English is good enough, although outside the UK any discussion could be in the students' mother-tongue.

Ex. 4

AIM
To discover first-hand the effect of different seating arrangements.

PROCEDURE

1 Discuss with a partner the seating arrangements on your training course for different types of sessions.

2 Choose at least one and give grades from 1–5 on a chart like the following:

Title of session (e.g. group work)

Approach   (e.g. discovery in groups)

Seating arrangement used (e.g. random groups of four

around desks)

I found it easy to

a) talk to the group   (5)

b) relax   (3)

c) see the board   (1)

d) see the teacher   (1)

e) work silently   (1)

f) concentrate on the
   activity   (4)

g) learn what was intended   (3)

---

3 Discuss how such sessions might have been improved by different seating arrangements.

COMMENT
The teacher can help such discussions by arranging the seating in a variety of ways; some of them may be eccentric (e.g. a straight lecture with trainees huddled in groups; group work in straight lines)! On occasions, it is worth the trainer hiding his intentions and only encouraging the trainees to evaluate afterwards. On other occasions it is worth letting them take notes during the experiment. Some trainers might wish to do this systematically over a number of sessions so that, for example, discussions are organized in three different ways, group work set out in four different ways and so on.

3.2 Giving instructions

As the teacher's instructions in a class are a means to an end, economy and precision are required, to avoid time-wasting and uncertainty. Frequently, showing what to do is more effective than telling what to do.

Setting up controlled practice activities

Generally speaking, what students should be doing during controlled practice activities, such as a drill, is so obvious that instructions are unnecessary. However, it may occasionally be necessary to demonstrate a new kind of drill, even a teacher-to-students drill, before using it, so:
– get everybody's attention, give the prompt, then move to make it clear you are in the role of the student and give the response. Do this at least twice, do it boldly, and check with eye contact that the students are following (see pp 7–8)
If demonstration is inappropriate then *explain* as clearly and simply as possible (see pp 25–27) and:
– try out the drill with one of the better students so that the rest of the class can see. If the better student cannot do it, you will have to simplify your explanation or break it up and do the drill stage by stage, explaining each bit as you go along.
or:
– write an example of the drill on the board and do the practice from that.

Directing controlled practice

Your instructions will need to be as simple as possible (see pp 10–13 and 25–27) in order to maintain the mechanical momentum of the drill. Students must know what they are expected to do immediately; if some of them don't understand the instructions then it will slow things up unless they can learn what to do by example from their colleagues.

Classroom instructions, however, are usually best learned directly as metalanguage for an exercise, rather than focused on separately. Here are some common ones:
Tell me   Repeat   Everybody   All together   Again   Try again
Look at the board   Look   Read   Say   Copy   Turn to page . . ..
The way you give instructions indicates the way you exercise control and your attitude to the group, yet, generally, students, even adults, would not appreciate you trying to be more polite. It would be time-wasting and slow things down and would involve you in more complicated language than they can readily understand.

Remember, impoliteness partly comes from an inappropriate use of language. Short instructions are entirely appropriate to this situation where the students accept your authority. Also, they usually realize that a firm, directive manner is necessary in order to make language practice efficient.

Besides, if your relationship with the class is right, almost anything said with a smile and the right intonation will be acceptable. Good humour in mechanical exercises, indeed in instructions generally, prevents you from sounding too militaristic!

Organizing seating arrangements

Make sure everyone knows what to do before the activity begins. This means giving simple instructions in segments and checking understanding of each segment as you go along, rather than giving out all the instructions in one go. This is particularly important at lower levels. Before a role-play, students will need to know who they are, what the context is, who they are to talk to and their motives for speaking. You might find it possible to elicit some of the instructions but don't spend too long on it.

Another alternative is to give only some of the instructions and allow time for them to be carried out before moving on to the next set of instructions.

To reorganize the seating arrangements you might tell Juan to sit next to Françoise and wait for Juan to move before dealing with the next couple. This process may take longer than other methods but it should cause less confusion. A reading or writing task might similarly be broken up, pausing to see that everyone has done what you asked.

Sometimes, instead of giving complete instructions to the whole class when the instructions don't concern everyone, you might give each student a number or some kind of symbol. In which case, it might be the number fives or the Aquariuses only (if you are using the signs of the zodiac) who listen for what they should do:

T: *Right, listen to your number. One, two, three, four, five* (pointing as the numbers are called), *one, two, three, four, five* (etc.). Juan, what's your number?

J: *Three*

T: *Abdullah?*

A: *Four*

T: *Right. Listen. All the fours are going to . . . All the threes . . .*

Setting written work

It's very easy, having practised, for example, a dialogue, to give a rather casual instruction, such as *Right. I want you to write a couple of similar dialogues substituting your own ideas where you can* and then wonder why the students are not able to do what you want.

If possible, demonstrate what you expect them to do either on the board or the OHP. This includes extracting ideas from them and writing some up for all to see. If not, explain some initial stages of the task, check the students have understood, get them working, and then rapidly check they are all doing what they're supposed to be doing (without worrying about correcting anything at this stage). Then, and only then, go round and explain the later, more complex stages individually or in pairs, giving the students a chance to ask questions.

What if students don't understand the instructions?

If you are teaching totally in English the language of the instructions must, of course, be understandable and you must check that the students know what to do. Nevertheless, they will need to be taught the appropriate expressions which tell you they don't understand e.g:

Sorry, I   don't understand
*   didn't hear*
Sorry,   could you speak more slowly?

They may also need to be able to ask for clarification through such expressions as:

Excuse me,   how do you say . . .?
*   what does . . . mean?*
*   how do you pronounce . . .?*
*   what's the English for . . .?*

Further hints

– Support instructions with pictures, physical guidance and gestures wherever possible.

– Be consistent, especially with lower-level classes: use the same set of words for the same instruction.

– Develop a signal, like the words *Right* or *Listen* which students will learn to recognize as the cue for an instruction.

– Make sure the students know when to begin an activity (e.g. say something like *Everyone. NOW!*)

Exercises

Ex. 1

AIM
To develop the ability to grade instructions to the level of the group, organize them, segment them and check comprehension.

PROCEDURE
1 Look at these role-cards for a fairly 'free' role-play:

A
```
AT THE GREENGROCER'S
You are the greengrocer.
Your prices:   Apples 24p per lb
               Oranges 8p each
               Bananas 20p per lb
               Grapefruit 10p each
               Pears 30p per lb
               Melons 55p each
You have no grapes.
You have no small change.
```

B
```
AT THE GREENGROCER'S
You are the customer.
You want: 2lbs apples
          6 oranges
          1lb grapes
          A melon if they're not
          more than 50p.
          Something else
You have a £5 note.
You don't want to spend more than £1.
```

2 Read the following transcription of how the activity might be set up with native speakers:

Well, we're going to do this role-play, see, and we're in the greengrocer's. Now there's a slight problem. The greengrocer hasn't got all the fruit the customer wants and he hasn't got any change. Not for a fiver anyway. Now, the customer's got a £5 note but he doesn't want to spend more than £1. OK? Look, I'll give out these cards. I want you to carry out this role-play in pairs. Right? Now, I think you'd better be the customer and you the greengrocer. OK? Right. Now, you know who you are? Right? Now, you'll see if you're the greengrocer a set of prices and, if you're the customer, you'll see a shopping list. I want you to stick to what's on those cards. All right. Are you ready? OK. Get on with it.

3 Underline the information students need to know in order to carry out the activity.

4 Simplify the vocabulary for an elementary class and cut out unnecessary language. Add instructions where it would clarify what the students have to do.

5 Number the instructions and arrange them in logical order.

6 Write questions which would check the students' understanding of each main instruction. (Remember they are elementary students, so keep the questions simple!)

7 Try out the activity on a group, checking understanding at the main stages or compare your instructions with the others.

COMMENT
Similar practice in instruction-giving can be done for such activities as making models from Lego sets, operating simple machinery (e.g. tape recorders), giving directions etc. It is often worth recording and transcribing the instructions as they would be given to (i) a native speaker and (ii) a low-level class. You might find you need give very little contextual information in your instructions, but make sure your students know all they need to know.

Ex. 2

AIM
To give practice in keeping instructions to a minimum and yet making them clear.

PROCEDURE
1 Take a course book and choose a page which has a variety of exercises on it.

2 Work with a partner. Discuss whether the written instructions are clear and sufficient for the students to understand without a teacher. If they are not, write out a set of instructions.

3 Discuss these written instructions and decide whether they are the same ones you would give to a class. If they are not, write out the instructions you would give and questions to check that the students understand.

4 Discuss where demonstration of the instructions might be more appropriate and how it might be done.

Ex. 3

AIM
To show how clear, simple instructions accompanied by gestures are both easily understood and learned rapidly by a class.

PROCEDURE
1 Make up a short dialogue in a fictitious language or in a language unknown by the rest of the group.

2 Make up some simple practice instructions to go with it (e.g. the equivalents of *repeat, everybody, again* and *write*).

3 Drill the dialogue line by line and get the group to write it down as best they can.

4 Discuss the lesson (if possible some time later) and see how far the instructions have been remembered.

COMMENT
It is probable that the instructions will be remembered better than the dialogue. The discussion can then most usefully focus on the reasons for this.

Ex. 4

AIM
To compare the level at which students understand instructions with their ability to write them.

PROCEDURE
1 Select a sequence of pictures which show clearly how to carry out a simple process, e.g:

2 With a partner work out a set of written instructions, suitable for a particular group, which do not refer to the pictures.

3 Ask a group of lowish-level students to do the same thing, giving them clear guidance as to what to do but not putting words in their mouth.

4 Compare your instructions with theirs, noting, for example, the use or non-use of phrasal verbs.

COMMENT
In discussion, it should be remembered that learners usually understand at a higher level than they speak or write.

3.3 Setting up pair and group work

One of the ways of giving the students more of the time they require to practise the language than is possible when you are 'up front' is by dividing the class into pairs or groups. The practice can be **controlled** or **cued**, as in a drill, or more **creative**, as in role-play or discussion, where the focus is communication rather than language practice. Having set up the practice, you can withdraw and monitor what is going on, giving help only when necessary.

As mentioned on p 32, pair work is frequently referred to as 'open' or 'closed', depending on whether just one pair is practising, usually across the class, to provide some sort of model for others ('open') or whether the whole class is divided into pairs and working for its own sake ('closed'). So, frequently, 'closed' pair practice is preceded by a small amount of 'open' pairs practice, in order to get it going. This process is particularly useful for many types of controlled practice.

Although almost any pair or group work takes the focus and the pressure off the teacher and gets the *students* doing, to succeed it has to be well-thought-through and well-organized.

1 Setting up pair work for different types of language activities

(a) Controlled Practice
    Where *you* decide on the language to be practised and control it accordingly, perhaps by the strict use of various prompts.

(b) Cued Practice

Where you decide on the language *areas* to be practised (e.g. 'Giving directions') but give the students a certain amount of freedom. The material you use should allow the students to make different language choices.

(c) Creative (or 'Free') Communication

Where you supply the motivation and the material but the students are free within the constraints of the communicative situation to say what they like.

Whatever form of practice you are employing, you must have a clear idea of what purpose it serves. It's no good giving pairs or groups a written dialogue to memorize and expect 'free' communication, except by accident; or character cards for role-play containing no language guidance and expect controlled practice.

Equally, you must organize the activity as sensibly as possible. It's no good setting up group work where only two of the group have anything to do or spend five minutes setting up group work and only give the groups enough to do for two minutes. (Usually, group work takes a long time to set up and do what it sets out to do. Pair work is often more suitable for short activities.)

Make sure that:

– your overall aims for the lesson necessitate the use of group work (i.e. you have a good reason for it)

– it extends logically out of previous lessons, or previous stages of the same lesson

– you allocate the right amount of time for the activity in your lesson plan

– you have enough materials for each pair or group

– where different pairs or groups have different tasks, these tasks will either take approximately the same time to complete or more capable groups are given the longer tasks.

How does pair work and group work vary according to the level of the class?

Low-level classes usually need more directive, 'up-front' teaching than higher-level classes; at the same time they find it tiring and boring if it goes on too long without a break (any activity with an elementary class should normally take no longer than twenty minutes). So, it is worth giving several opportunities in a class for paired practice simply to vary the activity. Of course, pairs practice also gives the students more valuable talking time.

However, group work at the low levels (both controlled practice and structured communication) needs careful planning and limited tasks: it can quickly defeat students without much language ability and force them into a worried silence.

At the higher levels, many classes are better conducted with large amounts of group work to enable the students to invest much more of themselves in the lesson.

Although low-level students will need more controlled practice than advanced students, they will still need opportunities to express themselves freely, just as advanced levels will need some controlled practice.

All levels can benefit from a couple of minutes of pair work before an activity to warm the class up and motivate it for what is to come (e.g. at lower levels you may give a quick revision drill, at higher levels you could ask students to give you ideas quickly which you put on the board without comment).

2 Planning the work

What size should the group be?

You need the right size for the right activity. A limited activity, with straightforward aims, will probably need pairs or small groups. If you want more ideas and you have more time you can organize larger groups. Be flexible, though. If you want four groups of five and you find you only have nineteen students, make do. Don't hold up your hands in horror!

How should it be constituted?

Sometimes you will find yourself wanting to decide on the exact composition of your groups and asking the following questions: *Do I want to 'stream' the levels? (What would be the aim/effect of this?); Do I want to mix up sexes?; Do I want to separate nationalities?; Do I want friends to work together?; Do I want people who never talk because they're on opposite sides of the room to sit together?*

Sometimes the groups can be constituted at random. Common techniques for doing this are:

– giving each student a number, 1, 2, 3, 4, 5, 1, 2, 3, 4, 5 etc. and then asking all the number 1's to sit together

– blindfolding as many people as there are to be groups who then in turn touch the people that are to be in their group (good fun, particularly with children!)

– dividing the class on the basis of horoscope groupings, likes/dislikes, colour of eyes, clothes etc.

– having as many pieces of string in the hand as there are to be pairs. Students take an end and find their partner

– giving out to each student at random a card with a word on. The students then have to go round and find words related to the subject matter e.g. *traffic light, road, car* would sit together.

What structure should it have?

You will need to ask the following questions: *Will the group manage itself and make its own structure?*; or *Will I say that each group must select a chairman and someone else to write down notes?* Possibly, *you* will decide on the roles of each member of the group.

3 Organizing the class

Explaining the task

Make sure that any pre-work needed for the pair or group has been done by you or the class. Possibly, get one pair or group to demonstrate. (For further considerations see pp 36–39).

Seating arrangements

Remember you may have to physically move people about the class so you will need to be both alert as to what is going on as well as positive in your approach. (For further considerations see pp 31–33).

Getting the timing right

You must get the timing right. If the activity lasts too long it'll drag. If it doesn't last long enough, it won't give any sense of satisfaction. If one group finishes early, give it a further activity, related to the task. Alternatively, you may wish to stop all the groups at that point. But don't let a group or a pair sit around with nothing to do. Generally, it's better to stop an activity when it's going well, provided it has achieved its broad aims, than to let it peter out. If there is a definite goal, like writing a story, the students might be encouraged to finish it after TP.

Students must know when they are to start and finish. Some teachers clap their hands, others shake a tambourine, some even blow a whistle! At the very least, you'll need to say something like *All right, everyone. That's it.*

4 After the activity

Evaluating and extending
It's often worth asking the students whether the activity was useful, what they learned etc. If you've asked them to *do* something like write an article, then *do something with it*, like pin it up, mark it, exchange it with other students, transfer the information to a graph etc. If the practice itself was the goal, then there may be no need.

Avoiding the use of the mother tongue in group work
In monolingual classes in particular, there's a danger that your students will use their mother tongue in discussions. It's not always possible to guarantee that they won't, even when you tell them not to, but you can make it easier for them to use English by:

– deciding where you place yourself in the classroom. The groups nearest you are more likely to use English than those further away. So, take an interest in what each group is doing and move around so that groups have less chance of switching back into their own language.

– making the work task-oriented. If the final product has to be in English, whether it is producing a story or a book report or just answering comprehension questions, a greater use of English is ensured.

– limiting the time available in practice-oriented work. It is better to have a shorter time than is strictly necessary for full practice of the language. Nothing is more likely to send students into their mother tongue than having time to spare at the end of group work.

– making sure that the students have the English to do what you ask. You might find it helpful to pre-teach some words and phrases.

– assigning roles. If everyone knows what they must do they are more likely to do it in English. Giving someone the role of 'language monitor' – someone to make sure English is used in the group – is possible with large classes particularly in schools where students are used to other students being given some authority.

Finally, don't be too *afraid* of students using their mother tongue. A lot depends on your attitude, although it's worth remembering that if you are doing group work as an alternative to whole-class work then even if only two people are using English simultaneously you have doubled the amount of student talk for that time.

Exercises

Ex. 1

AIM
To promote discussion of the uses and organization of pair or group work. This

exercise consists of a number of discussion points and should be carried out in pairs and groups. As a final discussion point, it is worth looking at the size of group you prefer to work in yourself for certain activities.

PROCEDURE

1 Draw up a list of classroom activities (e.g. interviews, drills, dialogue practice, role-play etc.)

2 Discuss which are suitable for pair work and which are better with larger groups.

3 Discuss ways in which those which seem best suited to pair work could be adapted to larger groups and vice versa.

4 Write down the organizational roles that students might be assigned within a group (e.g. rapporteur, chairman, secretary etc.)

5 Discuss which of the activities from the first list might require the assignment of roles like these.

6 Select an exercise from a course book and discuss how it could be dealt with in pairs, threes and larger groups. Discuss organizational roles that students might need to be assigned for each of these possibilities.

7 Discuss the problems of an odd number of students for pair work and how you can deal with it.

3.4 Monitoring

When students are engaged in an activity independent of you, you may need to keep an ear on what they are saying or glance at what they are writing. Your aim will be to assess how well they are performing the task and evaluate particular language strengths or weaknesses. Whether you help or correct will depend on the task and what effect it will have.

Monitoring what the students are doing is just as important a skill as teaching. Because the focus isn't on you, there is a temptation to believe that you aren't doing your job. However, giving the students appropriate tasks, knowing when and how to leave them alone and providing suitable follow-up requires sensitivity, intelligence and confidence. It is the show-off or the nervous teacher who hasn't a clear idea of why he has set the task that wants to interfere and mess it up.

An important aspect of monitoring is the discipline often necessary for less well-motivated students and monolingual classes, where the temptation might be to talk away unnecessarily in the mother-tongue. Often just being in the room and giving the students the *feeling* they are being supervised is enough.

Group work

The teaching aim of group work is often to encourage fluent, uninterrupted communication, even when the aim for the students might be to produce something like a dialogue or a story, so:

1 Stand back

Once you have set up the activity (see pp 41–44) allow a short time for the students to get on with it. This will give you a chance to see which groups seem to be working satisfactorily and which are having problems. It'll also give all the students a chance to get into the activity before you offer help to any one group.

Don't be too concerned if a group doesn't seem to be too sure of itself at first; some groups take time to get going.

2 Quickly check
If you decide to go round the groups, it's worth going to each one very quickly just to glance at what they're doing. This reminds them that you are there and allows you to check that they are doing what you intended.

3 Don't interrupt, unless:
   – the group has misunderstood what it is supposed to be doing (so put it right),

   – you are participating as part of a group (not as the teacher on high),

   – some of the groups seem to be on the verge of finishing (so either give them something else to do or stop the whole activity),

   – the group you are with seems to be a long way behind (so jolly it up),

   – you are asked to by the group (they may properly need some advice, but don't let them get too dependent on you).

4 Spread your attention
If you concentrate on one particular group, they will feel cramped by your presence and you won't get a very clear idea of how well the rest of the class is doing; the rest of the class, apart from feeling neglected, may well start drifting away from the activity without you realizing.

5 Don't correct, unless:
   – the aim of the activity is controlled language practice and it's breaking down,

   – a student asks you to. Occasionally, students will want you to help them say something correctly but don't hover so close to any one group that they get self-conscious and frightened of making mistakes. If you do have to get involved, do it discreetly, by crouching at the level of the group and allowing individuals to turn away from the rest of the group and talk to you. If the students need a lot of help and correction then the chances are that the task is inappropriate and/or beyond their capabilities.
   Sometimes, you might decide to only correct a certain *kind* of error.

6 Be easily accessible
All the groups should feel they have equal access to you and are being supervised equally.

7 If you need to feed in ideas
It is often better to subvert one member of the group and suggest to him a possible change of direction, rather than interrupt the flow of the whole group.

8 Jolly them, if necessary
At the beginning, groups often need encouragement to get them going; sometimes a group may start to lose interest. Always be positive. Never suggest that the activity could be less than totally useful.

9 Take notes
Although in group work you are often concerned to show students that you are more interested in *what* they are doing than in evaluating their language performance, specific problems do arise. Things may not be communicated adequately or there may be consistent and significant grammatical errors that should be noted. If there is a problem common to most of the group, then this

might be the focus of a future lesson, probably without any reference to the session in which you noticed it. Individual problems can either be dealt with face-to-face after TP (not always possible) or via a note handed to each student after the lesson. The note could contain something like: *These are some mistakes you made. Can you correct them? If not, see me* or *Here are some things you said and the things you should have said* or *Can you do the exercise on p x of* ____ *to practise* ____? Make sure you either provide notes for all the students (fairly easy in a small class) or make it clear you'll be getting round to each student before the course ends.

(Section 2.3 Position and movement should be read in conjunction with this section as well as Section 2.4 Attention spread and Section 2.5 Using the voice.)

Pair work

Most of what you need to consider when monitoring group work also applies to pair work, except that work in pairs can often be closer to the more controlled kind of work that might be set for individuals. This means that if, for example, the pair work is of the 'dialogue practice' kind, then you can correct more tightly.

Other differences between monitoring pairs and groups are:
– A pair is more likely to stop work when you approach than a group.

– In pair work it is easier for you to take one half of the activity for a part of the time to show the students what it is about.

Individual reading and writing tasks

Since students are individuals with different capabilities, different speeds and different work rates, the tasks set very often have to be individual. If all individuals are doing the same task, particular care will have to be taken as to when they will finish so you may have to have supplementary tasks up your sleeve to feed in to the quicker students.

With written work, giving help and correcting individuals will usually be on an individual basis so:
– make sure everyone has enough to do before you go round

– be discreet in your approach (i.e. not too loud or disruptive)

– try and be encouraging

– consider whether you will dot around the class unpredictably or move from one student to the next down the row (consider what the effect will be of either approach)

– make sure everyone has *some* attention.

If you've set a reading task, help might be given over the meanings of words and phrases or by showing how to use an English-English dictionary (in order to help the students do the task by themselves).

If it's a writing task, in some countries you might be showing some students not familiar with the Roman script *how* to write, helping others with spelling and phrasing, correcting and suggesting better ways of expressing things, perhaps even organizing some students' ideas.

Exercises

Ex. 1

AIM
To highlight the difference between errors and slips of the tongue.

PROCEDURE
1 Make a recording of students working freely on a task in pairs or groups, or ask your tutor if there is a pre-recorded one available.

2 Listen to it and divide the mistakes into two categories:
   (a) Those which will need working on

   (b) Slips of the tongue which can be ignored

3 Pass the list to a partner and see if his list agrees with yours.

Ex. 2

AIM
To show that immediate correction can lead to the teacher not focusing on the most appropriate areas.

PROCEDURE
1 From a fairly advanced group, take three pieces of fairly long written work.

2 With a pair of scissors, cut the work up according to what you think each student may have achieved after, for example, five minutes, ten minutes and fifteen minutes.

3 Distribute the first five minutes' work among three others in your group. They must decide which three items in their piece most need correction.

4 Distribute the second five minutes' work. They must now decide which three items most need correction from the two parts (after five and ten minutes) together.

5 Distribute the last five minutes' work and ask them to decide on the three items which most need correction from all three parts together.

6 Each should now compare lists and ask:
   (a) How many mistakes or errors occurred in the first five minutes?

   (b) How many were common to each student?

   (c) Which were the most in need of correction overall?

3.5 Using students' names

You can indicate who is to answer a question or respond to an instruction by eye contact (see pp 7–8) or gesture (see pp 10–13). Sometimes, however, it is better to use the students' names: it involves them in the class more closely and gives them the feeling that the teacher sees them as individuals, particularly important in a large class. Our name is terribly important to us; none of us like it when someone gets it wrong, or pronounces it incorrectly or calls us by our first name when it's more usual on that occasion to use a more formal type of address.

So:
– learn your students' names right from the beginning.

Do make an open and obvious effort. It is not essentially a difficult task but if the effort you make at the beginning is obvious to the students they will be more forgiving when you make mistakes. You can help yourself by:
– getting the students to introduce each other to you and then going round the class in random order two or three times, saying the names aloud to check that you remember. If you do this at the end of the first couple of lessons as well as the beginning it can act as useful revision.

– keeping a register. This will probably be required of you anyway, but checking a register openly at the beginning of a class is a useful reminder for you, particularly when you only see the class once or twice a week. It also serves as a good focusing device at the beginning of lessons.

– associating names with physical features. This is a useful trick with the occasional student whose name you find it impossible to remember, e.g. Jesus – brown hair, Maria – plaits. Say them to yourself two or three times. However, keep them to yourself as sometimes the physical feature could be one that the student doesn't want attention drawn to!

– using names consciously in the first few lessons to fix them in your mind. It's usually better to ask a student to keep his reply for a few seconds while you recall the name rather than allow the situation to continue where you can't remember his name. There comes a point where you should have learned the names and it becomes embarrassing to ask.

– in periods of pair or group work, checking the names to yourself.

– using name cards. Ask each student to write his name on a card and stand it on the desk in front of him. It's better if you can supply the cards yourself.

– drawing up a seating plan and keeping it with the class register. Make sure you alter it if the students change places though!

– using the return of written homework to help you remember. Trying to recall the student's face to mind when you're marking it is a help too!
Finally, if you can't remember a name, admit it and ask the person openly. It's better for you to seem to be not very good at learning names than for students to be left feeling their names are not very important. If necessary make sure they know each other's names too. You can do this by:
– writing their names on the board, perhaps asking them for the spelling

– saying your name, then asking the student nearest you to say both your name and his name, then asking the student next to him to say his name, the other student's name and your name, and so on round the class. It's quite a feat of memory for the later students, so it can be fun with everyone concerned to make sure their name is remembered correctly!

– particularly if you are teaching adults, be careful to use the right name. Ask the students what they want to be called, but it's usually better if you use a similar part of the name for each student (either all first names or all family names).

In adult classes, some will expect you to use their family names and some their first names. Usually, if a student sees everyone else is on first-name terms, though, he will accept it as a convention for that classroom. However, it may sound strange to him if he went to a school where everyone was addressed by their family name. In adult classes, many teachers prefer to use first names because it implies a friendly, informal attitude and a more equal relationship between the teacher and the students.

– if you don't speak their language very well, get them to teach you to pronounce their names correctly. You'll be spending a lot of time correcting their pronunciation, so you should be prepared to put in the effort to pronounce things correctly too!

– equally, if you are a native speaker of English teach them your name and how to pronounce it. Make it clear which part of *your* name you expect them to use: it might tell the students what sort of relationship you expect with them.

Using names when asking questions and giving instructions

The student's name is best used after the question has been asked or the instruction given. It is sometimes more effective to pause first:

T:　*Come on. Why did they go to London?*
　　(pause during which teacher retains all the students' attention with eye contact)
　　Ummmmm . . . Johannes?
S:　*To see the Queen.*

The reason for the pause is that it gives all the students the chance to work out the answer before they hear it from one of the students. Without such a pause, students may only get as far as hearing the question; if they know someone else is going to do the work they may make less effort. If the person who is to answer is nominated before the question is asked (T: *Johannes, why did they go to London?*), they may even panic and switch off without hearing the question.

– Be firm. Insist that the person you nominate should answer the question if at all possible. Try and hold back the others with a hand gesture if necessary. Nobody wants to dampen the enthusiasm of a lively class who want to shout out every answer or put a nervous student on the spot, but lack of control here can quickly irritate those students who are slow off the mark and don't get many opportunities to contribute.

Exercises

Ex. 1

AIM
To practise name-learning techniques.

PROCEDURE
1　Ask your group to each assume a foreign name.

2　Get the group to throw a soft ball or a screwed-up piece of paper from one to the other at random with the person throwing it saying his assumed name.

3　After a short time, get the group to change to saying the name of the person they are throwing the ball to.

4　Go round the class and check that everyone knows everybody else's name.

Ex. 2

AIM
To highlight the different uses of names in different cultures.

PROCEDURE
1 Find three students, if possible from very different cultures and language backgrounds (e.g. a Japanese, an Arab and a Mexican).

2 Find out their full names, how they are spelt and how they are pronounced.

3 Find out which name they use and when and whether any title goes with them (Mr/Mrs etc.)

4 Ask them in turn *What does your mother/sister/uncle/best friend/teacher/ doctor/boss/traffic policeman call you?*

5 Compare with others who have done a similar exercise.

COMMENT
This exercise clearly only . works as it stands in a multilingual classroom. However, a similar exercise can be done in a monolingual setting by you, the trainee, and your peers, listing the different names used for you in different circumstances, e.g. what your mother/boss/friends/colleagues/near-total strangers etc. call you. Decide what degree of latitude you would allow with each category and what the implications would be. For example, if your father called you Mr . . . would you respond, would you expect him to be angry. etc.? How would you react if the students in a children's class called you John?

Ex. 3

AIM
To check on the appropriate use of names in class.

PROCEDURE
1 Observe a short part of a lesson.

2 Using as a checklist a diagram of the class, make a note of which students' names the teacher used and when he used them.

3 Make a note of whether names were used at the end or the beginning of instructions and questions.

4 Discuss with peers the teacher's use of names, including pronunciation.

3.6 Starting the lesson

If you are teaching children in the state system, punctuality should be less of a problem but asking anything from half a dozen to thirty adults to be on time, in their seats and ready for a lesson to begin, is usually, if they are coming to the lessons voluntarily, to ask for the impossible. Just as we have to wait for buses or for a conversation with a colleague to end, so do they. The major difference between us and most adult students is that we have to be there for the lesson to begin, they often don't.

Wherever you are teaching, if possible, be in the classroom before the students, to set up aids, put things on the board, try out the tape recorder, and check seating arrangements. Aim to begin the class at the appointed time and not

just to be present in the classroom. This will:
– show the students that you have a positive attitude towards the lesson; it will make you look professional and inspire confidence

– encourage them to arrive on time; they won't want to miss anything valuable.

It might also discourage the teacher before you from over-running!

The students will take their habits from you. If you start late, so the students will arrive late. Five minutes out of forty-five is approximately ten per cent of their time. Consistently, it would make for a much reduced course.

How should you deal with late arrivals when they are adults and perhaps paying for their classes?

Some such students are bound to arrive late, no matter how positive your attitude
Your options are:
1 To exclude them
This is a bit extreme and rather disciplinarian. If they are paying for the classes it is better to try to motivate the students to want to come on time. The latecomer should be as genuinely upset as you that he is arriving late. If a student is disrupting the group by coming late and the group is unable to apply pressure of its own in order to get him there on time, then you might best give a warning with a.time limit attached (e.g. *If you arrive more than ten minutes late next time, you won't be allowed in*). Be sensitive and flexible, though, if the lateness is unavoidable.

2 To stop the class and explain to the latecomer what is going on
This, however, involves holding up the rest of the class for one student and may encourage persistent late arrival.

3 To allow them to creep in and sit down quietly
Probably the best solution for most adults. Acknowledge their arrival, if only with a nod, and when there is a break in the lesson for a change of activity, either briefly explain, or ask another student to briefly explain, what they have missed.
Some teachers prefer to state their policy on late arrivals at the beginning of a course. If you do that, you have to be consistent and stick to it.

In general, if you have a persistent problem you will need to increase the students' motivation if you are to get them to the classes earlier. One way which might be worth trying is to have, say, a five-minute vocabulary slot or a pronunciation exercise at the beginning of the lesson – in fact, any semi-self-enclosed exercise which you know the later arrivals will be sorry to miss. If you launch immediately into an activity on which most of the lesson depends, then it will cause problems if they are not all there. Equally, if you simply spend the first five minutes giving back homework or dealing with individual problems then there won't be any real compulsion to turn up on time – the students know they will get their homework back anyway, and the lesson won't seem to start until that is over. On the other hand, if your late arrivals are genuine and large in number then it might in fact be best to spend time doing something like that.

What if there are new arrivals to the class?

If new arrivals arrive late on their first day then stop the class and gently introduce them to the rest of the group or get the others to introduce themselves to the new arrivals, asking perhaps a few informal questions to find out something about them. Don't make too much of it or pressurize the students unnecessarily. Equally, don't expect too much in terms of the amount of language work you can give the new arrivals until they have had time to settle down.

How should you spend the time before the class starts?

Before the time appointed for the start of the lesson you might find yourself waiting with several of the students. It is an ideal opportunity to:

1 Socialize
i.e. to talk to the students individually. You could find out what English newspapers they read or if they saw such and such a film. If they are children, you might ask them if their parents speak English or, if you are teaching overseas, whether they have been to Britain.

Let them get to know you. If you are British, tell them something about your personal life in Britain. If you are not, you might tell them about your reasons for learning and liking English, about your English-speaking friends, or holidays you have had in Britain or the United States; anything which will arouse their interest in and make more personal their English work. It is the time when rapport, sympathy and confidence are really established.

2 Give back homework
You might discuss individual problems and the way a student is approaching his studies.

How can you make the starting point of a lesson clear?

The students need to know that they are to come together as a group and start work. You usually need to supply a signal such as:

– tapping chalk or a pen on the desk audibly

– clapping your hands loud and clear

– closing the door

– saying *Right, OK* or something similar.

Scanning the whole class will also help to focus everyone's attention on you.

Should you announce what the lesson is about?

Some lessons can be started straight away without explanation. Either the students know what to do and they can get on with it or with some language presentations you might simply lead the students inductively into what they are going to practise. For other lessons, it's often useful for the students to have a clear idea as to the aim of the lesson and what they are going to do (e.g. you might say *Today we're going to practise listening to English people speaking; then we're going to the lab. to practise saying those phrases we learnt last week* or alternatively you might write the topic on the board: *Apologizing to a friend*. Such explanations and titles need to be brief and easily understood by the students.)

3.7 Finishing the lesson

The last activity is the one that suffers if the timing of the other activities has gone astray. This can obviously be a problem if it is to be the highlight of the lesson or if homework is to be based on it. So good timing of *all* stages of a lesson is essential if the students are not to go away with the feeling that the lesson finished badly for them.

What's more, it's no good finishing at exactly lunch-time when the lunch queues are beginning to build up and then expect the students to wait attentively while you set homework and make announcements. You must allow time for these in the class.

How can you make the finishing point clear?

As with 'How can you make the starting point of a lesson clear?' on p 53 the students need a signal to indicate when they are to finish the final activity, e.g. *Well done. Close your books* or *Good. Look at me.* Maintain the class's attention by looking at them and speaking in a firm voice. You need to prevent the students drifting away mentally and physically.

Summarizing and evaluating

– Some lessons need a brief summary of what has gone on. If the timing of the lesson is wrong it may usefully be lengthened to fill out these final moments (e.g. by eliciting it from the students) or shortened if the bell goes!

– Telling the students what'll happen next time may also help to motivate them to return.

– Asking them what they found useful and what they didn't find useful not only fills gaps; it also provides vital feedback on your lessons.

Is it necessary to set homework?

Yes, usually, because it:
– provides the students with important opportunities to work in a directed way at their own pace outside the pressures of the classroom

– can consolidate or extend the classwork, if set correctly. This frequently, but not always, means the whole group should get the same homework. Alternatively it may be set according to individual requirements.

For 'whole-class' homework:
– make sure you have all the students' attention when setting it (see pp 7–8, 20–22, 23–24)

– clearly set the task, perhaps give an example, or start it on the board. Always check the students have understood what you expect them to do (see pp 36–39)

– make sure the students have their task written down before they leave, to act as a reminder

– if you set homework early in the lesson because it arose at the end of a particular activity, provide a last-minute reminder before the students leave.

For individualized homework:
– make sure the task is appropriate to the individual, that there is time for him to complete it, and that you follow it up

– allow time either before the lesson or during a break, or after the lesson, to set it. Make sure that if you set individualized homework *all* students are given some at some time during the TP.

Making announcements

Announcements are frequently best made at the end since the students will take the information away fresh in their minds.

Again, before making them:
– make sure you have all the students' attention

– give them clearly and understandably and check the students have understood. At advanced levels, just looking at their reactions may be enough.

Don't forget to fully exploit, through questions and comments, any notices you may wish to put up in English.

Farewells and socializing

Farewells are the final signal that the students can pack up and go. Make sure you say goodbye naturally; it's a good opportunity for the students to learn how to do it!

If you have a couple of minutes spare before they go, it's well worth asking them about their countries (if you are doing TP in Britain) or what books they're going to read in English. It creates rapport and helps extend their interest in learning English outside the classroom.

Exercises

Ex. 1

AIM
To highlight the structure of the beginnings and ends of lessons.

PROCEDURE
1 Observe as many lessons as possible for their beginnings and ends (say the first ten and last ten minutes of lessons).

2 Categorize each beginning and end in terms of the following activities:
 A Greeting the group
 B Greeting individuals
 C Socializing with the group
 D Socializing with individuals
 E Semi-enclosed 'waiting' exercises
 F Setting homework
 G Returning homework
 H Announcements
 I Checking
 J Time-filling
 You may need to add other categories.

3 Compare the beginnings and ends in terms of their appropriateness and success.

3.8 The group: its dynamics and the needs of the individuals within it

The teacher's attitude

It is not only the characters of the individual students and the way they relate to each other that determines how the group behaves but also the teacher's attitude. If you believe you are going to lose control of a group you probably will. If you feel that the material you are using is boring you are likely to end up with a bored class. So:

1 Be positive about the material you are using
   You are probably more critical than the class anyway. If the appearance of a text is not quite up to standard, (even though of course you should always aim for it to be) don't apologize for it. Emphasize how good it is for language practice or for whatever purpose you are using it.

2 Don't prejudge a class
   Other teachers' opinions are worth listening to but relationships with teachers vary and it's as well to assume that a bad class need not necessarily be bad with you and a good class, even if well-motivated, can be spoiled by poor guidance.

3 Look as if you enjoy your job
   A lack of enthusiasm and interest can only be a deterrent for those hungry to learn.

4 Don't assume that students share your low times
   Friday afternoons are notoriously bad for getting students to work hard. Frequently, however, this is more the teacher's feelings about the end of the week than the students' – particularly if they only come to the school for, say, two hours a week.

In the final analysis, it is more the teacher who creates the working atmosphere of a class. If you over-dominate, the students tend to invest little of themselves in the class and you are likely to have problems of discipline. On the other hand, if you fail to direct the students when necessary, and give firm guidance, they are likely to make an ineffective working group and suffer feelings of frustration and insecurity.

The same balance of participation and control should also be reflected in what you teach. In the end, you decide, but your decision must be based on both what you know the students need as well as what they say they need.

How do you balance what individual students in a class need with what the class as a whole needs?

At the beginners' level, it is possible to construct a course that all students find relevant. In multinational classes the distinct differences of personality, culture and educational background do matter in terms of how the group works together but the students in the main assent to a common purpose (in Britain, this may be to help them survive in an alien language environment; overseas, in monolingual classes, you are more likely needed to help students learn the language for vocational reasons or because it forms part of their general education).

At this level, too, the differences in how well the students perform in the main language skills of listening, speaking, reading and writing are perhaps less important, except in multinational classes where, for example, you may have some students who can write in the Roman script and some who can't.

As they improve, so all students are less satisfied with a blanket approach, particularly adults on a more intensive course, not only because their abilities become increasingly diverse but because they feel that their personal interests and the reasons they are learning the language should start to determine far more noticeably the content of the lessons.

As a result, even though there is usually enough a class has in common to be able to construct a common syllabus for at least part of the time, more time has to be given to individuals to be able to work on their own and more time given over to individuals by the teacher.

What can be done on TP?

Despite the constraints, for any level:

1 Plan your lessons to reconcile individual needs with group needs. Don't choose material or focus on points that only one or two students will find of interest.

2 During the class, don't focus disproportionately on individual problems, such as pronunciation difficulties in a multinational class, when you are commanding the attention of the whole group. Deal with them during breaks or group work.

3 Try and set small individual tasks geared to each student. As well as providing you with the necessary discipline of considering individual needs, it can provide extra motivation for the students and make them realize you take an interest in them.

4 Encourage the group to establish a positive working identity. Get students to help each other with problems, make suggestions for books to read and so on. Organizing out-of-class activities, such as small parties, can help to build relationships.

5 Spread your own interest. Don't spend too long on those students you like better than others or those who force their attention on you. Include everyone on as equal a basis as possible. This should apply to the breaks as much as to the classroom.

6 Avoid forming an opinion of the class, either as to its level or its interests, on the basis of one or two individuals.

Although for more advanced levels considering the individual becomes crucial in deciding what to teach, it is worth bearing in mind that in the end *every* class is made up of individuals. Students can learn from the knowledge and skills of other individual students just as they can learn from a teacher working on, say, the oral problems of a single student. But it is a question of balance. When individual attention ceases to be valuable for everyone and concentration wanders it should cease to be part of the work involving the whole class. Perhaps time will need to be set aside for individual attention while the group is getting on with something else.

How can you achieve balance when planning a lesson?

For a class to be effective, students need to be engaged in different ways, in varying amounts, throughout. Obviously, when some students are speaking others will be listening, and yet no one student can speak all the time if speaking is the aim of the others too. Ultimately, then, it is your job to make sure that most students are productive (speaking or writing) and receptive (listening or reading) on a more or less equal basis in the course of a lesson or in the course of a series of lessons.

When planning your lesson, then:

1 Make sure it has overall shape, with one activity as far as possible leading into the next. For example, a presentation and practice context might form the basis for a role-play. Or a role-play might highlight language problems that you then go on to deal with remedially.

2 Balance and integrate the language skills as much as you can, and place the emphasis where your students most need it. If possible, let the writing come out of the reading and the speaking come out of the listening.

3 Recognize that different activities make different demands on the students and try to arrange it so that an easy activity is followed by a more difficult one.

The sort of questions you might find yourself asking are: *Should I start the lesson or finish the lesson with that game*? *What will be the effect*? *If I give writing first how will I get them to speak afterwards*? *What happens if some don't finish as quickly as others*?

Further considerations when teaching

1 Remember different students have different learning styles; some may actually need the language explained to them a bit more than others; some might like to rely on dictionaries. Don't be too dogmatic about the way they learn. Accommodate their styles as much as possible into your general approach.

2 Pace your lessons so that everyone can keep up with them or add an activity to free you to help slower students.

3 Remember that although you influence what happens in the class it is often more a case of 'managing learning' than teaching; it is the pace the students work at that needs to be measured, not the pace you work at. You can exhaust yourself with a dazzling array of new ideas you are determined to try out and then realize the students are doing hardly anything. In fact, with some well-planned and well set-up activities you might need to do very little in the classroom.

What do you do with 'problem' students?

Looked at one way, all individual students are problems because learning a language is difficult. In a class sense, however, those personalities that stick out – the sullen, the impossible to control, the quiet, the over-enthusiastic – will have to be dealt with if they interfere with the learning effectiveness of the group.

Often students who are not a problem for you are a problem for other students. They are not always easy to detect although it occasionally comes out during informal conversations.

At least with small groups or adults, dealing with students like this need not be a heavy-handed affair:

– Often hinting that you recognize the trouble in front of everyone is enough but be tactful or humorous and try and win the problem student round.

– Sometimes a friendly chat helps, particularly when the real problem is that the student feels he's not being acknowledged enough by you. Listen to him. He might have a genuine complaint!

– Another tactic is to put the students into carefully constructed group work where their sense of responsibility is essential for its success. Often the problem is that students don't feel responsible enough for the progress of the class.

If in doubt, ask for advice from more experienced teachers. The problem may be a common one for which a simple solution exists. Although students frequently sort out problems for each other, don't ignore them or hope they'll go away. If the students seem to be sorting a problem out unaided leave it, but if not, intervene. It will only get worse.

If you are teaching large groups of reluctant children and you have no real control over the organization of the classes, you might have problems of discipline which are not the result of mere exuberance. Often if this is the case and you can't sort them out, it is essential you ask for advice from someone else in the school.

Exercises

Ex. 1

AIM
To focus on some of the ways in which individual students can be catered for within a group.

PROCEDURE
1 Find a group of adult language learners to help you.

2 Devise a questionnaire to help discover why they need English, how they learnt it in the past and how they think they should learn it in the future. Keep it short and easily understandable. (The sort of questions you might ask are: *What things will you write in English when you have finished the course? Have you used translation in your learning of English? Do you think this is a good way of learning?* etc.)

3 Work out a ten-hour timetable for the group based on what you have discussed, taking into account the needs of the group as a whole and including some work which allows you to give individuals different tasks and different roles.

4 Make a list of activities (preferably those which students can do by themselves) that could be given to each individual to carry out on his own either during the class if time were allocated or *after* the class and some activities which students can work on together in groups.

Ex. 2

AIM
To show how different teachers can view the same group in different ways.

PROCEDURE
1 Observe a class which is unfamiliar to you, if possible one containing a fairly 'free' activity.

2 Make notes on the more prominent students and the least prominent students in relation to their personalities, their approach to the class, their learning habits, their relationship with the other students and so on.

3 Show the opinions to the class teacher and discuss the extent to which he agrees.

COMMENT
This comparison can yield very fruitful discussion, particularly if your comments are committed to paper and, in the case of a discrepancy of views, both sides are fully argued.

4 Teaching Strategies

Introduction

This section includes:
- an introductory section on the writing of lesson plans

- brief reference to the principles behind the approaches frequently used in mainstream EFL teaching

- step-by-step practical guidance in how to employ the approaches effectively.

It does not include:
- reference to the theories of learning which have led to these approaches

- description of the many ways, other than group work, that students can learn independently of the teacher.

While the intention is to be helpful to trainees who have had little experience in the classroom, other teachers in training and practising teachers might find these pages a useful synopsis of the main strategies currently widely in use. The focus, however, is specifically on the TP situation and the demands it makes.

4.1 Writing lesson plans

The writing of lesson plans has three important functions:
(a) Writing down what you expect the students to be able to do by the end of the lesson, and what you intend to do to make that possible, helps you to think logically through the stages in relation to the time you have available.

(b) Having something to refer to in the lesson helps keep you on target (although it should never prevent you from responding to the needs of the moment, if necessary).

(c) Suitably amended after the lesson, a lesson plan acts as a record of what the class has done and might form the basis for a future lesson plan with a similar class.
Broadly speaking, any lesson plan can be divided into three areas: AIMS, METHODS and MATERIALS REQUIRED.

1 Aims

Questions you need to ask are:
What do I expect the students to be able to do by the end of the time available?
What will I do in order to make that possible?
How will I break up the time into main stages?
What will be the aim of each main stage?
How will the main stages be linked?
An outline lesson plan, in abstract, might look like this:

LESSON PLAN
Learning Aims for the Students: to be able to use the past simple more fluently and have improved listening skills.

Teaching Aims: to give further practice to the past simple and develop listening skills through a taped dialogue.

Time Available: 55 minutes

Stage 1:
Aim: Improve listening skills (20 minutes)

Stage 2:
Aim: Give controlled oral fluency practice using past simple
(10 minutes)

Stage 3:
Aim: Give semi-controlled fluency practice using past simple
(10 minutes)

Stage 4:
Aim: Give 'freer' practice of above (15 minutes)

2 Methods

Questions you need to ask are:
Which overall method will I use?
What series of steps will implement it?
The above plan would therefore be refined:

LESSON PLAN
Stage 1:
Method: Lead students to comprehension of dialogue
Step 1: Set scene; relate students personally to the topic
2: Set focusing questions
3: Play tape
4: Follow up focusing questions
5: Ask further simple gist questions
6: Break up dialogue into segments
7: Ask more difficult and more detailed questions to check comprehension
etc.

Stage 2:
Method: Practise pronunciation of past tenses from tape
Step 1: Stop tape before examples of past tense and try to elicit them
2: Choral repetition
3: Individual repetition
etc.

Stage 3:
Method: Drill using 'infinitive' prompts. Students convert into past tense
Step 1: Recap on context in dialogue
2: Choral/individual repetition of model
etc.

```
Stage 4:
Method:  Role-play
   Step 1:  Using same context, bring out characteristics of two of the
              characters
         etc.
```

3 Materials required

The question you need to ask is:
Which aids do I need to achieve my aims?
These can be included on the lesson plan.

```
LESSON PLAN
(. . . as above . . .)
Stage 1:  taped dialogue
 (i)  pictures to highlight context
(ii)  tape
(iii)  tape recorder
 etc.
```

Alternatively a lesson plan might be drawn up under the following headings:
1 The language you intend to present, practise, revise or focus on in a text

Without being completely familiar with the meaning, the form and the use of the language you are dealing with, you cannot hope to be confident in your execution of the lesson. It is important to be familiar with not only the language of any text, whether a dialogue, a listening text or a written text, but also with the language of any drills or questions you intend to ask. There is a necessary element of unpredictability in the language used in the course of any lesson, but you should still try to predict the language that might occur.

2 The activities that the students will be involved in
At first during TP the tendency might be for you to be overconcerned with what *you* will be doing during the lesson, particularly if you're doing 'up front' teaching. However, really it is what the students are doing that is most important. So:
– be clear in your own mind as to *what* you want them to, before you decide on *how* you are going to get them to do it. (Only then add notes like *pair work, listening, question and answer* or *individual writing*.)

– indicate the link between the different activities. (Write things like *students listening to find answers to questions; the answers form the basis of individual writing task* or *students listen; then they repeat the questions and answer; then they ask and answer in pairs*).

3 Reminders
These are basically instructions to yourself (e.g. if you have difficulty in, say, controlling the level of your language, you may script sections of the lesson, or it may take the form of simple reminders of announcements that you have to make.) It is also useful to write notes to yourself to help you correct faults that you know about in your teaching (e.g. *stop talking; zero the tape counter; question **then** name!*)

How neatly should a lesson plan be written down?

Ultimately how you put your lesson plan down on paper is up to you, since you are the one who has to interpret it both during the lesson and later on when you refer back. However, it should be legible and there are two kinds of legibility required. The first is for just before the lesson begins, when you want quickly to run over the aims of the lesson again, or you want to check the details of something (e.g. the lines of a dialogue). Normal-size writing is appropriate for this. However, there will be other things that you will need to check in 'the heat of the lesson' and if you don't want to appear to be reading from a script you will probably want to just glance down at your lesson plan on the desk. This means that you will need to be able to read these items from about three feet away or more. They need to be bigger, possibly with sections written with different coloured felt-tipped pens. Models for language practice purposes are also well worth underlining or putting in boxes to highlight them.

A lesson plan is rarely written perfectly clearly first time so count on making a couple of drafts before you write out the final copy. That will make sure that your plan makes sense when you come back to it in the future.

Should you write lesson plans in a book or keep them loose-leaf?

Some teachers prefer to keep their lesson plans in a book, with one book for each class they teach. In this way the plans are always kept in sequence and form an easy-to-refer-to neat record of the classes. If you do this, you may like to leave alternate pages blank when you are writing your plans so that after the lesson you can write in comments on the success or otherwise of each part of the lesson. This could form the basis of a very useful teaching diary (see p 16). You can of course do this if you write each plan on a separate sheet of paper and then file it afterwards. The loose-leaf format is easier to handle in class but there is a greater risk of plans getting lost or filed out of order.

Are there things about the students and the classroom circumstances that should go on a plan?

Yes. It's worth noting at the top of every plan things like the date, the level of the class, the coursebook they are using, the size of the class and something about its composition, especially if it is multinational. Sometimes it's worth making a note of your intended seating arrangements as well. You might also make a note of problems, language or disciplinary, that could occur with individuals during any of the activities.

What format should be used?

This is largely a matter of personal style and the type of lesson you are giving. However, by looking at other parts of this book you can see some examples (see e.g. pp 71,73–4.)

Two further examples are as follows:

Example 1

Aim:

Learning Aim: to be able to use, when prompted, *I've got* as a means of expressing family relationships.

Teaching Aim: to present and give controlled practice to the form *I've got.*

LANGUAGE	ACTIVITIES	NOTES
Questions		
Look at the picture	Students answer questions	ASK QUESTIONS
Where is it?	on context/situation	RANDOMLY
Who's this man?		
What's his job?		
What does he do ?		
Who's the other man?		
Dialogue	Students	
In the immigration dept.	– listen	
A: What about your family?	– answer general	CORRECT
B: Well, I've got a wife.	comprehension questions	PRONUNCIATION
A: Yes.		ESPECIALLY
And I've got two children.	– repeat line by line	CONTRACTIONS
	'Open' pairs practice	
	'Closed' pairs practice	

Example 2

Teaching Aim: to introduce students to concept of three different pronunciation forms of the regular past simple, give controlled practice and check understanding.

(1) PLAY TAPE OF 3 EXAMPLES:
   He watched TV last night.
   They wanted a Ferrari.
   I saved £100 last year.

(2) DRAW 3 COLUMNS ON BOARD
   ASK STUDENTS TO REPEAT VERBS AND WRITE IN COLUMNS

(3) GIVE OTHER EXAMPLES:
   carried   earned   walked
   worried   served   talked

(4) STUDENTS SUGGEST COLUMNS THEY SHOULD GO IN

Finally, on any lesson plan, don't write down too much detail. You need to make sense of it in the lesson!

Exercises

Ex. 1

AIM

To help ensure that your lesson plans work towards your stated aim.

PROCEDURE

1 Retrieve a lesson plan from your file.

2 Make a copy of it. On the copy obliterate or cut off the statement of aims.

3 Exchange lesson plan copies with someone else in your group.

4 Try to write down a clear statement of both the learning and teaching aims of the lesson from what is in the lesson plan.

5 Compare what you have both written with the originals.

Ex. 2

AIM
To highlight the different forms lesson plans can take.

PROCEDURE
1 Discuss a particular teaching point with someone else in your group. Agree on aims and activities for a particular group of students.

2 Both of you write a plan for the lesson you discussed.

3 Compare and discuss the different layouts you have used.

4.2 Presenting language

Presentation is one of the most important and the complex preliminary stages in the teaching of isolated, or related, items such as:

— GRAMMATICAL STRUCTURES (e.g. THE PRESENT PROGRESSIVE in 'He's cleaning his teeth.')

— FUNCTIONS i.e. ways of describing what an item does in a situation where communication takes place (e.g. 'Asking the way' might be one of the functions of the structure *Could you tell me where . . . . . . ?* Another might be: 'Asking the position of something'. Equally, the second conditional in *If I were you, I'd give it back* might be one of the grammatical exponents of the function 'Giving advice'. There are many other exponents such as *Why don't you . . . .* or *I think you should . . .* , some of which convey very similar shades of attitude but some of which are appropriate only to different situations.)

— ITEMS OF VOCABULARY (e.g. words for parts of cars: *choke*, *clutch*, etc.)

Presentation consists basically of helping students understand what they mean, what rules of form they obey (e.g. grammar, syntax and pronunciation) and, if appropriate, who uses them in what context (sometimes referred to as the 'rules of use'). In a lesson, it takes as long as is necessary for this to be achieved, in many cases only a matter of a few minutes at most. In fact, the time needed for presentation often depends on the similarity of the items to the equivalents in the students' mother tongue.

Whether or not, when and how often, students need to have items presented will depend on:

— the level of the group (the higher the level, the less the need for presentation)

— the aims of the lesson (e.g. if students only need to practise it because they already 'know' it, presentation won't be necessary)

— the long-term aims of the students (not all students need to learn many *new* items but they do need to use more fluently and correctly what they already know)

– the ability of the students to acquire an understanding for themselves, say from either listening or reading texts (usually more likely if they already have some understanding of English)

Usually, presented items are either new to the students or ones they haven't got a very good grasp of. Presented items are not necessarily isolated from other language: they may be embedded in examples or dialogues whose language is already known to the students (so if the presented item is *try + -ing*, the example might be *Try adding salt*, where both the words *add* and *salt* are known).

The next stage, where the students get on and practise the items (known as the Practice stage) takes much longer because the students have far more to do. In the early stages when the practice may be tightly controlled by the teacher, or by the material the student is working from, he may have to struggle to pronounce the models correctly, he may have to memorize the word order and he may not easily be able to copy it down correctly and so on. It is likely too that the internal processing associated more with the Presentation stage, where the students try to relate the new language to language they already know, work out rules and discriminate between items, will be continued through this stage as well, (see pp 83–95).

As the practice becomes less controlled, the students will be able to try out the items in a more experimental way choosing one and not another. Perhaps immediately afterwards, but perhaps several sessions later they might be given the opportunity to choose not only what they want to say but also whether or not they want to use the items at all (e.g. in a role-play or a discussion, designed to lend itself to the language areas practised) (see pp 133–141).

The initial stages, then, in the teaching of new items are the Presentation stage (where the students learn *about* the items) and the Practice stage (where they learn to use them in controlled and less controlled ways – some of which resemble real communication). Some practice will probably follow on from the Presentation in the same lesson but some will be split up and extended over several lessons, with other activities interspersed.

Breaking up the learning of individual items into stages, however, should not indicate a too-rigid approach to language teaching. So, for example, not all freer activities should be seen as belonging to a 'stage' in the learning of individual items. They may instead be intended to practice a wide range of the skills we use when we communicate with each other – in fact, not relate to specific items at all. Nor should all language teaching be seen as consisting of the presentation and practice of language items. If anything, it's better to look at it as an attempt to get the students to be able to *do* things in the language and to improve how well they listen, speak, read and write in different environments depending on what they want their English *for*, although that of course *does* involve learning new language.

One approach to presentation

Step 1: Deciding what to present
This is a complex area. On a training course, usually the trainer decides and will look for things that suit both you as a training teacher as well as the students you are practising on. In schools the decision is frequently made by a syllabus or a course-book, according to the students' level (often classified in such terms as *Beginners*, *Elementary*, *Intermediate* and *Advanced*). In some situations you may be able to analyse the specific language skills and needs of the students and work

out a programme of work for them. Although this is often preferable, it takes considerable time and experience and is not always practicable.

Step 2: Deciding on an overall aim

The first question to ask is: *Is the item completely new to the students*? If so, you will have to concentrate on its form, its meaning and its use, spending more time on the aspects problematic to your students. If the students are already familiar with it you will have to decide whether it actually needs presenting at all. In some cases, it may be best to start with the Practice stage. If, however, you decide that many of the students need some remedial presentation, then you'll have to decide where the problems of form, meaning and use lie and concentrate your attention there.

Step 3: Deciding on an overall approach

What is the general level of your group? If their English is very good, then you will approach your presentation very differently than if they are just beginning to learn English. If you don't speak your students' mother-tongue you can't *explain* much to them when they don't speak your language and you don't speak theirs. The students will have to learn how the form operates and what the meaning is from examples in some sort of context (this approach is known as the 'inductive' approach). At subsequent levels of proficiency, or with certain suitable items at low levels, such as question forms of tenses already learned, you might show or tell what the meaning, form and use are, provided the students understand your metalanguage (see pp 25–27) and then let the students go on to practise them (this approach is known, in contrast, as 'deductive'). When the students are familiar with most of the forms (say at middle-to-late intermediate level) you may spend far less time on separate items of language and concentrate instead on spoken and written texts where all the items interrelate and the students acquire understanding far more for themselves than from the teacher. You might explain things that are not known, but you might also send students to reference sources, such as grammar books and dictionaries, or ask the students to try to work out a meaning from the context. (At this level, though, you must still retain a clear idea of the language areas the students are expected to focus on.)

The teacher of a monolingual class who has a good understanding of the students' mother tongue can have a much easier time at the lower levels because he may know:

– what language associations between the two languages (target language and mother tongue) will be made in the students' minds

– what problems may be encountered

– what short cuts, such as translation, can safely be made.

Translation, however, is a dangerous habit for the students to be encouraged into (they normally need to be encouraged out of it!) There are numerous occasions when seemingly obvious structural or lexical equivalences are used differently in an English-speaking context. And also you want the students to speak and eventually think in English if possible and too much use of the mother tongue in class can inhibit that.

Step 4: Sorting out the item for yourself

GRAMMATICAL STRUCTURES (e.g. the SIMPLE PAST, the DEFINITE ARTICLE, ADVERBS of

FREQUENCY): you will probably need to refer to a grammar book, such as *A Practical English Grammar* by Thomson and Martinet (OUP) or, if you have some grammatical awareness already, *A University Grammar of English* by Quirk and Greenbaum (Longman). *Practical English Usage* by M. Swan (OUP) is particularly useful for areas of grammar problematic to students and *Discover English* by R. Bolitho and B. Tomlinson (Heinemann) gives you an excellent opportunity to learn about the language through a series of 'discovery' exercises and simple explanations.

FUNCTIONS (e.g. 'Invitations', 'Offering to help', 'Identifying oneself'): here the focus is on what the language actually does in terms of communication and help is not so readily available in a single reference source. *A Communicative Grammar of English* by Leech and Svartvik (Longman) might help – it's excellent if you already know your grammar quite well and feel able to interrelate grammar and functions. The Teacher's Books of various recent course books, such as the *Strategies* series (Longman) and *Quartet* (OUP), are also useful. Even if you can't find anything written on the function you need to research, it's always worth asking, say in relation to the function of 'Apology', such questions as *What expression do I use? Do other people use it frequently? Is it useful for my students to know? Can they use it in lots of different situations? What is the grammatical form of the function? Can I tie it in with another structure? What is the 'register' of the language* (e.g. formal or informal?) Grammatical structures are used to communicate with just as communicative expression has grammatical structure; however, we must decide which way of looking at the item is most useful for our students, even though we shall at some time probably want to indicate both.

VOCABULARY: Usually, best looked up in a dictionary. A useful dictionary for foreign learners that you might like to consult is the *Longman Dictionary of Contemporary English* (Longman). You need to identify the meaning of the word, how it is pronounced and when and how it is used. If the students are doing the research themselves they might need something simpler like the *Oxford Elementary Learner's Dictionary of English* or a good bilingual dictionary.

Aspects of any item:

A: FORM

1 <u>Grammar rules and syntax</u>: To work out what the important elements are of, say, the PRESENT PERFECT you might refer to *A Practical English Grammar* (OUP):

---

179 A   Form

The present perfect tense is formed with the present tense of to have + the past particple: *I have worked* etc.

The past participle in regular verbs has exactly the same form as the simple past, i.e. *loved, walked* etc. (see spelling rules 172 C. In irregular verbs, the past participles vary (see 317).

The negative is formed by adding not to the auxiliary. The interrogative is formed by inverting the auxiliary and subject.

. . . .

Contractions: have and have not can be contracted (see 115):
I've worked   you haven't worked   haven't I worked?   etc.

Individual grammar books, though, frequently don't tell you all you need to know as far as teaching the item is concerned, so you might have to refer to several or seek the help of experienced teachers. For example, with the PRESENT PERFECT it is also useful to know that the form is usually contracted when the stress is on the participle (I've seen him) or on the complement (I've seen the film). It's not contracted, for example, when someone has contradicted what has been said (I have seen him) and 'short-form' answers in the affirmative (Yes, I have).

2 How it's said: You need to work out not only the problems the individual sounds when connected might cause your students but also the main changes in pitch (intonation) and main stresses. So, in the case of *I've worked in France before* the *ed* ending in *worked* is pronounced /t /, the main stress is likely, depending on the context, to fall on the /ə:/ sound in *before* and the voice to fall in pitch after it.

3 Potential problems: Looking again at the PRESENT PERFECT in *You haven't told him*:
- French students might find the word order, with 'him' coming at the end, difficult to reproduce
- German students frequently find consonant clusters like / **hævnt** / difficult to pronounce
- the past participle *told* is irregular and thus has to be remembered as an individual item
- students need to learn to elide *told him* into / **towldɪm** / when speaking quickly.

Such anticipation of problems comes with experience.

4 What aspects to teach, e.g. of a tense: It is likely that many students will have been taught 'I've got' as an *idiom*. If, however, we are going to teach the PRESENT PERFECT as a *tense*, we would probably choose a regular form, since the students are able to memorize and internalize a 'rule' and generate other utterances from it (even though in speech we probably more often use irregular forms).
   There are several aspects to the form of a tense:

AFFIRMATIVE:	*I've worked in France.*
'WH' QUESTION FORM:	*Where have you worked?*
INVERTED QUESTION FORM:	*Have you worked in France?*
SHORT-FORM ANSWER:	*Yes, I have. No, I haven't.*
LONG NEGATIVE:	*I haven't worked in France.*
QUESTION TAGS:	*You've worked in France, have you?/haven't you?*
	You haven't worked in France, have you?
NEGATIVE INTERROGATIVE:	*Haven't you worked in France?*

Although this may constitute a possible teaching order, it's unlikely that you'd want to teach them all in quick succession, any more than you'd want to teach all the PERSONS *I, you, he, she, we, they* in one go. It's better to be systematic in covering all the aspects of a tense over a longer period. Perhaps delay some of the uses of the QUESTION TAG and the NEGATIVE INTERROGATIVE until you can put them together with those of other tenses, when the students are better at English. Probably you'd best start with the affirmative form and perhaps just one question form in one lesson and integrate the rest into the syllabus later on.
   If you intend to introduce some irregular PAST PARTICIPLES once the students have a grasp of the regular form, it's probably best to start with common ones (e.g. *seen, given, been,*) and avoid confusing ones (e.g. *had* which could be confused with the auxiliary *have*).

B: MEANING
Referring again to *A Practical English Grammar* we can see that one meaning of the PRESENT PERFECT is described as follows:

> 181   The present perfect is used for past actions whose time is not given and not definite.
>
> A   It is used for recent actions when the time is not mentioned:
>
> ....
> *Have you had breakfast? No, I haven't had it yet.*
> ....
> Compare with:
> ....
> *Did you have breakfast at the hotel?* (i.e. before you left the hotel—simple past).

Did you have breakfast at the hotel? is also an example of a past action 'whose time is not given and not definite' but because of the phrase *at the hotel* we know that the speaker is at least thinking of a specific occasion at a roughly-definable time in the past. The present perfect in *Have you had breakfast?* indicates that the speaker is not thinking of a specific occasion in the past: rather, he's concerned as to what should happen next (e.g. *Would you like some?*). The distinction between the past simple and this use of the present perfect needs to be carefully worked out and understood. Students frequently find it difficult to choose the appropriate form. There are other uses of the present perfect but it would be unwise to present those until the students have some grasp of one.

C: USE

All of us choose the above use of the present perfect when we want to express the temporal and attitudinal relationship to the event described above: *why* it is used being the important element of the total context.

If, however, you look at the following utterances, you can see that other elements can make up a context and determine choice of language:

1   *Oh, no! He's done it again!*

2   *I'm terribly sorry. Would you be so kind as to lend me a cup of sugar?*

3   *It's been decided to give all workers a cut in wages.*

4   *Trevor Francis scores again!*

5   *You're to sit there, twerp!*

Can you work out who is speaking to whom, when and where in each case? Can you also say why you think the grammatical structures used have been chosen by the speaker?

These considerations are important because:

– as soon as you give an example of the item you are presenting, you are suggesting the existence of a context

– language choices appropriate to one context are not necessarily appropriate to another and students will need to know what such 'rules of use' are (e.g. whether something is polite or impolite, formal or informal and so on)

– the context in which you choose to embed the model will need to be appropriate and widely applicable

– the total meaning that needs to be understood by students when an item is presented involves aspects of context (e.g. *I've had breakfast,* as an example of the PRESENT PERFECT, contains some contextual information but *You haven't given that £10 back to him, have you?* contains more. In the second example we know something of the possible attitudes of three people).

Step 5: Noting down important considerations on a lesson plan
The more that can be anticipated about the items presented, the fewer the problems there will be in the class. It is therefore a useful discipline, as well as a useful reminder, to synthesize everything into a few short notes at the beginning of a lesson plan:

Level: Elementary
Teaching Aim:
To present deductively from objects taken into the classroom five items of clothing vocabulary: *pullover, shirt, suit, shoes, socks.* Presentation and practice of items in isolation will be followed by practice in a 2-line dialogue in a shop situation.

Assumptions:
1 Some students will know some of the words so they may be elicited

2 All students will need to practise the pronunciation thoroughly

Form:
1 In isolation the words will provide only pronunciation, word stress and spelling problems:
pullover   – stress on first syllable (*pullover*)
        – written as one word
        – double 'l'
shirt   – might be confused with *skirt*
        – /ʃ/ difficult for some students to make
suit   – the sound does not seem to relate to the spelling
shoes   – /ʃ/ sound
        – sound/spelling relationship
        – remembering to write the 'e'
socks   – /ɒ/ sound
        – 'ck' difficult to spell
2 In context
    – *shoes* and *socks* are frequently preceded by 'a pair of'
    – the stress does not always fall on the item (e.g. 'No, not a red pullover!')

Meaning:
Conveyed by simply showing the objects but need for checking that any internal translation has been correct. Possible problems:
1 Confusion between *pullover, sweater, cardigan* and *jersey*

2 Not realizing that *suit* means both jacket and trousers of the same material and colour

3 Confusion between *shoes* and *boots*

4 Not realizing that 'a pair of' refers to both and that the singular is *a shoe* or *a sock*
Use:
possible need to know that, for the English, *suit* indicates formality

---

Although the above notes are probably more exhaustive than you will have time to write, they indicate the direction the sorting out of language should take.

Step 6: Deciding on a context, if necessary, for both 'Presentation' and 'Practice'.
For inductive presentation (see Step 3), you will need to establish a context. This can be done through a dialogue, a series of visuals, mime, a series of sound sequences, a song, a reading text or mixture of more than one of these. It will usually need to be
– one the student can relate to

– suitable for making clear the meaning and use of the item

– unambiguous (unless there's good reason to be ambiguous)

– vivid, with sharply distinguished characters, and a clear location

– generative (i.e. it allows students to practise the item in a controlled way by readily suggesting additional examples when cued by the teacher or the material being used).

So, if the function being practised is 'Polite requests' (e.g. *Could you lend me . . . . .?*) then a good context might be someone wanting to go on a camping holiday, who has none of the equipment so has to go next door to his neighbour:

> *(I know it's silly but) could you lend me a kettle?*

If you wish to teach the apologetic and hesitant-sounding lead-in *I know it's silly but,* provided it's not too much of a mouthful for your students, it can give an extra dimension to the relationship between the two characters as well as teach a very useful fixed expression for such occasions. The structure *Could you lend me . . . . .?* in a generative situation such as this can lead to such practice examples as:

> *Could you lend me a sleeping bag?*
> > *tent*
> > *penknife*
> > *torch*
> > *kettle*

Step 7: Planning the method of 'Presentation'

(a) *The method should always be appropriate to the item,* e.g. a verb like *trip* might best be presented by mime, the noun *elephant* by picture (provided all other possibilities are ruled out of the students' minds when understanding is checked) and the structure *going to* + INFINITIVE by embedding it in a short dialogue (the lower level of the class the more the need for an inductive approach for structures and functions – see p 67).

(b) *The model should always sound natural,* so make sure the context is natural. E.g. if you are presenting the function 'Spontaneous offers' the model *I'll help you!* if embedded in a dialogue should not come out as *I will help you* (i.e. decontracted and in a flat intonation) but should emerge in such a way that the students will constantly feel that when you give the model or when they practise it, the person speaking is actually making the offer.

(c) *Decide how much of the language around the presented item can be elicited.* As a basic rule, provided it doesn't take much time, elicit as much as you can because:
– it keeps the students involved

– it activates the 'known' language

– the students show how much they understand as you go along

– you are able to gauge the right pace at which to lead the students through to an understanding of the language model.

Usually, the contexts and lead-ins to the model are profitably elicited but sometimes it is more efficient in terms of the aim of the lesson and the time available to get to the point more quickly and *give* either the contextual information or the language you expect the students to use in their practice. Complicated structures that need more inductive assimilation (e.g. *must have* in *He must have gone out,* where the functional meaning of 'retrospective deduction based on evidence' is hard to convey) are worth spending time on, whereas isolated items of vocabulary, if not already contextualized, are rarely worth it. This doesn't mean that the contexts are more complex but that the students are guided through logically to the full meaning of the structure by careful cueing and eliciting.

Step 8: *Reminding yourself of the aims of 'Presentation'*
– to get across the meaning of the language and relate it to how and when the language is used

– to isolate and highlight the linguistic form

– to check the full meaning (including use) has been understood by the students.

Step 9: *Working out ways of checking understanding*
Both the context and the grammatical/functional meanings have to be checked so that you can tell how far your presentation is successful and whether it needs extending, repeating, shortening etc. For an example see the sample presentation lesson below under 'Execution'.

Sample sections of a lesson plan including aims and anticipated problems and Steps 6–9

Level: Elementary
Teaching Aim:
To guide the students inductively to an understanding of the item *too* meaning 'more than enough' (e.g. *He's too short*). Lead to practice.

Anticipated problems:
1 Conveying the negative force of 'more than enough'.

2 Likelihood of confusion with 'very'.

3 Possible confusion with 'to'.

4 Need to highlight stress on both 'too' and following adjective.

Context:
A short, fat man wants to join the army.
He has an interview and tests.
Context established from a picture:

Model: *Sorry, but it's too heavy*

EXECUTION
1 Check students understand and can pronounce correctly:
    heavy   high   narrow   difficult

Elicit and get students to repeat quickly in chorus and individually

heavy: try to lift a heavy table in the classroom
high: if the ceiling is tall try to touch it
narrow: point to a narrow street on a map
difficult: ask students if learning English is easy or difficult
Ask questions to check students haven't confused them with other words.

2 Show picture and elicit students' ideas about it as well as some words such as *short* and *fat*. Establish who the man is, where he is, what he wants to do. Tell them his name (Joe Small). Ask questions to check understanding of context.

3 Tell students that the army want to give him some tests. Put a picture of a weight in one of the top corners of the board. Pretend to be a soldier shooting at Joe.

4 Give the stimulus:
    LIFT THAT! (mime lift if necessary)

5 Pretend to be Joe and give the model naturally:
    SORRY, BUT IT'S TOO HEAVY
Let students listen to it two or three times.

6 Ask questions to check and reinforce understanding of
(a) Context
    Where is Joe?
    Is he tall?
    Is he fat?
    Does he want to join the army?
    Do you think it's possible?
    Who's talking to him?
    Does he want Joe to do something?
    What?

(b) Concept of the new language ('too')
    Is it heavy? Is it very heavy?
    Is Joe strong?
    Can Joe do (lift) it?
    Does Joe want to do it?
    Is Joe sorry?
    Very. Too. The same? Which is more?
    Is 'too' a good thing?

Notes

1 For this lesson plan, to keep it uncluttered, you might simplify the headings under EXECUTION to:

(a) Pre-check lexis

(b) Establish and check context

(c) Establish context of stimulus

(d) Stimulus

(e) Model

(f) Check comprehension of context and concept

2 Although, as you can see, the procedure is quite complex beneath the surface, it should seem simple and effortless to the students and last very little time. Providing it has been thought through logically and the item is appropriate to the students it should take no more than a few minutes (e.g. five) to go from 1 to 6. Not all parts of a lesson take so much working out for such little time spent in the classroom. Usually, the students will be more actively engaged producing language, with you playing less of a conspicuous role.

3 Although the students won't be producing language while they are listening to the new language, they won't be passive. Trying to understand language inductively involves a lot of effort and complex internal processing. It demands the utmost concentration.

4 The reason for pre-checking or pre-teaching lexis is to prevent you getting bogged down if you find that the students don't know the words after all. The new language needs to be embedded in known language to highlight it and aid maximum comprehension. There's nothing more irritating for you and the students if suddenly a crucial word is unexpectedly unknown. However, don't make too much of pre-checking language. Only do it if absolutely necessary (it can waste time unnecessarily). Ideally, you want to choose only language you know the students know.

5 For oral presentations where the main aim is to get the students to use the forms orally it is generally better to try not to write up your models until the students have learned to understand and say them. It's not always easy, possible or even desirable to do this (students generally like to write things down quickly to give a feeling of security at having captured the new language) but if you can it will avoid the muddle that sometimes occurs when some are writing, some aren't. If students are going to read and copy from the board it's better to have some control over the activity and do it properly.

6 It's well worth writing the main stresses, pitch changes (intonation) and problem sounds under your language models on the plan (just as it is on the board for the students when you come to write them up). It helps you become aware of them and anticipate the problems.

7 Sometimes it's worth highlighting the intonation pattern of the model by simply humming it and showing the movement with your hand.

8 Main stresses can be indicated to the students by beating them with your hand.

9 It is essential that when students are listening to and repeating a model the sounds belong to normal connected speech.
So:
I've been waiting here for two hours

might sound

/   aɪvbin weɪtɪŋ hɪə fətuː auəz   /

and not

/   aɪ hæv biːn weɪtɪŋ hɪə fɔː tuːauəz   /

Sometimes, though, problems need to be highlighted and sometimes students need to hear a slower version of the model to be able to recognize familiar elements in the structure. If this is done the students should hear the natural version before they are asked to practise it.

One way of executing the following lesson plan

Level: Low Intermediate (Multi-cultural adult class)
Teaching Aim:
To present and practise 'You could . . . . .' as suggested advice

Context:
Doctor talking to overweight patient.

Assumptions:
The phrasal verb 'take up' has been previously taught and is well known to all the students.

Aids:
Pictures of sports on cards. Blu-tack.
Tape recorder and tape.

Method:
1 Personalize topic

2 Pre-check the names of some sports

3 Taped dialogue with model in last line

Bill Big:	Hello, doctor. Sorry to trouble you.
Doctor:	Sit down. What can I do for you?
Bill Big:	Look at me. I'm so fat!
Doctor:	Mmmm, I see. *Well, you could take up cycling*!

4 Check understanding of context and language concept.

(Blu-tack is a re-usable sticky substance used for attaching visuals to boards and walls.)

TEACHER	STUDENT
What sports do you like, Khalid?	S1 *Sports? Eh . . . Swim*
Yes, the sport's called?	S1 *Swim*
Jose?	S2 *Swimming*
(looking at Khalid)	S1 *Swimming*
What about you, Dominique?	S3 *Tennis . . . . and, how do you say, with a ball . . . so . . .* (demonstrating)
Volleyball.	S3 *Yes. Volleyball*
(showing picture of man sports-cycling)	
What's this sport called? . . . Yuki.	S4 *Cycle*
Almost. Cy . . . . ?	S4 *Cycling*
Yes, that's right. Everyone (with gesture)	S1–10 *Cycling*
(beckoning to individuals to repeat)	S1, 3, 8, 4, 7 *Cycling*
(sticking picture in top corner of board with Blu-tack; showing picture of a game of table-tennis)	
And this?	S7 *Tennis . . . tennis-table*
(indicating with fingers that words should be reversed)	
(indicating approval; sticking picture underneath the other)	S7 *Table-tennis*
Everyone (with gesture)	S1–10 *Table-tennis*
(beckoning to individuals to repeat; correction if necessary, particularly with stress)	S5, 6, 9, 3, 2 *Table-tennis*

TEACHER	STUDENT
(showing picture of man running in race; sticking on board under the others; looking at Hans)	S8 *Athletics*
(gesturing everyone to repeat)	S1–10 *Athletics*
(beckoning individuals)	S8, 2, 1, 10, 1 *Athletics*
All right. Give me some names of other sports.	
	S10 *Motor-race*
	S9 *Motor-racing*
	S10 *Motor-racing*
	S2 *Skating, football . . .*
OK. Enough (showing picture of doctor)	
What's this man, Sami?	S10 *Doctor*
(drawing quick sketch of fat man on board)	
Is this man thin or fat?	S4, 6, 8 *Fat*
His name's Bill Big	S9 *Bill Big. Very funny.*
Thank you. Well, he went to see the doctor. Why do you think?	
(looking at Ali)	S7 *Not fit. Needs exercise.*
Yes, do you know the word? 'Fit' (noticing some incomprehension)	
Does he do a lot of exercise?	S5, 2, 6 *No*
(miming a fit person)	
Does this man do a lot of exercise?	*S1–10 Yes*
Which man is fit?	S8 *The second man.*
Yes. Listen: Fit. Everyone (with gesture)	S1–10 *Fit*
(beckoning individuals)	S2, 5, 7 *Fit*
Does a fit man do a lot of exercise? (looking at Hans)	S8 *No*
Are you fit?	(laughter)
	S2, 3 *No*
Am I fit?	S10 *I don't know. Perhaps.*
Well, Bill's not fit? Why not?	S8 *Because he's very fat.*
Why has he gone to the doctor?	S1 *I don't know. Perhaps the doctor want fit.*
Does Bill want to be fit?	S1 *Yes.*
OK. Now listen to what they say.	
Listen to what the doctor thinks.	
(pressing 'play' button on tape-recorder)	
	(listening to dialogue)
All right?	S2, 5, 7 *Yes.*
Who's talking?	
(looking at Yuki)	S4 *Bill and the doctor.*
Does Bill go and see the doctor?	
(looking at Dominique)	S3 *Yes.*
Why?	S3 *Because he's worried. He doesn't like to be fat.*
Right. Now listen again.	
(replaying the dialogue)	(listening)
Is Bill nervous? Does he sound nervous?	
(looking at Sami)	S10 *Yes.*
How do you know?	S10 *He says 'sorry to trouble you' (imitating the tape)*
What does the doctor tell him to do?	S4 *To take up cycling.*

TEACHER	STUDENT
No, tell him, not suggest.	S10 *To sit down.*
That's right. Does he say 'can I help you?'	S5 *No. 'What can I do for you?'*
Good. Now listen to the last line again.	
(replaying the last line)	(listening)
Does the doctor think he's fat?	S1, 7 *Yes.*
Does the doctor think it's a good idea for Bill to cycle?	S3, 9, 6 *Yes.*
Does he think cycling will make him thinner?	
Does Bill cycle now?	S2 *No.*
Does the doctor give him medicine?	S3 *No.*
Do you think the doctor's nice?	S4 (laughter) *No, he's rude. He's not very friendly.*
Would you like him to be your doctor?	S5, 6 (laughter) *No!*
Does the doctor think it's possible for Bill to start cycling?	S2 *Yes.*
Do you think it's a good idea?	S5 *Yes.*

A useful exercise for you would be to try and divide this sample transcript to indicate the Steps 1, 2, 3, 4, of the 'method' stated in the lesson plan and then answer the following questions:

1 Why personalize the topic of 'sports' with the students?

2 Why was it useful to pre-check the names of some of them?

3 Why was it helpful to present the language in a dialogue in this case?

4 Why was it put on tape, do you think?

5 Why was the model in the last line?

6 Why was understanding of the context checked?

7 Why was the language model *You could take up cycling* checked for understanding?

Commonsense will supply most of the answers. Reference, however, is made to them throughout this section.

Notes

1 Even though you are a central figure in this type of inductive approach, where the aim is to guide the students towards an understanding of the meaning of the language model, it is essential that you avoid dominating the class unnecessarily. This is partly done by keeping your own language to a minimum, eliciting when possible, and using eye contact and gesture.

2 Even during Presentation, student participation is essential. It not only maximizes what is known as student talking time (STT) and minimizes teacher talking time (TTT), thus activating what the students know, but it also gives you a good indication what the students are following, what is being offered and at what pace to proceed.

3 Even though the model has been presented on tape, each stage is built up simply and clearly, one thing leading into the next, to lead the students towards an understanding of the meaning of the new language.

4 Presentation dialogues:
  - are a good way of giving models of language a naturalistic communicative context or, in some cases, a vivid, imaginative unnaturalistic context (with at least two people talking in a specific setting).

  - They provide, in an economical way, information and contextual clues to guide the students to an understanding of the model.

  - They enable students to place the models imaginatively in a communicative context in the real world.

  - They show how the model arises and how it is led into, and, sometimes, how it is responded to.

  For the classroom:
  - they should be short if only one item is included (this is particularly true for lower levels; about four or six lines is the right length)

  - they need to contain simpler language than the language model so as not to impede comprehension of the model

  - they can usefully contain natural fixed expressions (e.g. *Sorry to trouble you*) that the students can become familiar with in a natural context

  - the model usually needs to be in the last line since it is an illustration of what the students have been led towards in the other lines and it can be used at the practice stage to generate practice from (e.g. *You could take up table-tennis/ athletics* etc.)

  - they don't have to be taped. Your students will find it useful to have different voices brought into the classroom on tape and have their imaginations stimulated by what is heard, but it's perfectly possible for you to act out the dialogue if you haven't got a tape recorder (differentiating between the characters by, say, changing hats, voices, where you're standing or simply pointing to drawn figures on the board).

  Whatever you do, the contexts and the language should be as natural as possible. They shouldn't be strained to fit the teaching, even if dramatic licence is employed to make the characters interesting and amusing.

5 Students relate to contexts better if you ask personal questions in relation to the topic of conversation. Just as the context of a dialogue needs establishing before the dialogue is presented, so the context is more meaningful if the students have been encouraged to think about the main topics beforehand (without you giving away what the actual dialogue is about).

6 Plan your board at the lesson planning stage. For example, for this lesson your board should look something like this when the pictures are up:

This arrangement leaves plenty of space for writing up the drill later, if necessary.

7 An important part of presenting new language is checking that the students understand what is going on. You need to check they understand:
   – who is talking to whom, when and where (this includes the sort of people they are, their relationship and the language they choose to employ for the occasion) (i.e. CONTEXT)

   – what's happening and what they're talking about (i.e. CONTENT)

   – the meaning of the new language (i.e. CONCEPT).

For a more detailed look at this complex area refer to pp 97–108. The questions you need to ask need careful preparation and to be included in your lesson plan.

8 Finally, if you're using a tape recorder set the counter to zero, note down the numbers on your plan for the beginning of the dialogue as well as the model, and then after putting the tape you intend to use in the recorder (if possible before the lesson) set the counter to zero and find the start of the dialogue.

Suggestions

1 Consider the level of your class and ask:
   Is the item best presented inductively or deductively?
   Which is the quickest and most effective approach (and the most memorable)?
   (see Steps 2 and 3).

2 This will go hand in hand with sorting out the item for yourself (see Step 4).

3 Ask yourself exactly what the aim of the lesson is (that is what you expect the students to be able to do by the end of it and how you will go about getting them to be able to do it) (see Steps 2, 8 and the sample lesson plans).

4 For inductive presentation, decide on the context and the best vehicle for it (e.g. mime etc.) (see Steps 6 and 7).

5 Decide on a model (i.e. an example of the target item).

6 Work out how you will check that students understand (see Step 10 and pp 98–101).

7 Above all think through the stages of the Presentation carefully, make useful working notes on your plan and ask: *What is the aim of each stage? (Why am I doing that? Is it necessary? Can I make it clearer? Is both the form and the meaning, and possibly the use, adequately conveyed?)*

8 Remember, although everything hangs on successful presentation for subsequent practice, it is only a prelude to the practice. The sooner you can get it done the sooner you can get on to helping the students use the new language accurately and fluently.

Exercises

Ex. 1

AIM

To help select a relevant language item for presentation and then choose a suitable context in which to present it.

PROCEDURE

1 Play about ten minutes of a recorded lesson (audio or video), preferably part of something like a role-play, where the students are doing most of the talking.

2 Select a structure or function the students show they lack or have insufficient grasp of. The weakness should be general and not just belonging to one student.

3 Discuss what everyone in your group has chosen in terms of how useful the items are in the group.

4 Choose a suitable generative context in which to present the item.

5 Discuss your choice of context with the others.

6 Write a four or five line dialogue which would clearly present the item.

Ex. 2

AIM

To help get used to working out problems of form, meaning and use.

PROCEDURE

1 Select a language item (e.g. *be used to + -ing*).

2 In two minutes make a list of as many problems of form, meaning and use that you can think of.

3 Find a partner and compare lists.

4 In two minutes come up with a new agreed list by adding and deleting.

5 Find another pair and do the same thing and with other pairs until the whole group has 'brainstormed' the topic.

Ex. 3

AIM

To give practice in selecting appropriate language and contexts.

PROCEDURE

1 Read the following dialogues and answer the questions below:
   (a) A: ● You're playing your stereo much too loudly again.
       B: Oh, sorry. I'll turn it down.
   (b) A: I wonder if you could help me?
       B: Certainly, sir.
       A: ● Could you possibly tell me where I could get a newspaper?
       B: Yes, just around the corner, sir. There's a newsagent's next door.
       A: Thank you very much.
   (c) A: You look awfully tired, darling.
       B: I'm whacked.
       A: ● Why don't you put your feet up for a bit?
       B: Too much to do.

– Where might each conversation be taking place?

– Who do you think the participants are?

– What language function does the utterance marked ● have in each dialogue?

– What other ways are there of expressing the same function?

– Would other ways of expressing the same function be equally appropriate? If not, why not?

– Would they be equally easy to teach?

– Would they be readily transferable to other situations?

2 Write a short dialogue (2, 4 or 5 lines) to present one of the items.

3 Ask the above questions of each other's dialogues.

Ex. 4

AIM
To help be as succinct and as logical as possible in Presentations.

PROCEDURE
A: 1 Ask one of your group to 'peer teach' an inductive Presentation (possibly in a foreign language), having submitted an estimate as to how long each stage will take.

   2 Afterwards, allow yourself five minutes to write down what you think the lesson plan would look like, indicating the main stages of the lesson, the aims of each stage, how long each would take and how one thing led or didn't lead into the next.

   3 Compare with the original.

B: 1 Do the same as A1.

   2 *Either* shout out the time e.g. every three minutes *or* make a gesture when the times have been exceeded.

C: 1 Make a lesson plan for either an inductive or a deductive Presentation of a language item (e.g. POSSESSIVE ADJECTIVES used for personal identification as in *My name's* . . . . . .) to include a simple drill. It should not last more than fifteen minutes.

   2 Number the stages of the lesson, indicating the aim of each, noting down the approximate time each will take and showing how each stage is linked to the next.

   3 Find a partner and comment on each other's plans.

Ex. 5

AIM
To practise the main stages of Presentation in an unstressful atmosphere.

PROCEDURE
1 Devise something simple in an unfamiliar or an invented language (e.g. the numbers 1–5: 1 = *dring*, 2 = *clowper*, 3 = *snit*, 4 = *throp*, 5 = *opper*).

2 Tell someone else in your group you are going to teach him some new language.

3 Using no English (only gesture) get across the meaning of the words, practise the pronunciation, check he understands the meaning, revise the whole set of numbers again and get him to write it down after he has read it aloud from the board in random order.

COMMENT
This exercise can, of course, also be done on several members of the group at the same time.

4.3 Controlled practice

Language that has been presented for the first time will normally need to be practised orally by the students. Even if the item is one that has arisen unexpectedly in the course of a lesson (e.g. the word *thermometer*) the pronunciation will need practising. Some remedial items – ones that the students understand but can't use very well – may not need *presenting* but will need *practising.*

Practice normally begins with straightforward repetition of the language model you, another student, or the tape have given. As such the students clearly have no choice as to which piece of language to use and it won't be serving any communicative purpose. A particular example of an item has been isolated and highlighted for practice and the students practise it. You probably don't respond to it as communication; you rather congratulate the students on doing it well or correct it if they don't. It is the first stage in getting the students to use the new language naturally as part of their repertoire. Its particular aims are:

1 to help students memorize the form (the 'rule' of the example – see pp 68–69) including the word order. It is essential then that it is the generative element that is focused on rather than the many examples of its use

2 to help students get the pronunciation right (the teacher will usually need to correct it if mistakes are made). It is sometimes helpful to think of pronunciation as another aspect of form

3 to consolidate the meaning of the item (providing that the meaning has been adequately demonstrated and the students are conscious of it throughout the practice)

Repetition practice helps to develop habits. However, in real life we are mostly able to *choose* which language to use and as we are largely non-mechanical beings this makes for a profoundly complex activity. Habit formation is only a small, if essential, part of learning to communicate in a language.

Later, perhaps in the same lesson, or perhaps in another lesson, the item will need to be set in other contexts in a wider range of language. The students may have far more choices as to the language they can use.

Later still, the students will need opportunities to use the language you have presented far more freely, in contexts which lend themselves naturally to its use. The students may in fact choose not to use the language at all.

Practice goes then:
        CONTROLLED
            ↓
    LESS CONTROLLED
            ↓
    CREATIVE

How much controlled practice is given depends on the level and abilities of the students. Normally, low-level students need a lot of controlled practice (often known as 'drilling') and advanced students much less.

A: Repetition Practice

This is made up of the following components:

1 Listening to the model

Oral models (i.e. examples of language items) may be provided by either the teacher, another student or an audio or video tape.

There is no fixed number of times that students should hear them; it may be once, twice, three times, depending on the students' concentration and how often you think they need to hear them. Concentration will lapse, however, if you give them too often, so it might be best to aim for once, or perhaps twice, unless there is good reason otherwise. If the new language is difficult to discriminate from similar items or commit to memory, it is more likely to be at least three times. To decide, you'll need to be sensitive and judge your students. Before giving the model:

– *Attract the students' attention.* Look at the whole class and alert them to the fact they are about to hear something important. For example, you might say 'Listen' and put your hand to your ear to emphasize the point (see pp 10–13).

– *If you are giving the model, don't change the stress and intonation each time.* Keep them constant. In fact, you might like to highlight the main features with your hand; beating the main stresses and showing the main pitch changes.

– *Say the model naturally.* Don't slow it down and distort it; although sometimes you can, with difficult structures, do it just once to give students a chance to recognize any familiar elements (i.e. words they know). The models the students *repeat*, however, should be spoken naturally. If the utterance is long and unmanageable, it's sometimes necessary to break it up e.g.:
    If I'd done it, I'd have got away with it.
In this case the two main parts may be practised separately. It is essential, though, that the students then practise the complete utterance, with the correct intonation. It is particularly difficult to keep the intonation natural when utterances are split up in this way.

Although this activity might be thought of as a kind of listening drill it is really as much a part of the Presentation stage as the Practice stage.

2 Everyone saying it together

It is often efficient and helpful to get students to say the model in chorus, either the whole class together or sections of the class divided up. This is particularly useful with lower levels although still possible at the higher levels. It:
– gives everyone a chance to rehearse the pronunciation of the item without having the spotlight put on them
– enables students to pick up how it's said from other students.

In large classes, there is very little opportunity for individuals to practise language with the teacher listening and correcting, so chorus practice often plays an important part.

At this stage you are like a conductor and the better your techniques the more efficient the practice. If the students all start at different times, not only is it difficult to judge how they are coping and how many times they need to chorus, they also tend to interfere with each other's production. Although they are rehearsing the item individually, they are also producing in chorus as part of a group. You'll probably need some definite hand or arm gesture to indicate when everybody is to start, perhaps accompanied by a word like *Everybody.* However you do it, you'll need to be decisive and clear, and use short, sharp instructions.

– Sometimes it's worth saying the model along with the students, sometimes it's better just to mouth it and sometimes you should just conduct and listen.

– Chorus repetition quickly becomes dull after about three goes and the language tends to lose its meaning. However, before that repetitions will need to be indicated by a gesture of some sort and a word such as *Again* (see pp 10–13).

3 Keeping the meaning uppermost in the students' minds and checking their understanding
To prevent repetition from reducing the item to a meaningless collection of sounds, it is sometimes worth:
– reminding the students of the context

– between repetitions, responding to the utterance as communication.
However, to check the students fully understand what is being said and indeed to reinforce that understanding, *ask questions* (see pp 97–101).

4 The students saying it individually
Sometime or another, perhaps after a chorus drill, you will probably want to give as many of the students as possible the opportunity to try to say the model correctly, if necessary with your help and the help of other students. To prevent the exercise from boring those students not getting the practice, you will need to involve the whole class and encourage the others to learn from the production one individual is attempting. So:
(a) make eye contact with the rest of the class and implicitly involve them (see pp 7–8).
(b) encourage and direct the others to help when a student is having problems like not knowing how to say it or getting it wrong. (You might say to the others something like *Help him* or *Is that right?* or *Where's the mistake?* rather than do all the work yourself. It is important first, though, to give a student every opportunity to get things right himself before calling on anyone else. Don't jump in too quickly!)
To prevent the practice from being laborious and predictable:
(a) spread it about in a random way! Dot around, instead of going round the room from one student to the next. It's a good thing if students have to repeat it more than once, so don't worry about asking a student twice. If the class isn't too big (say ten or twelve students) do try and include everyone, unless the item is clearly an easy one
(b) gesture or make eye contact with the person you want to do the work (see pp7–8, 10–13); using names can slow things down unnecessarily.

Finally, make sure:
(c) each student has sufficient attention (see pp 20–22)

(d) you don't give so much attention to one student that he gets discouraged and frustrated while the others are getting bored!

(e) the students get sufficient correction

(f) they don't get so much correction that they get worse and worse. (Although you'll try and help students to say things correctly, some students need to 'sleep on it' before they can get it right)

(g) the practice goes on long enough for students to have a reasonable chance of being able to repeat it when called upon

(h) it doesn't go on too long. There's no fixed amount of time; you have to respond to the needs of the class on the spot in relation to the difficulties they are having with the language. Once again, you will have to learn to be aware of how your students are reacting.

Remember, in a multilingual class, students from different language backgrounds will have different structural, conceptual and phonological problems. Again, you will have to balance the individual needs with the group needs. If the class is large, you will have much less time to work with individuals, so you'll probably want more practice in chorus, or more practice in pairs or in groups, to give everyone a chance to practise the item. Obviously, though, you will be less able to monitor what every individual says.

Your aim is to get the students both fluent and accurate when repeating the formal aspects of the new language you have presented: the structure and syntax, the sounds, the rhythm, the intonation and the stress.

Imitating models of language correctly, however, hardly ensures that students will remember them for a long period unless they are returned to on subsequent occasions. Even then, being able to remember them does not help the students communicate through them unless they learn to do that as well. However, imitation is a necessary first step.

The problem is, though, to reconcile the mechanical nature of the activity (and make it as efficient as possible) with the need to retain the meaning of the language that is being practised. The problem is also to maintain the students' interest and involvement at a time when they are able to invest very little of themselves as people (they are merely 'learning their lines').

B Substitution Drilling

If your context and model are generative (i.e. they are capable of yielding several relevant examples – see p 72) then you should be able to spin off a substitution drill to highlight the generative element of the structures as well as give extra interest to the practice, e.g:

Level: Elementary
Learning Aim: For the students to be able to memorize and produce accurately the structure: 'haven't got' and 'any'
Aids: Cheese, butter, a loaf of bread
Context: Shop
Drill: Sorry, I haven't got any cheese
                                    butter
                                    bread
                                    + students' own examples

The prompts can either be:
– the real thing (as here)

– a picture

– the word written on a card

– the word supplied orally by you.

You might do the drill something like this:
1 Check that students understand the vocabulary by showing the things (*cheese, butter, bread*). Make sure they can pronounce these correctly.

2 Remind students of the context used for presentation.

3 Repeat the model (*Sorry, I haven't got any cheese*).

4 Get students to repeat in chorus.

5 Get students to repeat individually and correct their pronunciation and word order if necessary.

6 Show the next object (*butter*). See if students can give you *Sorry, I haven't got any butter* without prompting.

7 Practise.

8 Go back and practise the original model (*Sorry, I haven't got any cheese*).

9 Show the next object (*bread*). Try and elicit *Sorry, I haven't got any bread*.

10 Practise.

11 Go back and practise the previous two substitutions.

12 Get students to give other examples that they can think of (e.g. *sugar*).

13 After sufficient oral practice, elicit the whole drill on to the board, asking students to show you where the main stress is and what happens to the intonation. Indicate it on the board as in the lesson plan above.

14 Indicate the 'rule' on the board:
   e.g. *haven't got* (negative) + *any*

15 Get students to read examples from the board.

16 Get students to copy the drill into their books.

17 Check that students have copied correctly.
(How you organize these last three stages would depend a lot on the reading and writing skills of the group. Poor writers will need extra time to write and this will have to be allowed for. Good writers will finish quickly and sit around with nothing to do unless you work out something for them.)

To make the practice more realistic and to open up the prospect of pair work it is often as well to supply a stimulus, e.g:

A pound of cheese please
   loaf   bread
   pound   butter

The procedure then might be:

1. Check that students understand the vocabulary by showing the things (first *cheese* then *a pound of cheese, bread* and then *a loaf of bread* etc.) Make sure they can pronounce them correctly.

2 Remind students of the context used for Presentation.

3 Indicate that you are the customer.

4 Say the lines of the stimulus (*A pound of cheese, please*) and get students to repeat – in chorus and individually.

5 Show the aids in order to elicit the other examples.

6 Indicate that you are now the shopkeeper. Distribute any aids. Get students to ask you for the things (e.g. *A pound of cheese, please*).

7 Reply with *Sorry, I haven't got any cheese*, etc. By the time you have replied several times students will have had ample listening practice of the form *I haven't got any* . . . .

8 Ask simple questions to check that students understand the meaning of the form (e.g. *Cheese? In the shop?*)

9 Repeat *Sorry, I haven't got any cheese* once more, and get class to repeat in chorus.

10 Get students to repeat individually. Correct if necessary.

11 Provide students with the other examples of the stimulus (*A loaf of bread, please*; *A pound of butter, please*). Get them to respond with the appropriate substitution, *Sorry, I haven't got any* . . . . . in chorus or individually.

12 If necessary, exchange roles, so that you are the shopkeeper and the students are the customers.

13 Give the aids to one student. Tell him he is the customer. Tell another student he is the shopkeeper. Let the other students hear the exchange.

14 Ask students to practise in 'closed' pairs. You may wish to give out several pictures, or words on cards, to each pair.

15 Elicit the whole drill on to the board. Get students to read from the board and copy it down in their books. Check they copy correctly.

Further practical suggestions
1 Keep drills snappy, efficient and fun.

2 Keep the meaning uppermost in the students' minds. Make sure they supply the right facial expressions, the right gestures and the right intonation. Check comprehension of both the context and the language from time to time. You might also occasionally ask questions to try and relate them to the content of the drill, not only in context (*Do you think the customer's angry?*) but also in terms of their experience (*Do **you** like cheese?*)

3 From time to time remind the students of the formal 'rule' (*haven't got + any*).

4 Unless the Presentation is deductive (when you might first write up an example, show the 'rule' and *then* practise) try to save the board-writing stage till after the oral practice and deal with it properly.

5 Make sure you leave adequate time for the pair practice; apart from during the chorus drill it is the one occasion when a large part of the class can practise at the same time.

6 Don't give more of the drill than is necessary, so:
   – elicit substitutions from students if possible by the use of non-verbal prompts and

   – beckon individual students or make eye contact with them to indicate who is to repeat.

7 Correct tightly but pay less attention to errors that do not directly relate to the target structure.

8 If possible try to allow students some freedom in less important details (e.g. they might want to add small bits on to the end – *Sorry, I haven't got any cheese. Come back tomorrow*).

Not all drills which students do in pairs need go through the teacher first. Providing they are set up so that the students know exactly what to do, the practice can be from:
– stimuli (or prompts for stimuli) written on one set of cards, with responses (or prompts for responses) on another set of cards

– model dialogues

– pictures

The problem with the drill illustrated here is that, even allowing for the fact that you are expecting the students to play a role (i.e. a shopkeeper) they probably won't have to play in real life, it is also in another way communicatively meaningless. The customer simply says he wants the things and the shopkeeper automatically says he hasn't got them. Both know exactly what is going to be said. While the practice usefully highlights the generative element of the form (*haven't got any*) and, through the different examples, allows for further pronunciation practice in a more interesting way than mere repetition, the students practising are not actually communicating anything to each other.

To make more realistic communication possible the students need to have:

– information about their situation which they withhold from each other until the drill is carried out, so there is something to convey

– a slightly unpredictable element built into the drill so that they have to make choices as to which language they are to use.

The drill in this case would not just be:
   C: *A (pound of cheese), please.*
   S: *Sorry, I haven't got any (cheese).*
but might at a very controlled level be:
   C: *A (pound of cheese), please.*
   S: *Sorry, I haven't got any (cheese).*
   or S: *O.K. Here you are.*

In other words, the shopkeeper has to say whether he's got it or not, and the customer doesn't know whether he's got it or not until he hears what the shopkeeper has to say. Although you may allow the customer to choose which things to ask for, the decision about whether or not the shopkeeper has got them

will still be yours, since *your* aim is to make sure the students practise the item. To help make the drill successful you might:
– give out to every student the following information, say on a card:

You are the customer. You want A pound of cheese A loaf of bread A pound of butter (+ 2/3 other examples)

– and then give out to the rest the following information, say on a card:

You are the shopkeeper. You have
    A loaf of bread
    A pound of sugar
    A packet of tea
You haven't got any
    Cheese
    Bread
    Butter
    (+ other things the customer wants)

It's vital, however, that the students don't show the cards to each other if they are going to communicate anything.
For this kind of drill you will need to decide how much of the above procedures you should follow. The students still have to have a model for the practice, i.e. they have to know what patterns they are to follow, although of course you can't give the game away as you might if you rigidly followed the procedure:

$$T \rightarrow S$$
$$S \rightarrow T$$
$$S \leftrightarrow S \text{ (open)}$$
$$S \leftrightarrow S \text{ (closed)}$$

By the time they got to the S ↔ S ('closed') stage they would probably know what was on each other's cards. If the students need a slow build-up before they can practise in pairs, it is often worth giving similar but slightly different information on the cards they use.

Further questions
1 When should I teach the response *OK. Here you are?*
   Clearly, if you are following the T → S/S → T procedure you can slip it in when you are playing the shopkeeper. Otherwise you will have to show them what to say when you have got something to give them and do a quick bit of individual repetition practice.

2 How do I check that the students have understood what is on the cards?
   You can briefly go round asking individual students questions about who they are, what they want, what they've got etc. while the others are reading.

3 What should my role be during the practice?
   In general, discreetly go round helping out once you are sure all the pairs have got going properly; correct bad mistakes, particularly in relation to the target structure (*haven't got any*); note how well they are coping with the language and the task. See pp 45–47.

At a later stage of practice or for a more able class this same exchange may be made more interesting and realistic by adding other elements: e.g:

1 Add the prices next to the shopkeeper's items so he has to reply *OK. Here you are. That's 56p.*

2 Make the exchange more than two lines. Two possibilities might be:

 A S: *Good morning. Can I help you?*
 C: *Yes. A pound of cheese, please.*
 S: *Sorry, I haven't got any cheese.*
 C: *Oh dear.*

(If the shopkeeper had got the items then the customer's final reply might be 'Thanks very much')

 B C: *A loaf of bread, please.*
 S: *Sorry, I haven't got any bread.*
 C: *Never mind. Have you got any tea?*
 S: *Yes. Here you are.*
 C: *How much is it?*
 S: *64p.*
 (C: *Really. That's expensive!)*

Obviously, in your planning, you must take into account what the students will say if they've got the shopping item as well as what they will say if they haven't got the shopping item. Two bases for practice might be:

1 memorizing the dialogue structure with the variable elements missing (you might wish to modify the procedure on pp 114–115).

2 giving out cards with the dialogue structure written on them and the variable elements missing.

Less controlled practice

The gap between a drill and real communication has been narrowed by offering the students choices. There is less chance of the drill seeming meaningless and boring because the students are not simply being asked to reproduce a series of sounds but to actually use the item to say something which in turn affects what the other person says.

A drill though remains a drill and thus surrounded by constraints imposed by the teacher, the material and the classroom situation. Most items don't become fully absorbed into the students' productive language until:

(i) they have appeared in a wider language setting (see pp 110–120, 121–125 and 126–132) than the language and the context used for the drill.

(ii) the students have been given the opportunity to use the item in a freer, more creative language situation geared to the items (see pp 133–139).

Drills though can contain creative elements which expect the students to do more than choose between presented items, for example taking the above drill again, if the customer has on his card:

You are the customer. You want A pound of cheese A loaf of bread A pound of butter (+2/3 other examples) You don't want to pay more than 30p for any item You only have £1

and the shopkeeper:

> You are the shopkeeper. You have:
>   A loaf of bread: 20p
>   A pound of sugar: 35p
>   A packet of tea: 40p
>   (think of other prices of things you have)
> You haven't got any:
>   Cheese
>   Butter
>   (+ other things the customer wants)

and the dialogue is

> C: *A pound of cheese, please.*
> S: *Sorry, I haven't got any cheese.*
> C: *Never mind. Have you got any tea?*
> S: Yes. Here you are
> C: How much is it?
> S: . . . . (SAY)
> C: (CONTINUE)
> S: (CONTINUE)

then clearly the language at some stages of the exchange, particularly the end where it can develop freely, is being left to the students to decide on. This type of drill takes time to set up and lasts longer than other types but the students find them more interesting because they have to put more into them.

Using 'the real thing' as a basis for controlled and less controlled drills

Railway timetables, theatre programmes, entertainment advertisements, horoscopes and such like things all make good bases for drills. Here is an example of some specially prepared material designed to approximate 'the real thing' and cue language practice (for published examples see *Cue for a Drill* by Harkess and Eastwood, OUP):

		Anna's Diary:			Bill's Diary:
MONDAY	Morning	Get car back from garage	MONDAY	Morning	Free
	Afternoon	Free		Afternoon	Dentist
	Evening	Dinner with parents		Evening	Squash with Jane
TUESDAY	Morning	Go to hairdressers'	TUESDAY	Morning	Free
	Afternoon	Do school work		Afternoon	Do school work
	Evening	Free		Evening	Cocktail party at school
WEDNESDAY	Morning	Free	WEDNESDAY	Morning	Free
	Afternoon	Pick children up from school		Afternoon	Cinema with Mary
	Evening	Tickets for the theatre		Evening	Tickets for the theatre
	etc.			etc.	

A: For controlled practice

Aim: To practise ways of making suggestions:
        What about . . . .?
        Why don't we . . . . . .?
1 Set the scene for the following dialogue:
    Anna: Hello, Bill. How are you?
    Bill: Fine, thanks. Listen, we must meet this week and talk about our holiday.

Anna: O.K. Why don't <u>we see each other on Monday afternoon</u>?
Bill: No. I can't because <u>I've got a dentist appointment</u>.
Anna: What about <u>Wednesday morning</u>? I'm free then.
Bill: That's fine. See you then.

2 Get students to practise it. Possible ways of doing this are:
   (a) elicit each line and give choral and individual repetition practice (see pp114–115)

   (b) give choral and individual repetition practice from a tape or after you have acted it out

   (c) rehearse it with the students in pairs with the dialogue written on cards

   (d) rehearse it from the board or the OHP (in pairs or as a whole class directed by the teacher)

3 Ask the students to work in pairs, each with his diary hidden from the other, and make arrangements for the week to include: going to the cinema, playing tennis, etc. The underlined phrases should be substituted with meaningful choices.
If you wish, the same dialogue can have built-in 'free' elements:
   e.g. write on both cards the instruction 'The second time you try to make an arrangement you can't find a convenient time. You get annoyed. Continue the dialogue as you like.'

B: For less controlled practice
1 Set the scene (e.g. two friends are trying to arrange a time to discuss the climbing holiday they want to take).

2 Give out the diaries, so that one has Anna's, the other Bill's, round the class. Ask the students to read them silently.

3 Check that the students have understood what's written.

4 Either draw a chart like this on the board, show it on the OHP or give it out on cards:

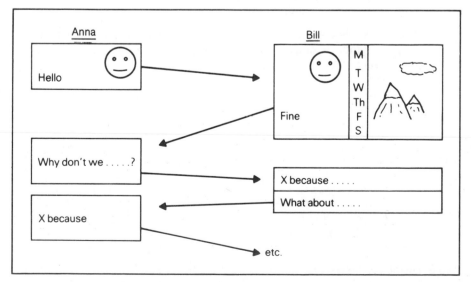

5 Do a 'run-through' of the dialogue with one of the students (don't do it too often with fixed lines or the students will memorize one version rather than speak with relative freedom).

6 Finally, ask students to practise a dialogue in pairs along these lines. They can use what language they like provided they are guided by the cues on the chart.

C: For 'creative' practice
1 Set the scene.

2 Give out the diaries. Check comprehension.

3 Tell the students they must try to find some free time they have in common to talk about their coming holiday. If they can't, they must try and persuade the other to make time before or after one of the things they have already planned to do.

The language here is almost entirely chosen by the students, so this would only work as a suitable follow-up to *What about . . . . . ?* and *Why don't we . . . . . ?* if the structures have already been practised thoroughly.

Chain drills

In large classes it is often helpful to split the students up and do a drill in groups; so the interaction pattern of a simple repetition drill might look like this:

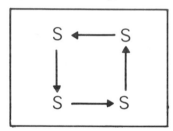

Figure 16

In the following example, the aim is to give further practice of the structure *So . . . . . . I (e.g. I like swimming/So do I).*

Step 1 With the whole class elicit from visuals and practise the vocabulary to be used to prompt the drill e.g.:
      swimming
      a bicycle
      a policeman
      the cinema
      headache
      etc.

Step 2 Elicit and practise a whole series of prompts e.g:
      I like swimming
      I ride a bicycle
      I'm a policeman
      I go to the cinema a lot
      I've got a headache
      etc.

Step 3 Distribute the visuals.

Step 4 Ask individual students to say the prompt to you; you respond with the response *That's funny. So . . . . . . I:*

      T: *Tell me.*
      S1: *I like swimming.*
      T: *That's funny. So do I.*
      S2: *I ride a bicycle.*
      T: *That's funny. So do I.*
      S3: *I'm a policeman.*
      T: *That's funny. So am I.*
      etc.

Step 5 Reverse the roles so that you say *I like . . . . .* etc. and the students say *So . . . . I.*

Step 6 Do one or two examples in 'open pairs' (see p 41).

Step 7 Divide the class into groups and give each group a set of pictures.

Step 8 Indicate how you want the chain to go (S1 → S2 → S3 → S4 etc). It is of course possible in smallish classes to have the whole class as one chain and you feed in prompts to several strategic positions, provided that you indicate that the chain is to go in the same direction!:

      S1: *I like swimming.*
      S2: *So do I.* (turning to S3) *I like swimming.*
      S3: *So do I.*
      etc.
      (by which time S1 has gone on to the next prompt)

An interesting and amusing alternative to this, although freer in its choice of examples, is: instead of visuals get S1 *miming* anything he likes; S2 then has to make a statement beginning *I* (e.g. if S1 has mimed someone tripping, S2 has to say *I'm always falling over*); S3 then has to give the response (e.g. *So am I*).

Exercises

Ex. 1

AIM
To give practice in producing consistent stress and intonation.

PROCEDURE
1 With others in your group compose a simple substitution drill around an utterance showing a very strong attitude e.g:

    Did you really drink all that?
                 eat
                 buy
                 spend

2 Stand in front of your group and say the model.

3 Get the others in turn to hold up cards with the prompt written on them (e.g. *drink*).

4 Say the whole utterance containing the substituted item, keeping your stress and intonation consistent.

5 Record the exercise and comment on any distortion.

COMMENT
The strong attitude gives much more marked stress and intonation to utterances which is far more difficult to maintain consistently.

Ex. 2

AIM
To improve chorus drilling.

PROCEDURE
1 Chorus-drill an utterance with your group, making sure:
  – everyone starts together

  – the rhythm and major pitch movements are indicated by gesture.

2 If there are problems of maintaining correct stress, substitute the model (e.g. *He's gone to the bank*) with sounds (e.g. Da DA dada DA). If there are problems with intonation, a humming sound might be better.

COMMENT
This exercise is often more usefully done in a foreign language or a nonsense language.

Ex. 3

AIM
To learn how to do quick, efficient drilling, using a variety of different prompting techniques.

PROCEDURE
1 Prepare a simple substitution drill around a structure or a function (e.g. *Have you got any . . . . .?/Is there a . . . . in the house?/Do you like . . . . -ing?*) using one of the following prompts:
  – objects

  – visuals (e.g. pictures to be held by you or stuck on the board; board or OHP drawings)

  – spoken words or words on cards

  – simple mimes

  – noises

2 Try out the drill on your group concentrating on:
  – giving a clear model

  – clear efficient prompting

  – using simple metalanguage and talking as little as possible

  – spreading your attention, so that every student gets plenty of practice

  – maintaining a good pace

  – keeping stress and intonation consistent and not distorting sounds

  – making clear gestures for choral work, individual repetition, 'nomination', beating stress, indicating pitch movement, etc.

3 Discuss with your colleagues how efficient you were. If you were recorded, particularly on video, this will help.

COMMENT
Frequently, this exercise is best done piecemeal, concentrating on one aspect at a time (e.g. gesture).

Ex. 4

AIM
To give practice in clear, efficient prompting.

PROCEDURE
A: 1 Take turns at drilling your peer group using prompt words on cards, visuals or objects.

2 Ask a colleague not taking part in the drill to shout out every time a prompt is not clear, too small, upside down, only visible to part of the class, etc.

3 When you are shouted at justifiably, sit down!

4 Someone else then takes over. The object is to complete the drill without having to sit down!;
B: 1 As in A, but the observer is looking for speed and only allows a certain time for each prompt and response.

2 If the time limit is exceeded, the observer should shout and someone else take over.

COMMENT
You will need to guard against these exercises becoming chaotic and comprehensibility being sacrificed for speed.

Ex. 5

AIM
To reduce the amount of 'teacher talking time' while drilling.

PROCEDURE
1 Prepare a simple substitution drill.

2 Drill the group. However, you are not allowed to speak once you have given the model. Colleagues can 'score' the number of times you speak!

COMMENT
Good for developing eye-contact control, use of gesture and if correction is necessary, correction techniques using fingers (see p 149). The drill might best be done in a foreign language.

4.4 Checking

1: Checking how well the students produce language

Every time a student produces, in oral or written form, a stretch of language, he is providing evidence of his productive abilities. If what is said or written has been carefully set up and controlled by you — e.g. you might want a student to repeat something or make specific utterances from picture prompts – then what is being revealed is largely his imitative abilities i.e. can he make the right noises (if speaking) or the right signs (if writing) and put them in the correct order?

So, your assessment of how well the student can 'perform' is done by measuring the student's utterance against your model (provided either by you or by a tape). If it's approximately accurate you can either accept it silently or make some encouraging comment ('good', 'almost' etc.); if it isn't, you can get the student to try again, help him to correct it himself or simply correct it for him and *then* get him to try again (see pp 149–151).

That, however, is a very different thing from being able to use that same type of utterance naturally, selecting it, probably unconsciously, from an infinite number of language choices in order to express oneself or to negotiate one's way through a communicative situation. In the classroom you will need to consider two types of activity to allow for this:

(a) Activities with a predictable language focus
For example, you have decided you want the students to experiment freely with, e.g. IMPERATIVES since you have already given controlled practice of the form on a previous occasion. So you might put them in pairs, one with a picture which he hides from the other. The student with the picture then has to tell the other how to draw the whole picture (e.g. *Draw a big man*). Since the activity naturally encourages the use of instruction-giving language you will not need to direct the students to use the imperative form but you will need to assess how well the students manage to communicate what they want to say, noting things like:

(i) *choice:* Did the students call upon the appropriate forms of the imperative or did they avoid them? Did they know the range of forms that could have been employed?

(ii) *accuracy:* Did the students get the grammar right? Did they pronounce the words correctly? Was the stress and intonation right? Was the word correct?

(iii) *fluency:* Did the forms come out naturally and easily or did the students stumble and hesitate?

(b) Activities with a less predictable language focus
In, for example, a spontaneous discussion where what is actually said is less likely to be predictable, then your assessment of how well it was performed will also be less likely to have a specific language focus, even though you might decide to concentrate on only one general criterion of performance (e.g. accuracy).

In either case, make notes (taping the students and playing it back later can be a help), either on a class basis (e.g. by writing down what seem to be the commonest problem areas) or on an individual basis (for a general assessment you might need headings like GRAMMAR, VOCABULARY, PHONOLOGY). If you are interested in the problems of the whole class, then you'll need to consider whether to deal with them at a later date in a specially-prepared lesson or immediately after the activity. If you are more concerned with individual problems, then you will need to give individual guidance and direct students to exercises and material that will help them.

2: Checking how well the students understand language

(a) Checking structural concepts
All teachers need to know that students have understood any new language they are presenting. This is most obviously revealed by whether the students use it

appropriately when the choice is theirs.

However, you will probably need to know whether they've understood it before you give them opportunities in the class to use if freely. There is no point in controlled practice being done if the students don't understand what they're saying.

So you will need to set a task or ask a series of questions that *check* that they understand. e.g:

Teaching Aim:	To introduce 'used to' to express a discontinued past state.
Model:	'She used to be fat!'
Questions to check understanding of meaning of new item (i.e. 'Concept' questions):	
	Is she fat now?
	When? Past? Future?
	Was she fat one day? Two days? More? Some time?

In this case the questions go to the essence of the item and check understanding of the components that make up its meaning. Here *used to* expresses a discontinued past state so the questions refer to those elements: *Is she fat now?* (No, not now – discontinued) When? Past? Future? (Past) *Was she fat one day? Two days? More? Some time?* (One day, two days and more – state). There is no reference to the context (the person speaking, the person spoken to, the place and the occasion) although sometimes questions about these aspects can help you check the students' understanding of language concepts. However, they don't *necessarily* help.

(b) Checking 'functional' concepts

The techniques used to check the understanding of the 'functions' of utterances are the same as for structural concepts in that you need to break the concept down into the essential elements. Because, however, the functional concept relates to how the language is used, it will always be inextricably related to important elements in the context, e.g.

Language aim:	To introduce 3rd conditional type sentences used as a reprimand.
Model:	Manager to worker: If you'd done it on time, we wouldn't have lost the order
Concept questions:	
	1. Who's speaking?
	2. Who's he speaking to?
	3. Is he pleased?
	4. How can you tell?
	5. Was the worker right or wrong?
	6. What will happen to the worker?
	7. Will he be late again?
	8. What will happen if he is?

These questions are aimed at establishing the fact that the worker has done something wrong (5), that the manager is in a position to reprimand him (1 and 2) and that he is doing so (3 and 4). Questions 6, 7 and 8 confirm that the reprimand could be followed up with the threat of dismissal, particularly if the problem occurs again.

With a structure like this, of course, you may need to include structural concept checks as well.

(c) Checking lexical concepts

If your aim is to check understanding of an individual vocabulary item such as the noun *building*, the questions would have to determine what the word doesn't signify as much as what it does signify. In other words you are checking (and in a sense clarifying) the limits of the meaning of the item, e.g.:

> *Is it a big thing?*
> *Is a school a 'building'?*
> *a hospital?*
> *a house?*
> *a tent?*
> *What's the difference between a house and a tent?*
> *Who makes a 'building'?*
> *Who makes a tent?*
> *Is what a bird makes a 'building'?*
> *Is a police-station?*
> etc.

You cut away those things (e.g. manufactured shelters and animal-made homes) that could be confused with a 'building' and leave the students with a clear impression – just as you have *assessed* that they have that impression – of what a 'building' actually is (i.e. something constructed by a builder with walls in which people live or work).

Any questions that check language 'concepts' usually need to be:

(i) Simple and short
   i.e. below the 'level' of the student. One word questions, e.g. *Past?* and gestures such as a thumb over the shoulder to indicate pastness together with a questioning expression, are not only acceptable they are *preferable*. Remember the aim is simply to check that the students understand the meaning of the language you are focusing on, not to develop their listening skills!

(ii) Varied and numerous
   In fact more than one question is needed for each aspect so that more than one student can be asked without anyone picking up the 'right' answer from the first student.

(iii) Asked often and spread around the whole class

(iv) In language that does not include the language being checked
   If students don't understand what you are checking, then your question will be meaningless and will not guide the students towards understanding.

(v) Constructed so that you do not expect the language being checked to appear in the answers. That might encourage more repetition of the language being presented.

'Concept' questions can obviously be asked any time you wish to ensure that the students have understood any items of language you want them to work with. However, they need to be automatically included when new language is presented. Asked after a listening drill (see pp 83–85) they not only ensure that you are not asking the students to repeat what they haven't fully understood – a frustrating and boring exercise – you are also helping to reinforce the meaning you have tried to get across in your Presentation. In inductive Presentations, it provides the explicit understanding of what has been conveyed implicitly. They need to be asked until you are sure that all students have understood fully, but no longer. They may come before a listening drill, as well as after; they may come during a repetition drill, or during a substitution drill. As often as necessary, but sometimes that is hardly at all.

'Concept' questions are a complex aspect of language teaching and demand firstly that you have a full understanding of what you are teaching. They are difficult to think up and it is as well to work on them when you are researching your language points. **Until you have had considerable experience, you will need to write them into your lesson plans.**

Of course, you can also check that the students have understood not only the meaning of the item, but also how is it used by setting up a freer, more 'creative' activity (such as a short role play, structured so as to encourage use of those items) soon after the Presentation (see pp 60–80).

3: Checking whether the students have understood what is going on

Understanding of other more general features of a context also often needs to be checked, not only who is talking to whom, the place and the occasion but also what they are talking about and what's happening. It needs to be done:
– during Presentation, any time a textual environment is needed for new items of language. This may be a dialogue or a newspaper article.

– during skills work, when a text is used (e.g. a listening text such as a station announcement or a reading text such as a letter).

– when setting up 'creative' activities such as role-plays, when characters and their relationships are being introduced.

What types of questions should be asked?

Comprehension questions need to be organized and serve a clearly thought-out purpose. You will need to ask yourself: *What do I want the students to understand? What is this question really asking? Does it ask what I want them to understand?* Different types of questions expect different types of answers, e.g:
– look at the following dialogue from *English in Situations* by O'Neill (OUP) where the overall teaching aim might be to give further practice to the frequency adverbs *often, never,* and *always.*

Tony and Susan are a young married couple. Tony writes advertisements for a large advertising agency and Susan teaches French. They are at home now. It is evening and they are sitting in the living-room.

Tony: You know, Susan, I think we're becoming vegetables . . . cabbages!
Susan: What a strange thing to say! What do you mean?
Tony: Well . . . just look at us! You're sitting there and I'm sitting here . . . we aren't talking . . . or reading . . . we're just staring at the wall!
Susan: Turn the television on if you're bored!

Tony: Television! That's the trouble. We never go out in the evenings. We always watch television. It's terrible. **Susan:** All right. What do you want to do then? **Tony:** Hmm ... I don't know ... the Academy cinema is showing a new Swedish film this evening. **Susan:** Swedish films! Ugh! I don't like them! All that sex and religion. **Tony:** How do you know? You never see them! **Susan:** Oh all right! We can go to the cinema this evening if that's what you want. Where's my coat? **Tony:** Oh! Just a second. It's Thursday today isn't it? **Susan:** That's right. So what? **Tony:** Well ... I want to watch the boxing on television this evening. I always watch it.

(In the following sections try to answer the questions yourself.)

1 'Gist' questions or 'detail' questions?

(a) *'Gist'*   gist questions check the general context and the general content

               – Are they watching television while they are talking?

               – Is Tony happy watching television every night?

(b) *'Detail'* *– Does Susan suggest they turn the television on?*

               – Does Susan like Swedish films?

Gist questions are normally asked first, to check general understanding, before you break a text up and try for a full understanding of its parts. They are sometimes asked before the students are given a text so that they keep them in mind while they are listening or reading in order to give them something to listen and read *for*. Sometimes *only* gist questions are asked (e.g. when you want to exploit the topic, or when you use a difficult text with elementary students) or *only* easily-answered 'detail' questions, where the students are expected to recognize only certain *outstanding facts* rather than understand the whole text fully (e.g. when using a news broadcast with beginners).

2 Questions which can be answered from the surface of the text and those which cannot.

(a) Information which is directly retrievable from the text:
     i.e. obvious facts about the context or content
     – What are the names of the two people?

     – How often do they go out in the evenings?

(b) Information not directly retrievable from the text:
     i.e. where the students interpret what is happening, make inferences and speculate what *will* happen. The 'answers' won't be obvious and students may disagree and want to discuss alternatives:
     – Does Tony change his mind often?

     – Do they love each other?

     – Will they go to the cinema or watch television?

     – What sort of person is Susan?

Type (a) questions often involve the students giving straight repetitions from the text and as such can often be replied to without real understanding of the content. Comprehension checking should not often involve too many such questions although a certain amount of direct retrieval is necessary. However, because students will have to think and draw upon on their own language, questions of type (b) are more demanding and more interesting. It's as well to get on to interpretative work as soon as you are sure the students have understood the text reasonably well.

The two broad categories above (gist/detail; directly retrievable information/not directly retrievable information) are the most valuable way of dividing up question types. However, you should also consider the following:

3 What are easy questions and what are difficult questions?

(a) *Easy:* Since the students might find the replies they are expected to make to questions often more difficult than understanding the text itself, you will need to grade your questions in terms of how easy or how difficult they are to answer. 'Easy' questions might expect the students to answer simply *yes* or *no* (*yes, they do; no, they don't*) or to give a one-word answer to an *either/or* construction.

– *Do Tony and Susan watch television?*

– *Are they watching television now?*

– *Does Susan teach French or Spanish?*

– *Is she teaching French now?*

These questions, though, might be constructed using a form of *do* or *be* or *have* or a model such as *can* or *should*, all of which your students may find difficult to understand, so be careful! (The question *Should he have told Susan they are becoming cabbages?* is easy in the sense that all students have to say is *yes* or *no* – or *Yes, he should/ No, he shouldn't* – but the form of the question is not easy to understand at all and demands the students have an opinion about what is happening in the text.)

(b) *Less easy:* These might be questions beginning with a question word (*What, When, Where, Why, Who, Whose, How, Which*) where the answers can be found in the text. These clearly relate to 2 (a) in the previous category.

– *What do Tony and Susan do every evening?*

– *How often do they go out in the evenings?*

– *Why doesn't Susan like Swedish films?*

– *Who decides to stay at home tonight?*

Although the last question in this case is effectively only a choice between two alternatives, this type of question is usually felt to be slightly harder than those in (a). Obviously, though, there can be degrees of difficulty within the category and some will in effect be easier than those in (a).

(c) *More difficult:* These questions might be those where the student has to draw upon his own language rather than the language of the text. Obviously, they overlap with 2 (b) above. Such questions often begin with *Why* or *How*.

– *Why does Tony think they're becoming cabbages?*

– *Why do you think they never go out in the evenings?*

– *How often do you think Tony sees Swedish films?*

– Why does Susan agree to go to the cinema?
Clearly these categories are not rigid. The important thing is to ask yourself *Is the question I am asking easy or not?* and, probably, ask the easy questions first.

4　Which questions give short answers and which give long answers?

(a)　Questions giving short answers:
Clearly this category overlaps with the 'easy' questions above but it could also include
– What's the name of the cinema showing the Swedish film?

(b)　Questions giving long answers:
This category overlaps with 3 (c) above and 2 (b) above. They might expect interpretation or description, where the students are expected to draw upon their own language and ideas.
– What sort of person is Tony?

– How differently do they feel about television?

This distinction is important when you are deciding how far you want the students to use the language. Obviously, particularly at the higher levels, questions which encourage long answers help to keep your own talking time down. However, 'speaking prompts' such as *Tell me about . . . . Describe . . . . .* are often better for this e.g.:

Describe the relationship between Tony and Susan.

The students will have to be able to interpret the text, and recast it in their own words in a reasonably long flow.
To summarize, then, the scales are:

```
(a)  Gist → Detail
     Information retrievable from text → not retrievable from text

(b)  Easy → Difficult
     Short answers → Long answers
```

Scales of questioning should not be rigidly translated into a teaching order. They can quickly make your teaching mechanical and predictable. You will need to vary the *types* of questions asked according to:
– the aim of the lesson

– the stage the lesson is at and what level or type of understanding you expect

– what your students are capable of at any one point.

It is important at all times to be aware of what a question expects and to be sensitive as to how much a student needs it to be asked. So:
– be flexible
Don't stolidly wade through all the questions you've written out on your lesson plan if you find they're not necessary

– grade within the types
generally you should ask easy questions before you ask difficult questions, but mix them up and *vary* the types. On your lesson plan it's well worth breaking them up into categories for easy reference but don't just read through a list in the classroom.

– deal with the text differently at different stages of a lesson

So while a first exposure to a text often demands easy gist questioning, subsequent exposures, say to small segments of it, can be dealt with in different ways with these questions on this segment expecting short answers and those questions on that segment expecting interpretation.

Remember, asking questions *after* a text is a checking process not a teaching process. If you wish to *teach* listening and reading you will need to give students a reason for doing so. In which case you will have to set the questions beforehand geared to the type of listening or reading you expect (e.g. listening for gist or detail). Other tasks such as chart-filling (see below) are often more suited to the purpose.

Can you get students to ask the questions?

Yes. It is a way of passing the checking process across to the students once the basics have been covered by the teacher. It removes you from the limelight a little and gives the students extra practice in question formation. It might develop like this:

T *What are they doing now?*
S1 *Staring at the wall.*
T *Good. OK, Moktar. Ask Juan a question with 'Why' and 'Swedish films'.*
S2 *Why doesn't Susan like Swedish films?*
S3 *Because they have too much sex and religion.*

Can you check understanding without asking questions?

Again, yes. You can ask the students to fill in forms, compose charts and the like. The aim is for the students to transfer some of the relevant information from the text you are dealing with to a simple graphic format, something they can't do properly if they don't understand it; e.g. read this letter:

Saturday

Dear Mary,

Well, we arrived on Thursday evening. We travelled all day. We were very tired so we went to bed early. On Friday we went shopping in the market. That was in the afternoon. In the morning John went fishing and I went to hire a car for the week. After shopping we drove into the hills to a little restaurant for supper. Very good it was, too.

This morning we're not doing very much, just writing postcards and planning the rest of the week.

I'll write again soon.

Love,
Martha.

Now, in the right space write down what Martha and John did.

	Thursday	Friday	Saturday
Morning			
Afternoon			
Evening			

They take quite a lot of thinking up and examples can be found in many modern materials (e.g. *Exchanges* by Garton-Sprenger et al, Heinemann). Of course, they are mainly used to *teach* the skills of listening and reading. In the early days of TP you might wish to stick to two other simple techniques:

1 *True/False statements:*
   Write some statements on the board or OHP, or give them out on a work sheet e.g.:
     Susan likes boxing
     Susan changes her mind about going to the cinema
     Tony is bored
Tell the students to write 'True' or 'False' next to each.

2 *Multiple-choice statements:*
   Write up choices such as the following:
   Susan doesn't like Swedish films because
     she never sees them
     she doesn't like the Academy cinema
     they are full of sex and religion
   (there should be a maximum of five alternatives).
Then tell the students to tick the statement they think is correct.

Such exercises perform a vital function in providing variety to the type of work done, particularly if they are in worksheet form and the students are given the opportunity to compare their results. Where and how often you use them will depend on what you want the students to be able to do. If you are assessing how well the students have understood something, you might give the students such exercises *after* they have read or listened to the text but if you wish to concentrate their minds in order to help develop that understanding then you might well get them to do them *while* they are listening or reading. (You must check that the students have understood how to do the exercises first – and be careful not to include unnecessarily difficult language in the task itself).

How do the principles of checking relate to the stages of Presentation and Practice or new language?

1 During the presentation of new language you should
   – prevent the students from being forced to repeat language they don't understand by checking whether they have or not (roughly at least) understood the 'concept' (i.e. the meaning) of the language you are presenting. If they don't understand have another go at getting it across

   – assess how well the students are following the logic behind any inductive presentation by checking their full understanding of the context and what's happening within it

   – generally assess how well the students can speak and how much they know when you elicit information, ideas or language

2 When giving controlled practice
   – for example during a drill, check that students have understood the language they are practising and assess how well they can reproduce it. Remember, though, you cannot at this stage judge how far they can select it appropriately in a situation outside your control

– if you are trying to develop the students' listening and reading skills or giving less controlled language exercises such as narrative and dialogue building (see pp 110–119 and pp 121–132) you will need to check comprehension of what is happening as well as check language concepts when unfamiliar and important items come up.

3 *When the students are communicating freely during an interaction activity*
– you should assess the students' ability to *use* the language accurately and fluently, as well as note how well students get across what they want to say and how well they understand each other.

– assessment is likely to be 'diagnostic' rather than lead to immediate correction (see pp 133–134); what you discover may modify what you do with them in the future.

What is the difference between checking and testing?

At the end of a section of a syllabus or a timetable, perhaps every week, you might want to give the students a more formal 'achievement' test to see how well they have absorbed the body of language material that has been taught and how well they can now do the things they couldn't do before. It'll help you decide what to do next, what to repeat, what to consolidate, what to develop.

Testing can be a complex area and is normally outside the scope of most TP situations, whereas checking is part and parcel of every lesson. However, if you do give students an 'achievement' test bear in mind the following principles:

1 *Only test what the students are supposed to have learned or what you think the students can reasonably do*
In other words, if the students have only learned to understand the meaning of an item, only test understanding. If you have also taught the students to use an item orally in a controlled way, then you can test whether or not they can use it orally in a controlled way. In the main you shouldn't test what the students haven't learned to do unless it is a test designed to check on the students' general language level which will help decide which class to put them in and what to teach them. Don't test how well they write something when they've only been taught to say it. If you haven't taught them to use an item of language freely you shouldn't test that ability formally.

2 *Students must be familiar with the form of the test*
Some students perform badly because they don't know what to do. Many students are not familiar with conventional testing techniques. Many tests are far harder than they seem, as you can see if you try some unfamiliar types in a language other than your own. For example, to fill in a gap in a sentence (e.g. Susan . . . . like English films) or to complete a sentence (e.g. Susan agrees to go to the cinema because . . . .) a student needs not only familiarity with the appropriate written forms, a good knowledge of grammar, an ability to predict what is expected, an awareness of what can and cannot fit in the gaps but also familiarity with what he is expected to do!!

Are dictations a good way of checking what the students can do?

Dictations are far harder than they seem. To do them successfully, students have to be able to:
– identify sounds when run together in connected speech

– understand what they represent in terms of words

– understand and to a certain extent interpret what the words mean when grouped together

– transfer what they hear into the written mode

– write quickly with few spelling mistakes.

There are also usually severe limitations on the time that can be taken to do these things!

Dictations, however, can test a lot (in fact the ability to do all things just mentioned). At the lower levels you usually only dictate what the students have had both oral and written practice in. In general terms:

– dictations shouldn't defeat the students

– you should have a clear purpose for giving them.

One conventional way of giving them is by doing the following:

1 Establish a context and check the students understand it fully.

2 Relate the students personally to the topic of the dictation.

3 Read it through once at normal speed, with the students only listening, not writing.

4 Check they have a general understanding of the text.

5 Read each group of words – they will need to be divided up on your lesson plan – at normal speed as many times as it takes the students to be able to write them down. Don't slow down or 'decontract' your language.

6 Read the whole dictation again giving time for the students to make corrections at the end of each sentence.

7 Ask the students to read it again silently.

8 Ask one or two more questions to check general understanding.

9 Get students to discuss and compare their dictations in groups.

10 Give out, write up or show on OHP the correct version. Get the students to correct their own in a different colour ink.

11 Assess how well they did the task.

12 Ask students to write out a neat copy at home.

Dictations needn't be passages. They can be numbered sentences, small dialogues, incomplete sentences which the students have to complete for themselves, or jumbled sentences which they have to order according to the sense.

A final note

Testing can be motivating or defeating depending on what you give and how you give it. It can give a sense of achievement, show how much needs to be done, diagnose problem areas for your attention in future lessons, but it can be terribly demoralizing if pitched too high and given without purpose.

Exercises

Ex. 1

AIM
To give practice in writing questions to check that students understand new language.

PROCEDURE
A: 1 Write 'concept' questions to check presented language items, e.g:
   I wish he'd come.
   He used to go fishing every week.
   She must have gone out.

   2 Swap questions around and get each set modified or developed by others in your group.

   3 Discuss.

B: 1 Write 'concept' questions.
   2 Ask colleagues to try and guess what is being checked.

C: 1 Get each person in your group to prepare 'concept' questions for different items.
   2 Shuffle the items and questions.
   3 Get the whole group to match them.

Ex. 2

AIM
To give practice in deciding on the usefulness of comprehension questions.

PROCEDURE
1 Choose a piece of dialogue, two or three lines long, e.g:
   A: *So I said I didn't want to go.*

   B: *What on earth did you do that for?*

   A: *Well, I didn't really like him.*

2 In pairs, write down as many questions as you can about what is in the dialogue and what it implies. Do this quickly without worrying about how good or bad the questions are. A strict time limit will help you concentrate.

3 Divide the questions you have written down into the categories given on pp 103–104 i.e. 'Easy', 'Less easy', 'More difficult'. You can either discard irrelevant questions or put them to one side and discuss later in what way you think they might be of use.

Ex. 3

AIM
To give practice in other means of checking comprehension.

PROCEDURE
1 Look at the chart on p 105.

2 Find a text which describes a process, e.g. the production of steel or what happens to a letter after it's been posted.

3 Try to draw up a chart to check understanding of the different stages. Do this with a colleague and discuss whether you should ask the students to tick boxes, write in single word answers, label diagrams or write sentences. Try to decide on the advantages and disadvantages of each.

4.5 Eliciting dialogues and narratives

You try to elicit ideas, information and language when you build up Presentation contexts in order to:
1 get students participating fully in all stages of the Presentation

2 help you assess how far the students understand the *logic* of the Presentation and how far they understand the language you are using.

It will in the end determine how much you can assume and how fast you can go.

However, you can only elicit what the students are able to give so you shouldn't spend time trying to elicit what it is clear the students don't know (see pp 143–145).

Whole dialogues and narrative can be elicited for Presentation purposes but the activity can be a bit time-consuming and deflect you from the main aim of introducing new language if they are too long.

Eliciting long stretches of language is better done when you want to:

– give further practice in another language setting of language recently introduced.

– reactivate language that the students *know* but less frequently *use*.

– get the students to practise ways of responding to a specific item when it is used in conversation (e.g. having taught *I'd like . . . . .* as an item you might want to show that when the person gives you what you want you can informally respond with *Thanks*).

The techniques that are frequently employed when dialogues or narratives are elicited are difficult to master because they require you to maintain a balance between the students using language freely in response to your cues and controlled language practice.

Two approaches to building dialogues

Context:
John Adams, a student from Manchester, has come down to London. He has to stay in a hotel but hasn't much money.

Approach 1

Aim: to give further practice to the function of making a suggestion through the structure *Why don't you . . . .?*
Dialogue:

John:	*A single room, please.*
Receptionist:	*They're £20 a night.*
John:	*£20! Sorry, I can't afford that.*
Receptionist:	*Why don't you try next door? They're cheaper there.*

(Here, you have written your dialogue out in your lesson plan, in accordance with your aim. You then try to elicit these lines from the students even though in the end you may not stick to them exactly.)

Approach 2

Aim: to give further practice to the function of making a suggestion. Possible forms: *Why don't you . . . .? How about . . . . . .? Have you thought of . . . .?* Useful vocabulary: *vacancy.*

Dialogue:

Between John and the hotel receptionist.

Line 1: John asks for a room
2: The receptionist says how much they are.
3: John can't afford the price.
4: The receptionist suggests alternatives.

(Here, you decide on the sequence of exchanges and what they should contain in a general way but you allow the students to select the actual language used, provided it is grammatically correct and appropriate to the situation. You give guidance, you compare and assess their contributions, you evaluate and finally you accept *one* version for practice even though others might be as good. It is a subtle exercise and not easy to do until you have had experience. To give you some security it might be worth using a chart of the type illustrated on p 93.)

For both approaches the aids might be drawings on the board, or pictures mounted on card, to represent the hotel, John and the hotel receptionist. To establish the context the teacher will give *some* information and try and get the rest from the students:

T: (putting picture on board) *OK. What's this?*
S1:   *Hotel*
T: *An expensive hotel?*
S2:   *Maybe.*
T: *Why do you say that?*
S2:   *It's very big.*
T: *Are all big hotels expensive?*
S5:   *In England, yes! Especially London.*
T: *London, all right. This hotel's in London and it's very expensive. Tell me about this hotel, Juan.*
S7:   *It's a big, expensive hotel in London.*
T: *OK. Now, this is John Adams* (drawing a man and writing 'Manchester' on board). *Do you think he lives in London?*
S3:   *No. Manchester.*
T: *Yes. And where is he now?*
S3:   *London.*
T: *Yes. What else do you know about him?*
S6:   *He doesn't have any money.*
T: *Why do you say that?*
S6:   *He has poor clothes.*
T: *OK. Now he goes to this hotel and he sees the man behind the desk. What do we call him in English?*
S4:   *Receptionist.*
T: *Yes. Everybody: Receptionist.*
S1–9:   *Receptionist.*
S2:   *Receptionist.*
S4:   *Receptionist.*

> T: *He wants a room. Do you think he can afford it?*
> S8: *No.*

So the essential elements are built up. The teacher gives information such as his name and where he comes from but elicits ideas such as his financial state and words such as 'receptionist'.

The first approach, however, is likely to continue as follows:

> T: *OK. John wants a room. He's by himself. So . . . . . A single or a double room?*
> S9:   *Single.*
> T: *Yes. How does he ask?*
> S1:   *Excuse me, madam, but could I have a single room?*
> T: *Madam? Probably not 'Madam'. Not to the receptionist.*
> S1:   *Excuse me, but could I have a single room?*
> T: *OK. That's all right. Very polite in fact. But let's keep it short.*
> S3:   *Single room.*
> T: *Yes, but more polite.*
> S3:   *Single room, please.*
> T: *Single or . . . . .?*
> S4:   *A single room, please.*
> T: *Good. OK. Now listen. Again.*
> S4:   *A single room, please.*
> T: *Everybody.*
> S1–9: *A single room, please.*
> S8:   *A single room, please.*
> S6:   *A single room, please.*

Notice, here, that because the teacher is trying to work towards a specific line of dialogue, alternative contributions where the English is correct (*Excuse me, but could I have a single room?*) are acknowledged as correct and commented upon (*Very polite in fact*) but not accepted for the repetition stage. By getting the students to repeat it in chorus and individually, you are indicating to them which line you want them to memorize. It's very important, of course, that the students get the pronunciation and intonation right at this stage.

The second approach, however, because you haven't exactly pre-decided which language to practise, is more flexible. You have to listen even more carefully and process the students' contributions without giving the impression that you have the right answer in your head. The whole group, including the teacher, is collaborating as it decides which lines to choose for rehearsal:

> T: *OK. John wants a room. Let's think of some ways he can ask.*
> S9:   *I'd like a room.*
> T: *Yes. How polite is that?*
> S9:   *So-so. Better with 'please'.*
> T: *Yes. Much better. And you need more range in your voice. Like this: 'I'd like a room, please'* (exaggerating the intonation slightly).
> S9:   *'I'd like a room, please'.*
> T: *Good. Let's write it up so we don't forget it* (writes up as though starting a list of possibilities)
> S7:   *Have you got a room?*
> T: *Yes, it's a hotel. There are rooms. But are there people in them?*
> S8:   *Spare room?*

T: *Do we say that for hotels when we ask for a room?*

S2:   *No, only in houses. When we ask the landlady if we can use a room.*

T: *Yes. Possibly even in hotels if we want to use a room which isn't a bedroom for something unusual.*

S5:   *Free room?*

T: *Yes, possibly, but not 'Have you got any free rooms?' Why not?*

S1:   *It means the rooms don't cost any money.*

T: *Yes, it could do, though not necessarily. What should we say then?*

S1–9:   (silence)

T: *Have you got any rooms free?*

S2:   *Have you got any rooms free?*

T: *Let's write that up.* (Write up) *Any other ideas?*

S9:   *Have you any vacancies?*

T: *That's good. Come and write that up.* (S9 writes it up)

T: *All right, let's choose one to practise.*

S8:   *Have you any rooms free?*

T: *OK. Everyone.*

S1–9:   *Have you any rooms free?*

Obviously before this exercise can work successfully the students must be prepared to contribute a lot of ideas so there has to be a good co-operative atmosphere in the classroom. They must also have a sense of the language appropriate to a situation and language which isn't ('vacancies' and not 'spare rooms') and which words might go with one another in which order ('room free' not 'free room'). Inevitably too, because some of the explanations by the teacher demand a good standard of English, it is likely to be more suitable for advanced classes.

For either approach, however, the teacher must be prepared to:

– give some ideas on how the language is used

– acknowledge that 'correct' English contributions are correct and that rejection is only on the grounds that they are either not appropriate or not suitable for the dialogue you are building up

– help correct or get the students to correct incorrect contributions

– provide language that isn't known by students. It's very easy, but unhelpful, to spend ages trying to elicit what the students don't know!

– give lots of encouragement. If you appear to be rejecting too much it can seem as though you are in sole possession of a secret the students have to prize out of you!

How do you practise the dialogue once you have elicited it?

In fact you need to get the students to memorize the lines as they are elicited so that in time the whole dialogue can be acted out. After you have elicited *possible* ideas for what the line could be the students have to understand which line it is you are settling on to include in the dialogue. This is sometimes known as 'standardizing' the lines and usually involves you in giving a quick 'listening drill' of the line, or you may get the student who contributed the line to provide the model. You then get the whole class to chorus the line and give as much individual practice as is necessary for all of them to be able to memorize it and say it correctly.

(If you are building narratives, this stage is likely to differ in that longer stretches of language need to be built up in bits and then joined together. Also, being monologues they can't be acted out.)

Continuing, then, using the first approach to dialogue building, we were at the point when the teacher had focused on the line he wanted, given chorus practice and individual practice (probably substantially more than indicated in the transcript.):

S2:   *A single room, please.*
T: (drawing '£20' on the board) *How much do they cost?*
S8:   *£20.*
T: *Is that expensive?*
S8:   *Yes, very.*
T: *OK. How does the receptionist tell him?*
S9:   *It costs £20.*
T: *Possible, but 'it' sounds funny. How many rooms are there?*
S4:   *Lots.*
T: *So not 'it' but . . . .?*
S3:   *They . . . . they cost £20.*
T: *Yes. But he isn't selling the room. So not 'cost'. Listen: 'They're £20 a night'. Everybody.*
S1–9: *'They're £20 a night'.*
T: *Marion.*
S5:   *They're £20 a night.*
T: *Is he selling the room?*
S5:   *No.*
T: *OK. I'm John. You're the receptionist. 'A single room, please.'*
S6:   *They're £20 a night.*
      (repeated with several students)
T: *Now, I'm the receptionist. You're John.*
S2:   *A single room, please.*
T: *They're £20 a night.*
      (repeated with several students)
T: *Now, Juan – Marion.*
S7:   *A single room, please.*
S5:   *They're £20 a night.*

This last stage, known as 'open pairs' practice, can now be extended into 'closed' pairs practice in the same way as the paired substitution drill was built up on pp 86–88. The next two lines could then be elicited in the same way and added on. The amount of actual practice always depends on the degree of difficulty your students are having and how well they can memorize the lines.

The procedure just mentioned could be outlined as follows:

1 Elicit line 1.

2 Give chorus and individual practice.

3 Elicit line 2.

4 Give chorus and individual practice.

5 Teacher gives line 1/students respond with line 2.

6 Students give line 1/teacher responds with line 2.

7 'Open' pairs practice.

8 'Closed' pairs practice.

9 Elicit line 3.

10 Give chorus and individual practice.

11 (Practise all three lines together on an individual basis) – optional.

12 Elicit line 4.

13 Give chorus and individual practice.

14 Teacher gives line 3/students respond with line 4.

15 Students give line 3/teacher responds with line 4.

16 Teacher gives lines 1 and 3/students respond with lines 2 and 4.

17 Students give lines 1 and 3/teacher responds with lines 2 and 4.

18 'Open' pairs.

19 'Closed' pairs.

20 (Some pairs act out in front of class) – optional.

21 Elicit for the board.

22 (Students read from the board) – optional.

23 Students copy into workbooks.

There are many variations. Sometimes you might cut out many of these stages and go more quickly into 'closed' pairs. You should always relate what you want the students to gain from the exercise with how you get them to do it and how much you expect them to do it. Remember, as with all controlled practice, too little can be frustrating, too much can be irritating and boring.

Whatever, don't get bogged down in procedures. Any complicated techniques like the above need sensitive and flexible handling. They also need practice. It is embarrassing for both you and your students if you are too hesitant. But remember, there is no 'right' way of giving practice. If you get too wound up in either your lesson plan or your techniques your students will suffer. It is far better that you listen and respond to your students than you worry about making technical mistakes.

Further suggestions:

1 Write short, manageable dialogues, with a clear focus and good contrasting characterization.

2 Keep the language natural. Include 'social' language like 'How are you?' and expressions like 'Oh dear' when possible. It may be the only time you'll get the students to practise them!

3 Relate the moods and attitudes of the characters to the intonation patterns you expect.

4 Keep the students' imagination alive to what is happening in the dialogues.

5 If necessary, check understanding as you go along. Because one student can supply what you want, it doesn't mean the rest understand.

6 Use 'hooks' that the students will remember, such as the visuals that you used in the lesson where some language you want to elicit was first presented.

7 Give the students clues; if they can't seem to give you what you want give the first sound, the first letter or the first word to help them. Don't leave them floundering!

Narratives

Like dialogue-building, narrative-building, when it leads to practice, is not a 'creative' exercise because the teacher has final control over the language being practised. The contributions elicited, however, although guided by tight questioning, are in the main in language that the students choose.

Basically, both types of language building can be dealt with in similar ways. For example:

1 Set the scene with the students and establish the time frame (e.g. in the past).

2 Elicit the first segment of the narrative (probably the first part of a sentence).

3 Modify and shape the students' responses as you go along but select only one utterance for the practice.

4 Practise a polished version with *all* the students.

5 Repeat steps 2, 3 and 4 for the next segment of the narrative.

6 Connect it to the previous segment and get at least one student to retell the story from the beginning.

7 Continue until the narrative is more or less memorized.
Narratives, as well as dialogues, can be elicited using:
– mime

– picture sequences (as in cartoons and board drawings)

– sound sequences (usually on tape)

– lists of words on the board or on cards

– different-sized and different-coloured sticks used to represent people and things and suggest events.

Why narratives?

Telling stories and jokes and describing things that have happened to us are things most of us do frequently. They are essentially monologues and normally don't require the sort of complex negotiation required in two-way conversations.

So while one of the aims of your narrative-building might be to give further practice to language presented, or to provide a contextual environment for some items of vocabulary, a subsidiary aim might sometimes be to develop the skills of storytelling. Of course, it may also be the *main* aim.

For that reason the stories will often be in the first person singular rather than the descriptive third ('I saw this man . . .' rather than 'John saw a man') and include, particularly at the higher levels, special constructions such as 'What he did was . . . . .'. When storytelling is the main aim it is often better that the narrative is not *too* rehearsed so that the hesitations and imprecisions that occur when we grope for ideas and language are also allowed to be included.

Have they any other advantages?

Yes.

1 They provide an opportunity to practise and sometimes present connectives (e.g. *and, but, however*). Other 'cohesive devices', such as the use of the third person singular (*he* or *she*) after a person has been named, can also be illustrated.

2 They show how a stretch of language is *organized.* How sentences come together as a paragraph can be shown and the function of paragraphs generally can be illustrated.

3 Most importantly, though, they give students the opportunity to practise saying long stretches of language in one go.

Here is an example:

Level: Elementary

Aims: – to give further practice with the PRESENT SIMPLE

– to give further practice with PREPOSITIONS of place and time

– to present *where* as a connective

Aids:

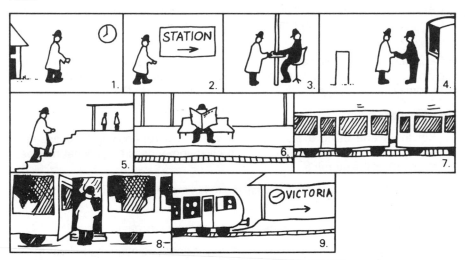

(taken from *Modern English Teacher* M.E.P. Publications Vol. 5 No. 2)

Context:
Mr West doesn't like his job. Every day is the same. He is talking to a friend.

The story:
Every day I *leave* my house *at* 8 o'clock. I *walk to* the station *where* I *buy* a ticket. I *show* my ticket *to* the ticket collector and *then go on to* the platform *where* I *read* a newspaper and *wait for* the train. At 8.30 the train *comes into* the station. I *get on* and *arrive at* Victoria *at* 9.10.

What planning is necessary?

1 Write the story beforehand, making sure the English is appropriate to the level of the class and that the tenses relate to the time-frame you have selected.

2 Decide how to present the picture sequence:
e.g. – draw or photocopy the pictures on to an OHP transparency and reveal them one by one

– draw the pictures on large cards, stick them on to the board with Blu-tack or magnets and exploit each one as you go

– photocopy the sequence, cut the pictures up and ask groups to put them in order

– give out a copy of one picture at a time and elicit what it shows.
If possible, try not to give students the whole story in the correct order before you start; it tends to reduce motivation.

3 Decide which words might be a problem. For example, what a *ticket collector* is should be clear from the picture, although you should check that you and the students 'see' the same person. However, they might well find the pronunciation difficult. Verbs like *get on* are always difficult because of what does or doesn't follow them in the sentence.

4 Write the whole story out in the lesson plan, underlining the key words or highlight them with a fluorescent pen.

5 Decide what gesture or sign you will use to get the students to employ connectives (e.g. you might link index fingers for *and* or write 'and' beneath two pictures: 1 and 2.

6 Consider such problems as 'How will I transfer the students' descriptions of the picture (*he gets on the train*) to Mr West's own description (*I get on the train*)?' At some time they will have to *imagine* themselves as Mr West.

A possible procedure

1 Set the scene using a picture of Mr West, a bored-looking businessman, talking to a friend. Give his name and elicit some ideas about what he does every day in the morning.

2 Tell the students that Mr West is talking to his friend about how he doesn't like going to work.

3 Establish the time frame (e.g. *he is talking about every day*).

4 Establish any gestures you may need (e.g. a finger pointing to the floor might indicate that you want them to use a present tense). This is particularly important for mime stories.

5 Elicit some ideas for the first picture. Mould the answers into a polished opening (e.g. *Every day I leave my house at 8 o'clock*). Make sure all the tenses, prepositions and the like are correct.

6 Give practice (possibly in chorus before the individual practice).

7 Do the same for picture 2.

8 Do the same for picture 3.

9 Show that pictures 2 and 3 are connected (e.g. by linking index fingers). Try to elicit *where*. If necessary, give the opening sound /w/ or the letter 'w'. If they don't know the word, give it and indicate that it refers to place.

10 Get one student to say the whole sentence (*I walk to the station where I buy a ticket*).

11 Get students to repeat individually.

12 Ask another student to tell the whole story from the beginning.

13 Build up the rest of the story in the same way.

Reminders:
– Keep the tenses constant unless there's good reason not to.

– Check that students understand the context fully and the language used.

– Keep the mood of Mr West's boredom alive. Get them to sound bored (i.e. with a bored intonation).

– Drill the narrative in segments, add another segment, link it with what has gone before and so on. Get a student, and probably only one, to recap *occasionally*. It can get boring if it's done too often.

– There are many ways of doing this type of exercise. You might think up variations to suit you and your class.

How can you consolidate the story?
At the end, it can be elicited on to the board or handed out on copied sheets. To highlight important language areas and help the students to memorize them you can rub out bits and re-elicit them. Seeing how much the students can remember the next day is sometimes worthwhile.

Can you extend out of it?
Yes. Don't waste good material! Try to extend it into other activities, for example:
1 Interruptions
   To simulate real anecdotal monologues get one student to tell the whole story and the others to interrupt by either challenging what is being said or asking for clarification (e.g. *Doesn't the train leave at 8.32? What **newspaper** do you read on the platform? I leave **my** house at half-**past** eight*). The students may need to have some suggestions written on cards to get it off the ground. (It can of course be done in pairs.)

2 Paired role-play
   (e.g. One student is Mr West, the other the friend. The friend has to give advice to Mr West, who wants to leave his job. See pp 134–137 on how to set up role-play.)

3 'Transfer' activities
   Get the students to ask each other what time *they* do things. This will give further practice in using the present simple.

4 Questionnaires
   Show students how to compile a questionnaire about work-routines. Get them to ask each other and possibly other people outside the classroom.

Exercises

Ex. 1

AIM
To give practice in eliciting a stretch of language.

PROCEDURE
1 Distribute different short dialogues and narratives among the group.

2 Get everyone to prepare appropriate prompts and write down questions which will elicit their dialogue or narrative.

3 Take turns in eliciting (either use a mixture of methods or decide beforehand to concentrate on one only, e.g. mime, visuals, board drawings).

COMMENT
1 Teachers who talk too much should concentrate on mime stories!

2 Make sure there is sufficient practice and recapping.

3 This exercise might be better done in a foreign language.

Ex. 2

AIM
To give practice in recognizing and accepting some deviations from a pre-scripted text while rejecting others.

PROCEDURE
1 Distribute different short dialogues or narratives among half the group.

2 Distribute a selection of sentences close but not identical to the ones written in the dialogues or narratives among the other half. Some sentences will be acceptable because they do not disturb the logic of the text, but others won't be:
   e.g. Pre-scripted story:

   (1) Last week Mr and Mrs Jones were eating dinner. (2) Mr Jones was talking boringly and Mrs Jones was not enjoying herself. (3) She suddenly fell to the floor and lay there motionless. (4) Mr Jones ran to the phone to call the doctor. (5) While he was ringing, Mrs Jones got to her feet and crept out of the room
   . . . . . .
   One person might have *(3) She suddenly died.* This would not be acceptable. Another might have *(3) She pretended to faint.* This would be acceptable because it fits in with the rest of the story.

3 In turn, those with pre-scripted narratives or dialogues then try to elicit them, from the others in the group; those with numbered sentences call them out at the appropriate stage.

4 Those 'teaching' must accept or reject accordingly.

COMMENT
The effect of this exercise can be enhanced by giving out role-cards so that each member of the group 'plays' someone with a specific character and a specific attitude towards the 'class'. Your colleagues might be encouraged to keep their roles over several exercises.

Ex. 3

AIM
To show the need for both speed and thoroughness.

PROCEDURE
1 Get two of your colleagues to each prepare a short narrative or dialogue.

2 One is asked (secretly?) to elicit his very slowly and thoroughly from the whole group getting every 'student' to repeat every sentence in chorus and individually.

3 The other is asked to elicit rapidly, asking only two or three 'students' to practise the lines.

4 The two attempts are discussed and compared. Ideally, the conclusion will be that a middle way is desirable. (i.e. That a slow pace is boring but a too-quick pace is inefficient.)

COMMENT
This exercise is best done in a foreign language.

4.6 Using Dialogues

What do dialogues consist of?

Any dialogue will normally consist of two speakers (in a particular place, at a particular time) engaged in some form of communication of which language is likely to play a significant part. The speakers will have some individual identity (i.e. a background and a character as well as features more specific to the occasion such as a mood or an attitude) and a social identity (e.g. a specific role such as a bank manager or a more general status such as a boss), both of which might affect what language is chosen (the **register**) as well as how it's said.

So, obviously, the relationship between the speakers – their degree of intimacy as well as their relative social positions – affects the interaction. Also, the stage the exchange is at and what both speakers are trying to do at that stage are also important. In real life, the interplay is likely to be subtle and complex.

Nevertheless, the lines of a dialogue obey certain rules of form, relating to grammar, phonology and choice of lexis, as well as certain conventions as to which forms are chosen and how they operate as part of an interaction (e.g. there are accepted ways of starting conversations, interrupting someone and emphasizing points).

Why are dialogues important for the language classroom?

They are important because although language can be broken down into isolated items (words and structures) or be seen to operate according to at least one system (i.e. the grammatical) we have to teach students *how* it is used. Parroting items in isolation is not enough! When students hear dialogues they can hear some of the ways native speakers communicate with each other and take the first steps in learning to participate.

The problem with real-life dialogues is that they are often confusing, culturally specific and difficult to understand. As a result, you need to employ not only real dialogues to illustrate and help students with what *really* happens but more 'idealized' dialogues (particularly at the lower levels) which simplify and clarify certain specific language features and highlight certain items.

Dialogues for presentation purposes

Specially-written dialogues, with many of the muddling features of real speech omitted, containing language appropriate to the level of the students, are ideal vehicles for the presentation of new items of language because they:
– provide a natural but controlled setting for the items

– illustrate their communicative role

– help students to understand their meaning.

Finally, but very importantly, they are much more memorable!

If you use dialogue for presentation remember:
1 Students need to understand as much of the *context* as is necessary for them to understand the dialogue, including such features as *who* is speaking to *whom, when, where* and *why*. Either elicit the details using your aids or if time is short tell them to the students (but don't forget to check that they understand!)

2 Presentation dialogues ideally should be about four to six lines long, with the target item included in the last line (this allows you to use the previous lines to guide the students towards the meaning of the item and then provide a generative basis for practice).

3 Although more idealized than real conversation, dialogues can usefully contain such social phrases as *Sorry to trouble you but . . . .* and such expressions as *Oh dear*, i.e. things which otherwise might not get taught!

4 The non-presented language used in the dialogue should not usually be new to the students (unless you have a good reason for it to be).

5 Warm the students up to the topic of the dialogue, perhaps by asking some personal questions or by giving away some personal information. (So, in a dialogue about smoking: *Juan, how many cigarettes do you smoke a day?* or *I don't smoke.*)

6 Don't give away what's in the dialogue before the students hear it, otherwise they won't have any reason for listening to it! (You might try and ask them to find out something specific from it by giving them a question beforehand to see if they can answer).

7 Check the students understand what they have heard (i.e. first the general context and what's happening, and then more specifically the item of language – see pp 97–108).

8 On TP, you might find it useful to act out the dialogue with another trainee teacher. Otherwise play it on audio or video tape or act it out yourself, distinguishing sharply between the characters.

Dialogues for practice purposes

Dialogues can be used for all sorts of practice. If real conversation is used, your main aim will probably be to develop the students' listening skills and help them understand and interpret what they hear. Specially-written dialogues (you can find them in most course books or you can write them yourself) pitched at about the students' language level, can, however, be used to:
1 Consolidate and give further practice to an item of language already presented.

They can provide a fresh setting in longer stretches of language. The dialogue will first give practice in helping the students to *listen* and then provide a basis for controlled practice exercises (see pp 83–95).

2 Give repetition practice to stress and intonation patterns as well as problem sounds.

3 Provide a context and a topic for another activity, such as a discussion or a role-play.

Obviously, any dialogue will need to be understood by the students (either the general drift or every single detail). Therefore you will need to deal with it as a listening exercise first. The first time the students listen you will probably expect an **extensive** understanding (i.e. the general drift) or simply a recognition of one or two simple features. Depending on what you are using the dialogue for, you may expect a more detailed (i.e. **intensive**) understanding and so you will have to break it up and scrutinize parts of it. To move from an 'extensive' to an 'intensive' exploitation of a dialogue, the procedure might be as follows:

1 Select or write a suitable dialogue, making sure it is appropriate to the aim of your lesson and the level of your students.

2 Relate the students to the main topic of the dialogue (perhaps by asking one or two questions or giving them some personal information on what *you* think of it.)

3 Build up the context (see p 72 and pp 76–78.)

4 Pre-check or pre-teach any vocabulary that the students won't be able to work out the meaning of from the context and which might hinder what you are trying to do with the dialogue (the students will then see how those words operate in context, although you should only do this if absolutely necessary.)

5 Make sure the students know they are not expected to understand everything and don't discourage them by saying it's difficult!

6 Give them a task to help them to listen out *for* things – either for what's happening in general or for some easily-identifiable things like the names of people. You might write some questions on some sentences on the board which the students have to decide are *true* or *false*.

7 Act out or play the dialogue once. Make sure everybody is able to hear, particularly in a large classroom!

8 Follow up the task you set in 6.

9 Check how much the students have understood. Start by asking easy, general questions (for types of questions see pp 101–105.) and then go on to more difficult and more detailed questions. When the students begin to find it impossible to answer, stop!

10 Present a segment of the dialogue again (which segment depends on what you want to achieve: sometimes you might deal with the whole dialogue in this way; other times you might just take one or two separate segments).

11 Check on detailed understanding. Try not to deal with each segment in exactly the same way; it can get boring!

12 Extend out of the dialogue, encouraging the students to interpret it, perhaps by setting up a role-play or a discussion.

When the dialogue has been understood, the parts you want the students to repeat can be used for practice. Some further pointers:

− Don't get students to repeat an item for its own sake. Make sure you have a very clear purpose. Remember, too much of it can be boring.

− Repetition can be in chorus, by individuals or practised in pairs.

− If you use a tape, make sure the students repeat from that. If you 'bridge' the tape it destroys its validity and makes students overdependent on how *you* say things.

− Acting out a few lines, after some rehearsal, can occasionally be fun; if everybody does it every time, it can get dull.

− Developing on from memorized lines freely can lead to more creative spontaneous exchanges.

− It is sometimes worth consolidating a dialogue by giving out the text and getting the students to read as they listen. (This is usually best done after it's been exploited orally first).

− As revision, it's sometimes a good idea to give out a skeleton text with, say, key words only written down and then get the students to fill in the missing parts orally.

Dialogues always need bringing to life. Once they've been understood, the students can quickly lose interest. Interesting questions to see what the students think and feel about what is happening can be a stimulus. You might also exaggerate the intonation a little to bring out the attitudes of the characters.

Taped dialogues

Course book dialogues on tape provide students with examples of the voices of different native speakers, Make sure that if you use a dialogue from a course book that it is suitable for *your* class. Find out from the Teachers' Book why it has been included and how it can be used. Ask yourself such questions as: *Should I use all of it or only a part of it? Should it be exploited intensively? Are there lines that can usefully be rehearsed?*

Occasionally, though, you may wish to make your own taped dialogue instead. If you do then make sure:

1 The language level is appropriate to what you want to use the dialogue *for*.

2 The language, even if 'idealized', *sounds* natural although it shouldn't be mumbled, gabbled, distorted, or spoken unnaturally slowly − particularly if the students are expected to understand it fully! Make sure background sounds used to make the dialogue more realistic don't dominate what is being said or distract the students.

3 The participants are clearly characterized.

4 You build in drama − even conflict.

5 The exchange is not *too* long and the characters don't speak *too* much.

6 There's a good final line to stop the exchange.

Acted dialogues

If you don't have facilities for recording a dialogue or you can't get another teacher to act it out with you, there are several tricks to enable you to differentiate characters, e.g.:
– Using different voices with different pitch

– Putting up pictures of the characters on the board and standing under the one supposed to be speaking (don't put them too far apart!)

– Indicating different physical heights by moving slightly to one side when a character speaks and looking up or down

– Making simple puppets (from tennis balls and cloth!)
Remember, the fewer the characters the easier it is for everyone!

Authentic spoken language

Using unedited, unscripted conversation is worth doing *regardless of the level*. The lower the level, of course, the less complete the understanding and the more encouragement and tact you will need to keep your students interested. Your role will be to give friendly help and direction rather than check up on how much they have understood. The sort of tasks you can do at the lower level will relate either to a general understanding or to particular fragments of information, such as the names of places, times and so on.

Always make sure you:
1 Choose texts that the students can relate to and do not require too much knowledge of what is outside their experience (in Britain, the television or radio news is often a good source).

2 Make it clear you don't expect complete understanding. Until the students learn *not* to listen to every word they will instinctively try and pick up everything.

3 Get them to relax and build up their confidence.

4 Grade the task according to the level. Don't try and do too much, particularly at the lower levels. Simple tasks like matching pictures with what they hear might be enough.

5 Play the text as often as the students need it, although they should never feel they need to understand every word (again particularly at the lower levels.)

If the students are not used to listening to natural language they might well be daunted at first. However, if you really *can* help them understand something, it is a marvellous confidence-booster. Also, it's amazing what they can pick up incidentally!

Exercises

Ex. 1

AIM
To give practice in the preparation necessary for using a short dialogue.

PROCEDURE

1 Select a four to six line dialogue from a course book.

2 Write two or three questions which would get the students thinking about the theme of the dialogue.

3 Decide which features of the context are essential to an understanding of what the dialogue is about.

4 Decide whether they can simply be deduced as the students listen to it or whether they need to be given beforehand. If the latter, decide whether they can be elicited from the students or whether they need to be illustrated.

5 Write two sets of questions, one to test general understanding and one to check understanding of detail.

COMMENT

This exercise is worth doing without the pressure of having to use the dialogue in class afterwards. It is often best if it is done by a number of people and the results compared.

Ex. 2

AIM

To show how necessary a context is when illustrating the meaning of a target structure.

PROCEDURE

1 Write and/or choose a short dialogue which presents a structure in the last line.

2 Conceal the last line from a colleague, who should then try to guess the structure from the evidence of the dialogue. If unsuccessful, add contextual information of the kind that you think would be useful.

3 Get your partner to do the same exercise with you.

4.7 Using Texts

The word *text* usually refers to a stretch of written discourse intended to be read or a stretch of spoken discourse intended to be listened to. Texts may be *idealized* (i.e. prepared especially for the classroom) or *authentic* (i.e. taken from the real world). Sometimes, idealized texts are constructed to seem authentic.

What can texts be used for?

1 *To present new language*
   New language items can be embedded in a text. The text provides a context to help students infer the meaning of the items. So, to present the structure *going to* + INFINITIVE to an elementary class, the following specially-written news bulletin might be used:

> Good evening. This is the BBC 9 o'clock news. The Queen left England this morning on a visit to Italy. She is due to arrive in Rome at 11 o'clock. Some newspaper reporters think the Pope is going to meet her and they are going to drive to the Vatican in an open car but nobody really knows because the plans are secret.

The phrase *due to* may be new but should easily be inferred from the context; the word *reporters* may need to be checked beforehand. The force of *going to* to express the Pope's intention is highlighted by the fact that the arrangements hinge not on what happens as a matter of known procedure (in which case the structure *will be + ing* might have been used) but on the unknown plans of the Queen and the Pope. The context is generative and can lead to a drill of the sort indicated on pp 86–88. e.g:

The Pope is	going to	meet her
They are		drive to the Vatican
		shake hands
		discuss politics

Basically, the principles of using a text for Presentation are the same as when you use a dialogue for Presentation (see pp 65–80, 83–95 and 122–124.) You select the item, find a suitable textual context to help convey its meaning, then provide a natural example of it and check that the students understand both the context and the concept (see pp 97–109.) Finally, of course, you give the students plenty of practice in saying it.

When writing such a text for your class you should:

(a) Make sure the language you are using is appropriate to the medium (i.e. it is better to construct listening texts in language that people speak and reading texts in language that people write.)

(b) Try not to overload the text with examples of the item (one or two should be enough). Think instead of the text as providing as many clues as possible to the *meaning* of the item. The actual example might best come towards the end of the text.

(c) Make sure the surrounding language is at a lower level than the language presented (i.e. make it easier), although some incidental items you might leave to be inferred.

Although authentic texts can usefully be used at the lower levels (see p 125) they are rarely suitable for Presentation purposes. At the higher levels, where your lesson might be constructed around a topic and a text rather than individual language items your approach would be different. e.g:

Mr John Parsons, 41, saw a 20-year-old girl fall from a crowded platform at East Penge, South London, as he was on his way to work yesterday morning.

Recovering from his injuries in bed at home last night he said: 'I just knew I had to help. Everyone was standing there staring at the poor girl. I hurled myself across the platform and jumped on to the line. Out of the corner of my eye I could see the train coming round the bend. All I could think of was saving her life before she was crushed.

'I wrapped an arm round her and scooped her under the over-hanging platform. All the time the train was getting nearer. I think she was unconscious. I just pushed her face into the gravel and shouted 'Lie still; don't move'. I tried to scramble up the platform but the train was on top of us and it hit my left side. It threw me on to the platform. Unfortunately the girl's bag got caught in the train . . . . .

From the *Daily Mail* (courtesy of *Words*, Maley and Duff, CUP)

Here, you might:
(a) Relate the students to the context.

(b) Ask them to read the passage silently.

(c) Check they understand what it's about.

(d) See if, in pairs, they can work out the meaning of the words underlined.

(e) Discuss with the whole group, giving the meaning if necessary, or referring the students to an English-English dictionary.

(f) Get them to practise the pronunciation of both the infinitive and the past tense forms.

(g) Drill some of the difficult words in another utterance (making sure the meaning is the same).

At the lower levels the item will determine which text you choose, whereas at the higher levels you can (to a certain extent) allow the text to determine which language will be dealt with. As can be seen, such a procedure is particularly useful when developing the students' vocabulary because a text often brings together words with related meaning (in this case the words relate to dramatic movement).

It also allows students to acquire language naturally, according to their own needs, without having everything highlighted by the teacher.

2 *To practise presented language*
   If an item of language has been presented in, say, a dialogue and then drilled, it is often worth reinforcing it later in a text because:
   (a) The text can provide a new setting

   (b) It can be embedded in greater stretches of language than is normal when isolating an item for presentation purposes

   (c) The text provides important reinforcement using some other language skill (i.e. if it has been practised orally then a reading text can highlight the written form).

   (d) A text has different points of interest so exposure to the previously presented item can be more incidental, more unconscious and more natural.

Again, a text should not be unnaturally loaded with examples of any one item. It is better to deal with it as primarily a listening or a reading exercise to prevent you from giving another lesson where the only important language is the item itself.

In the main, Practice texts will be longer than Presentation texts, simply because the focus is not *necessarily* on an individual item. Frequently, texts can be used to revise several items presented in several previous classes.

If your aim in using the text is to develop the skills of listening and reading, then the text may not contain any specific items that you have recently presented at all. In that case the text will be either:

– slightly above the students' level (i.e. a little difficult). Your job then would be to guide the students towards full comprehension, moving from a general understanding at first to a more detailed understanding as you work further on it.

– or authentic (i.e. real and ungraded, therefore almost certainly well above the students' spoken and written level). The sort of work you would do on it would depend on what sort of thing the student would be expected to do with the text in the real world (i.e. a railway timetable would be looked at in order to help the students use one effectively at a railway station, not to get them to understand every single word written down on it).

With an authentic text it is the tasks the students do or the questions you ask, not the material, that would be graded according to the students' level. At the lower levels, you may expect them just to have a general idea of the text but you may expect them naturally to *do* something as a result of having read it (e.g. they may have to fill out their personal details on an application form). Do you want them to simply acquire language as best they can, unhindered by the teacher?

Using a text

The procedure for aiding and checking comprehension of dialogues on pp 122–124 is basically that which can be used for all reading and writing texts, although of course you will have to adapt it to your class and the material you are using. You will also want to vary it on different occasions to prevent your classes from being predictable and dull. (There are many ways you could do it). The most important thing is to decide what you expect the students to be able to do with the text. Do you want full comprehension? Do you want them just to have a general understanding? Do you want them to retrieve some specific information? Do you want to give further practice of a specific language item?

Giving the text to the students

1 *Reading texts*
  Authentic texts should really be authentic (i.e. if taken from a newspaper, it is better to photocopy the text or give out sufficient copies of the newspaper than to try to type it out). Specially-written passages, however, can be typed out and photocopied, put on an OHP transparency or written on the board before the class. 'Authentic-like' texts should try to look like the real thing. If you write it out by hand, make sure it is clear, leave plenty of space between the sentences, and add visuals somewhere if possible.

2 *Listening texts*
  You can use tapes or read aloud. For the use of dialogues see pp 121–126. Authentic texts might include such things as railway announcements (which could complement timetables). Specially-written texts are likely to be dialogues or anecdotal monologues of some sort.

Can you motivate students to improve their listening and reading skills?

Yes. We listen and read most efficiently when we either need or want to. In the real world, the need is created naturally by circumstances: we need to read the newspaper to find out what is going on, we need to listen to the football results to check the pools, and so on. In the more artificial situation of the classroom, there are inherent general compulsions, like the need to please the teacher, or the need to improve one's English but still you, the teacher, have to create specific needs for specific exercises. For example:

1 To create the need to read a text, one technique is to relate the reading to the achievement of another task. You might tell the students – it can be real or simulated – that they are going to plan a weekend trip. Before they can book their hotel, however, they have to read some hotel brochures and compare the conditions to find the one that meets their requirements.

2 A related idea is to get students to transfer the main content of what they read or listen to into some other format, such as a graph, a chart or a picture, so that comprehension of the text is checked by looking at the results, e.g:

Aim: to give practice in understanding street directions.

Method: (a) Warm students up to the topic of asking directions.

(b) Give out the map and check that students understand the pronunciation of street names, place names etc . . .

(c) Play tape once. Check general comprehension.

(d) Play tape again. Students mark the route.

(e) Students check and discuss route in pairs.

(f) Play tape again, in segments, to check answers.

Text: The bus station? Let me think. Ah yes I know, go out of the Post Office and directly opposite you across the road is a street, Albert St I think it is. Well you go down there, all the way to the end, then you take the road opposite again, that's King St, straight down there to the end and turn right, then take the first left and the bus station is a few hundred yards along on your left.

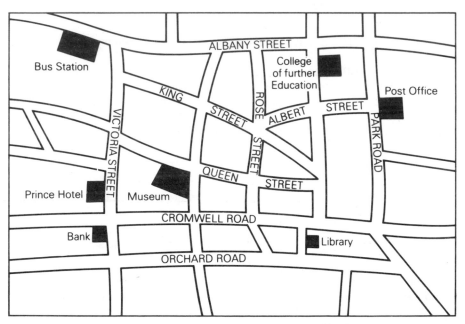

Adapted from *Listening Links*: Gill Sturtridge and Marion Geddes (Heinemann)

(In the class you might want to make the text longer and include more natural-sounding expressions and hesitations. One way of doing this is to get the person recording it to speak from only looking at the map and not reading a script.)

3 To help focus attention and to give the students a purpose, give out questions (you might put them on the board) which students have to answer when they are exposed to the text. Be sure that they serve the intended purpose: Do you want students to understand the gist or retrieve specific information?

4 Motivation can be created by working on one segment of a text before revealing the next. The students should be left hanging at the end of each segment.

5 Jumbling the paragraphs of a reading text and getting the students to put them in the correct order can also be stimulating. Before they can sequence them correctly they have to understand what's happening. Students can either do this individually and then compare their results with the others or, in a small class, it can be done with everyone round a table discussing it. A variation on this exercise is to give each student a different paragraph and, through discussion only, find out and sequence what the others have.

6 'Jigsaw' texts (either listening or reading) are also an interesting idea; this is where individual students or groups of students are given slightly different texts concerning a single event so that they have to exchange information with each other before some final task can be completed. This approach is best demonstrated in *Reading Links* by Geddes and Sturtridge (Heinemann).

7 Giving students the first segment of a text and getting them to discuss what they think comes next is not only a useful exercise in prediction, it also stimulates interest.
Of course, the students may also want to listen to or read the text because you have chosen one which genuinely interests them. It is not always easy to predict this interest or guarantee that all the students feel it, so you may need to:
– get a discussion going on the topic beforehand

– relate your texts to a common theme, so that the interest generated by one text carries over into the next.
A topic-based approach is very common at advanced levels, since it not only helps maintain the students' interest but it also gives coherence to a series of lessons.

Are there any further hints on how to make sure the students understand a text?

First pp 97–108 should be fully read. However, there are a few other points:
1 No matter how comprehension questions are organized (if that is how you are doing the checking), no matter how subtly they develop, if you simply read through a series of questions from your lesson plan it will be a rather dull activity for the students. You need to be sensitive and flexible. If it's clear they do understand, change direction. Make sure any questions you ask give everyone enough to do both in the amount of language expected in the answers and in the degree of interpretation, and therefore involvement, needed (after more simple questioning that is.)

2 It's often better to sit down in a relaxed manner if you are asking comprehension questions; don't make the exercise sound like an interrogation!

3 Remember that asking questions after a text is only to help you determine the extent to which the students have understood it; it does not focus attention and encourage improvement in the skill itself. It's worth bearing in mind, too, that, in one way, it is not possible to *teach* listening and reading. Really, one can only make the conditions right for the students to *learn*. (In some respects, this is true of the whole of language teaching! Quite a thought!)

4 Vary the activity. Sometimes, try getting the students to ask the questions (see p 105) or write 'True' or 'False' next to a series of statements. Try to deal with different segments of a text in different ways.

Are there any special problems associated with reading?

Yes. The fact that most reading is silent and each person reads at his own speed makes it a difficult activity to control within the context of a group. Some teachers set a time-limit, which (at the intermediate level) might be three times the time a native speaker would take. A time-limit can help (it also encourages slow readers to concentrate more on the whole rather than the parts) provided that:
– the time-limit is explained and adhered to

– some encouragement is given to slow readers

– the approach is consistent over a series of lessons

– the text is put away before any oral work is done on it to prevent slower students from carrying on reading.

However, time-limits are insensitive instruments and frequently discourage rather than encourage slow readers. Reading should not be something to fear. In general, it is better to give everyone time to go at their own speed. You can always give the quicker readers longer texts or more complicated tasks to get on with. If there are serious differences between the students' reading abilities, the weaker readers might be given a text to be read at home or during the breaks. Students with no reading ability at all need extra remedial help.

Extension work

A text is a marvellous source of further activities. Don't drop it too quickly. Consider, for example, whether it could provide the elements for a good role-play; if there is some useful pronunciation practice that could be done; whether some written homework would be useful. And so on.

Exercises

Ex. 1

AIM
To develop awareness of the possibilities of reading texts.

PROCEDURE
1 Distribute among your colleagues a selection of texts, some idealized for EFL use, some authentic.

2 In groups, indicate the levels and types of classes each could be used for.

3 Indicate in the margin, or by underlining, any items that could be focused on and what the teaching aims behind using the text could be:
   – presentation (underline)

   – practice (underline)

   – vocabulary development (underline)

   – developing reading skills

   – extracting information (underline the information)

   – prediction.

4 Indicate what types of reading would be most desirable (e.g. intensive, extensive, skimming, scanning, etc.)

5 Exchange your text with another group. Discuss.

6 Individually or in groups, prepare an outline lesson plan for one of each other's texts.

4.8 Setting up communication activities

In 4.2. it was shown how, particularly at the lower levels, items of language which are new to the student (e.g. the structure *need + -ing*) can be isolated from the language as a whole and held up for attention. However, the language chosen for examples of how they are used (e.g. *your hair needs cutting*) is usually selected by the teacher.

In 4.3 it was shown that when items are practised (e.g. in a drill), the teacher introduces more varied language and some of it may be contributed by the students. This helps to set items in a wider language context to make the practice more interesting and to show some of the versatility of the items.

Students, however, still need to be given the opportunity to experiment with any item, to see how far they can communicate with it in situations where all the choices of language used are made by the people speaking. Of course, any situation the teacher sets up in the classroom for such experimentation will to a certain extent determine the language used (for any limited communicative situation one can predict some of the language functions likely to occur), but students should still be free, if they wish, not to use any new presented items at all. The communicative needs of the situation and the language which comes more or less naturally from it is far more important.

Inevitably, lots of grammar mistakes are made (native speakers make them too!). However, they must be seen as part and parcel of learning to communicate. In general, being clear, fluent and convincing is more important than being grammatically accurate (although frequently you need to be accurate to be understood).

Activities set up to encourage such freely chosen language are normally known as communication activities or seen as the free stage of a lesson. They are usually designed to give either:
– creative practice opportunities for predicted language areas, or

– general communicative practice, where the specific language focus is less relevant.

In general, they both increase the students' motivation, since the students talk for themselves, and help bridge the gap between the rather artificial world of the classroom, with its controlled language practice, and the real world outside.

Your role as a teacher is to:
1 Decide clearly what you want to do and why.

2 Work out how long the activity will take and tailor it to the time available.

3 Prepare the materials.

4 Set up the activity so that the students know what to do (this means giving clear instructions and checking they've been understood).

5 Monitor the activity, to help out if necessary, to jolly it along and give advice when asked.

6 To observe and note areas of difficulty, although not to give instant correction.

7 Leave the students alone, unless you have good reason not to!

Does each lesson then consist of *presentation*, *practice* and a *'free stage'* in that order?

It is tempting to think that each hour could break down into three neat slots like that, so for the first fifteen minutes you might present a structure, for the next twenty minutes you might drill it, and for the last twenty-five minutes you might set up, say, a role-play to see whether the students can use it or not. In reality, classes aren't like that. You might present the structure for a few minutes (not necessarily at the beginning), then set up a mini-role-play to see the extent to which the students have grasped it, then give some controlled drilling, through several sessions if necessary, integrated with other work the students might be doing, such as work on their listening or writing abilities.

Shouldn't you give any assessment of the activity at all?

Yes, of course. Because you're not giving instant correction it doesn't mean that your class doesn't need you to evaluate it. The students might well want some idea of how they did, so:

1 Indicate how each communicated, comment on how fluent each was, how well they argued as a group, and so on. Sometimes you might tape the activity and play it back for discussion.

2 Note down glaring and recurrent errors in grammar and pronunciation. Ones which are common to the class can be sorted out and practised another day when you've had chance to prepare a suitable remedial lesson, whereas individual ones can be discussed with the individual students concerned, perhaps during a break or after the lesson (you might recommend a suitable remedial exercise in a course book to do at home).

How long should the activity last?

Well, usually stop it before the last student peters out, although some activities might need the time to be played through completely. As a rough guide, at elementary and intermediate levels, they will possibly be short and simple, lasting, say ten to fifteen minutes, whereas at the higher levels a freer activity might last at least an hour.

Example A: Role play

Role-play is when students play the parts of other people in a situation. It is unscripted, although general ideas about what they are going to say might be prepared beforehand. Role-play can be used to:

– diagnose the strengths and weaknesses of the students' English and so calculate which areas need working on

– give the students an opportunity to try out language recently presented and practised

– help the students, through a wide range of language, to talk freely in a variety of moods and attitudes and 'negotiate' with other speakers.

TYPE 1

Simple role-plays where students are put in situations they may be faced with when they stay in an English-speaking country (e.g. buying things from a shop, asking a landlady the rules of the house etc.) are very useful, particularly at the lower levels. In such role-plays there is no need for detailed character definition or a lot of biographical information. The activity also works best if there is:

— no fixed conclusion to be reached

— something awkward in the exchange: so, for example, if someone is buying things from a shop, then certain items might not be available or the shopkeeper might have no change, e.g:

Step 1 Prepare the following cards:

STUDENT A	STUDENT B
At the station	At the station
You want to get to London by 6 o'clock. It is now 3 o'clock.	You are a ticket clerk. To get to London, passengers must change at Cambridge. There is a train at 3.10 and 6.10.
Before leaving, you must buy your friend a birthday present. Find out how to get there.	The 3.10 might be very late.

Step 2 Build up the context of the railway station but be careful not to give away to all the students vital information written on the cards.

Step 3 Divide the class into pairs. Each pair consists of student A and student B.

Step 4 Student A and student B then read their card silently and digest the information written down without giving away anything to the other.

Step 5 Check that the weaker students have understood on an individual basis.

Step 6 Get the students to act it out in pairs. Monitor unobtrusively.

Step 7 Possibly get one or two pairs to act it out in front of the others.

Step 8 Provide general feedback.

TYPE 2

More complex role-plays are usually more suitable for the higher levels. For example, the students might play the various characters at a trial, or the various members of a town-planning committee. In these cases, much of the work on the context needs to be done more slowly and in greater depth, perhaps over a series of lessons, particularly if the whole class is to be involved in an extended discussion. The students will also need to prepare certain aspects of their role beforehand, perhaps for homework. In order to stimulate the imagination and interest, the situation may of course contain certain elements of fantasy.

For this type of role-play the students need to have clearly in their minds as much knowledge as possible about:

— the full context. This should include the characters, what they look like, their age, their mood, any mannerisms etc.

— the reason for the interaction. This will often have some conflict built into it somewhere.

Such role-plays can be found in published form, e.g. *Act English* – Peter Watcyn-Jones (Penguin), *Q Cards* – Saxon Menné (Paul Norbury Publications), *It's Your Choice* – Michael Lynch (Edward Arnold).

One simple way of building up a role-play with a class of adults studying in Britain, which would include the whole class, might be as follows:

Step 1 Prepare the following cards

CUE CARD

Situation: The customs. Two characters: an immigration official and a Peruvian doctor trying to enter the country.

Props: A date stamp. A desk. A passport. A walking stick.
Problem: The doctor's passport is out-of-date and his money has been stolen on the plane. He has to persuade the customs official to let him in.

CHARACTER A

You are an *immigration official.* You are working overtime because one of your colleagues is sick. Your wife is ill and you want to get home. You like everything to be simple and straightforward. You are irritated by the doctor and his problem. You have the habit of running your hand through your hair.

CHARACTER B

You are a *Peruvian doctor.* You have come to England to attend your son's graduation at University. You have had a long journey. You are fed up and cold. Your passport is out-of-date and you have had your money stolen on the plane. You want to see a policeman. You have a bad back so you need a walking stick.

Step 2 To warm them up to the topic, discuss with the students the problems of going through immigration.

Step 3 Check they understand one or two words like *out-of-date* and *stolen*, if you think they don't know them and they are crucial to the role-play.

Step 4 Give out a copy of the Cue Card to each student. Get them to read it silently. Check they understand what's written on them by asking one or two comprehension questions.

Step 5 Put the students in pairs. Give out the props – or objects to represent the props.

Step 6 Give out the Character Cards. Check that individual students have understood who they are without giving the whole game away to the other students.

Step 7 Get them to rehearse the situation in pairs.

Step 8 Ask one pair to go through the role-play again in front of the others.

Step 9 Discuss with the whole class how it might continue and what other characters might be needed (e.g. a policeman, the son etc.)

Step 10 Build up a picture of the characters with the whole class, perhaps writing notes on the board.

Step 11 Assign roles, so that everyone has at least one role.

Step 12 Continue the role-play as a 'whole-class' role-play.

Step 13 Discuss the role-play. However, don't get into too much detail and kill it dead!

Further suggestions
1 Try to predict the language likely to emerge. For example, in Type 1 much of the language will relate to asking for information (*Could you tell me* . . . . .?). You might wish to do some prior language practice to facilitate communication but not so much that the role play turns it into another drill.

2 If you have a 'dummy run' or a rehearsal, perhaps make the 'real thing' something you tape (audio or video). Doing role-plays twice can be deadly, unless there is special incentive the second time. Remember that the language should be spontaneous and interest maintained by the students not knowing where they are going. A second run-through usually means the direction has been worked out.

3 All instructions should be segmented and checked (see pp 36–44).

4 Simple props, such as hats and umbrellas and character cards with pictures on them, can help bring role-plays to life.

5 Cut a role-play short rather than let it peter out. Make sure in paired role-play that pairs are not left idle if they finish.

6 Don't force students to perform. If you set up the right task and it's both interesting and amusing then you should create the need to speak and the interaction can take place in small groups.

7 Be careful about who you allot roles to (e.g. some boys can get silly when they have to play girls' roles!)

8 Keep out of the activity yourself. Don't allow the students to constantly refer to you.

Example B: Discussions

Discussions with a class are frequently unsuccessful because of one or more of the following reasons:
1 Students are not interested in the subject or have few ideas on it.

2 The activity does not have sufficient motivating factors in its structure to create the need to speak.

3 Students haven't been prepared for the discussion (i.e. they haven't organized their thoughts).

4 Some students dominate, whereas some are unwilling to give their ideas.

5 Some students haven't the language skills to discuss what they are supposed to discuss.

The result is the teacher ends up doing the talking and the discussion flags!

Most fully-fledged discussions (as opposed to small ones that arise naturally in response to something immediate like the day's news) take a lot of preparation if the teacher is not going to dominate. The time they take also rules them out of many TP situations.

Some simple techniques *are* possible, however, in longer TP situations, e.g.

1 Modifying statements

The students are given a list of, say, ten controversial statements around the topic of 'parents' (if that is a relevant theme), e.g. *Parents should teach boys to sew and girls to mend the car.* Groups are then asked to modify the statements so that all the members of the group agree with them. Time willing, groups can then compare their statements with other groups.

2 Sequencing statements

The students are given a list of, say, ten *non*-controversial statements, e.g. *It's important to put children to bed early if they have school the next day.* They are then asked, in groups, to sequence them (1–10) in order of priority for the successful bringing-up of children in the home.

3 Defending statements

Different controversial statements are written on pieces of paper and then put into a box, e.g. *Children should be encouraged to leave home at sixteen.* The students are told to pick out a statement and then spend a few minutes preparing arguments to defend it. One of the students can be made chairman. All the students then have to present their arguments in turn, answer questions and defend themselves from attack.

It is likely that free discussion will quickly break out but possibly in the end there can be a vote as to the most convincing defence! This method is often more effective than formal debates which can be rather cumbersome. (These ideas are explained more fully in *Modern English Teacher* Vol. 9 No. 1 (MEP Publications), 'Structured Conversation' by Roger Gower. Other useful ideas for discussions can be found in *Discussions that Work* Penny Ur (CUP).)

Obviously, these approaches are more suitable for late-intermediate and advanced classes. Even so, it is worthwhile trying to predict the language that is likely to arise and see whether you need to rehearse any useful phrases beforehand. Make sure the students can discuss what you ask and don't find they haven't the language to express their ideas! (One way of predicting the language is to give the activity to some teachers first, noting down what they say.)

For elementary classes, discussion can be stimulated in a multinational class by asking the students to give a mini-lecturette (perhaps only for two minutes) on one aspect of their country (e.g. wedding customs, food etc.) The other students might be encouraged to interrupt and ask questions. Obviously, the student giving the talk will have to prepare it a little beforehand.

Example C: Games

Many conventional games can be adapted to foreign language teaching. As with any communication activity, the areas of language produced may be predictable, depending on the sort of interaction demanded, or less predictable and therefore less suitable as a free stage for presented language.

Type 1 Predictable language

> TWENTY QUESTIONS: For low level classes, to give further practice of inverted question forms (e.g. *Is she alive?*) and short-form answers (e.g. *No, she isn't*).
>
> Instructions: A student chooses a place, a famous person or an object and the rest of the class has to guess what or who it is by asking a maximum of twenty questions that demand the answer *yes* or *no*.

1 Make the game competitive. In most classes competition increases motivation and interest considerably. Divide the class into teams and have a scoring system to record the wins and losses of each group. The group with the most points wins.

2 Have a quick run-through with you writing down your choice secretly first. This will provide the students with a model for the activity. Then pass the game over to the students as far as possible. You might even get them to do the scoring.

3 Make sure you have checked all your instructions sufficiently (see pp 36–44).

4 Make sure you have allowed the right amount of time for the game. It's very difficult to have to follow on from one that has petered out! Equally, it's very frustrating for the students to have to finish before the game has come to an end.

5 Get all the students involved.

6 Make the game fun!

Type 2: Less predictable language

> THE BALLOON GAME: For intermediate and advanced students.
>
> Instructions: Each student in the group is given a profession (one might be a doctor, another an architect). The class is told that the balloon they are travelling in is too heavy and one of them must go. Each member of the group has to convince the others that their survival is essential to the survival of the group. A vote is taken as to who must go.

1 Make sure the students enter their roles and don't vote according to the students' popularity in the class!

2 Give credit for creative expression!

3 Don't worry about grammatical inaccuracy here. The aim is for the students to persuade each other of a point of view, not to produce accurate utterances.

4 The students might need time to prepare the discussion and the language of one or two conversational openings (e.g. *Listen, I'm sorry I don't agree* . . . .).

In multinational classes, all games of this sort can be a problem if some students know the game and others have never heard of it. The latter are at a disadvantage at first. Be careful, generally, that if you have Europeans and Arabs in the same class the game does not depend on too much general knowledge. Frequently their general knowledge does not overlap!

Example D: Interaction activities

These have minimum rules and are non-competitive. They are carried out in pairs or groups and usually depend on one or more students either having incomplete information or no information at all, and the other(s) having the information needed to complete the task. The aim is either for the 'haves' to communicate their information to the 'have-nots' or for the 'have-nots' to extract it.

Seating (also see pp 31–33)

Pairs can sit opposite each other, with the material they are using between them. It is usually important that each student does not see the material of their partner so it is sometimes best concealed in a folder. In large classes, with minimal resources, pairs sitting opposite each other may look at the facing wall where the material may be hanging or projected.

Two examples

1 *Describe and draw*
Aim: to give free practice to the language of instruction (e.g. *You draw a . . . . Put a big . . . . .* etc.) One student with a picture (e.g. a picture advertisement) mounted on a card or stuck in a folder tells the other student how to draw it. At the end the two drawings are compared.

2 *Fixing an appointment*
Aim:. To practise use of the language of suggestion, rejection, acceptance and confirmation as used in making an appointment with someone.

Sheet 1.

You are a teacher and you want to meet the father/mother of one of your students. You must make an appointment with them. Here is your diary for next week. Do not show it to your partner.

	Morning	Afternoon	Evening
Monday	teaching class 3		opera
Tuesday		teaching class 2	
Wednesday		teaching class 3	dinner with headmaster
Thursday	teaching class 2		
Friday	teachers' meeting	teaching class 3	going away for the weekend

---

Sheet 2.

You are the mother/father of a student. You want to talk to the teacher. You must make an appointment with him/her. Here is your diary for next week. Do not show it to your partner.

	Morning	Afternoon	Evening
Monday		driving lesson	
Tuesday	dentist		dinner with boss
Wednesday	interview for new job		
Thursday			theatre 'Macbeth'
Friday			

The aim of all interaction activities is to get the students to bridge what is known as an ***information gap*** and so genuinely communicate with each other.

Exercises

Ex. 1

AIM
To develop awareness of the sort of language likely to arise from a 'free' activity.

PROCEDURE
1 Divide the group into pairs and give each a structure or function (e.g. PRESENT SIMPLE, 'Making Suggestions').

2 Each pair is then asked to decide on a game that should yield the item naturally. They must also write down instructions for it.

3 The names of the activities and the instructions are redistributed with no mention of the language item.

4 Each pair should then perform the game in front of or with the whole group.

5 The group is then asked to decide on the language area that the game has been designed to focus on.

COMMENT
If you can, it is often worth recording native speakers performing an activity and analysing what they say. This gives you an idea of the areas of language that might naturally be used.

Ex. 2

AIM
To give some idea of the kind of language necessary to carry out an activity.

PROCEDURE
1 Select an interaction activity suitable for pair work (e.g. one exploiting the 'information gap').

2 Work with two other colleagues, one whose task will be to jot down what language he expects to be used and then take note of the language used during the activity.

3 Carry out the activity and compare what was expected with what was used.

4 Decide what language areas the activity could usefully give students practice in.

COMMENT
1 Don't be too discouraged if you find a huge gap between what is expected and what actually occurs!

2 Noting the language down on paper as the activity is carried out is less time-consuming than going over tapes; on the other hand, taping can rule out many fruitless arguments.

Ex. 3

AIM
To show the value of a carefully structured approach to discussion.

PROCEDURE

1 Write down six controversial statements about EFL teaching (e.g. *Students will be easily understood if they don't use contractions; Students find contractions hard to understand so they shouldn't be taught; Vocabulary teaching is more important than the teaching of grammar* etc.)

2 Give the list to your group and ask them individually to modify the statements so that they can agree with them.

3 Modify them for yourself.

4 In pairs, compare the modified statements and modify them again so that you can both agree with them.

5 Repeat this procedure in groups of four.

6 Double up the groups until the discussion involves the whole group.

COMMENT

The most clearly demonstrable fact from this exercise is that discussion takes place, involving all members of the group. Even if the topic is not very interesting to the group (e.g. 'Etiquette') it is surprising how much more discussion takes place than in conventional discussion forums.

Ex. 4

AIM

To give some idea of the length of time a role-play will take.

PROCEDURE

1 Select two role-play activities, one at an intermediate or advanced level and one at a more elementary level.

2 Work in groups of three, with two carrying out the role-plays, the third timing them.

3 Repeat the role-plays more than once.

4 Discuss the time each took and estimate how long it might take with learners of the appropriate level.

5 Discuss the preparation needed to set it up and the length of time it would take with a group of students.

6 Discuss whether it was useful to do the role-play more than once.

COMMENT

This activity might be more useful if done in a foreign language which would mean grouping yourself according to languages you speak.

GENERAL COMMENT

Communication activities are by their nature something involving thought on the part of the people involved. They can all therefore usefully be tried out in pairs or groups of teachers before being given to students.

5 Teaching Techniques

5.1 Eliciting

As was seen in 4.5, whole dialogues and narratives can be elicited as a way of getting a group to collectively compose the language they are to practise.

Eliciting a few ideas from the students about a context or some vocabulary related to it is also a useful part of setting up an activity, whether it be a role-play, a game, a listening task or the presentation of a new language item. It has the advantages of:
– getting the students involved in the context and bringing relevant information to the front of their minds

– increasing the amount they talk

– telling you how much they know and can say in relation to it.
More generally it gives a class the necessary and motivating feeling of being encouraged to invest part of itself, give some of its opinions and contribute some of its knowledge so that what happens seems to depend partly on the students themselves.

At the advanced level, eliciting might consist of something like: *Tell us what you know about the production of rice* or *Look at this picture and describe the man as fully as you can*. At the lower levels, however, the eliciting often needs to be guided by the teacher, particularly if it serves a specific aim as it would when you are building up a context in order to direct the students inductively towards the meaning of a new language item. (Some indication of how to do this has already been given on pp 110–119).
So:

Aim:	to present and practise the structure 'NEED + –ING', as in *The roof needs mending*
Context:	Mr and Mrs Roberts are looking at a house they want to buy. It's in a very bad state at present.
Aids:	A picture of Mr and Mrs Roberts. A picture of a delapidated house.

Instead of saying to the students *This is Mr and Mrs Roberts. They are newly married. They are looking at a house for sale. It's not in good condition. There's a hole in the roof . . .*, you might approach the task of building up the context something like this:

 T: *Right. Now, do you remember Mr and Mrs Roberts?*
S3: *Yes, last lesson. They married.*
 T: *Married? Is that right: They g. . .*
S3: *Got married.*
 T: *Yes, again.*
S3: *They got married.*
 T: *Fine. When? Ten years ago?*
S1: *No, no. Two days ago.*

T: *Yes, where are they here?* (Showing a picture)
S6: *A house. An old house.*
T: *Yes. Is it theirs?*
S4: *No, it's for sale.*
T: *So, why are they here?*
S2: *They want to buy it?*
T: *Maybe. Do you think they will buy it?*
S1: *No.*
T: *Why not?*
S1: *It's old. No good.*
T: *Tell me more.*
S5: *Roof no good.*
T: *Yes. There's a ____ in the roof.*
S6: *Hole.*
T: *Yes, good.*

Most of the students can be involved in a build-up like this and you can get a rough idea what language the students more or less know and can use in relation to your very limited context. You also know how far they are with you and following your logic.

However, eliciting takes time. *Don't* do it when:
1 Time is short and you have an aim you quickly want to achieve (in which case, it's usually better to *tell* the students the context and quickly check they understand)

2 The students don't know something. If they can't give you a word or an idea, don't spend ages trying to elicit it!

Now look back at the extract and note the following points:
1 The teacher makes use of characters and information about them from a previous lesson, thus reducing what has to be done in *this* lesson.

2 Using a first-sound prompt (/g/ to elicit *got*) helps the students remember a word they know. It gives an important clue as to what you want. *Eliciting should never be a guessing-game about what's in the teacher's head*!

3 An obviously incorrect suggestion by you (*ten years ago*?) can sometimes provoke the right response. Use this technique sparingly and only when you are sure the students know the answer. Otherwise it might sound as though you are mocking them!

4 Giving a sentence with a blank in it, filled in perhaps by a grunt or the first letter of a word (the grunt having the same number of syllables and the same stress pattern!) allows the students to hear where the word is expected to come in a whole sentence.

5 Here, both individual language items (e.g. *got married, hole*) were elicited as well as ideas and opinions (i.e. *Why are they there? Do you think they will buy it?*) Usually in low-level Presentations you will want to elicit both. You should be aware, though, that when eliciting language you usually only expect a single word or phrase (e.g. *So the roof needs . . .?/Repairing*) whereas ideas and opinions are far more variable and numerous and often come in more complicated language. With specific language you might, if necessary, provide correction and pronunciation practice, but with ideas and opinions you probably

won't correct what the students say since it's the idea rather than the language that is important.

A final word. Eliciting is a difficult skill. It needs practice and experience if it's not to be time-wasting and embarrassing. The most important qualities you need are the ability to really listen to the students and the ability to respond quickly and flexibly, both of which are difficult if you are being observed on TP! Sometimes, even at the lower level, it's worth starting with the *Tell-me-about-this-picture* approach and trying to build up as the students come up with things.

Exercises

Ex. 1

AIM
To establish which types of questions are most suitable for eliciting information.

PROCEDURE
1 Choose a picture which could be interpreted in different ways (e.g. there are several in *The Mind's Eye* by Maley, Duff and Grellet, CUP.)

2 Decide on *your* interpretation.

3 Write a list of five or six salient facts about the picture as you see it.

4 Write a number of different questions which might elicit those facts.

5 Work with a partner and try and elicit your interpretation. Discuss which questions were most effective and why.

Ex. 2

AIM
To give practice in asking questions to elicit information.

PROCEDURE
A: 1 Work with a partner.

2 Select a topic like 'Schooldays'.

3 In two minutes ask your partner as many questions as possible about his memories. Your partner should answer with one-word answers wherever possible.

4 At the end write down as many facts as you can remember.

5 Reverse the roles and go through the same procedure.

6 Compare both sets of facts for completeness and discuss each other's question techniques.

B: 1 Divide the group into two teams.

2 Ask each team to write a short story (or if time is short select the title of a book or film).

3 Get one person from each team to change place and elicit what his team has written without giving any direct information.

Ex. 3

AIM

To practise relating the students personally to a topic before eliciting facts about it.

PROCEDURE

A: 1 Choose an unlikely topic (like 'filling in holes in the road' or 'toothpick manufacturing'!)

2 Try and get your group to relate personally to the topic by asking suitable questions.

B: 1 Ask the group to think up a topic they have no interest in.

2 Get them to relate to it by asking interesting questions.

Ex. 4

AIM

To practise eliciting vocabulary.

PROCEDURE

1 Select a text.

2 Identify five key vocabulary items.

3 Try and elicit them from your group.

COMMENT

As with many of these exercises, this exercise benefits from your colleagues having assumed a definite role that has carried on over a series of exercises.

5.2 Correction

Correcting errors that students make when they speak or write can be one of the most difficult tasks in language teaching. General questions that need to be asked are:

1 Has the student made a simple slip or does he in fact not know what the correct form should be?

2 At what stages of a lesson do I correct?

3 How much correction should I give?

4 How can I get to the root of the student's problem?

5 How can I correct in such a way as not to discourage the student?

6 What should the other students be doing while I'm correcting?

7 How can I follow up my correction so that the student will get the form right next time?

Error correction is usually thought of as relating to the form of the language but obviously students can say something incorrectly because they have misunderstood the meaning of something or they choose an inappropriate thing to say on a particular occasion. Students can equally get things wrong (i.e. they misunderstand or misinterpret) when they listen or read a text. For advice on how to check whether students have understood correctly or not see 4.4.

How do you decide whether the student has made an error or a mistake?

A mistake is really a slip of the tongue or the pen. The student is able to correct it himself, either completely unprompted or with the guidance of the teacher and other students. Native speakers make mistakes all the time even though the correct form is usually known.

An error is much more deeply ingrained. The student might:
– believe what he's saying is correct

– not know what the correct form should be

– know what the correct form should be but can't get it right.

Errors are usually produced regularly and systematically, so asking the student to try again is often the best way of helping you decide whether the incorrect form is an error or a mistake.

Very little time need be spent on mistakes but errors will need attention at certain stages of the lesson.

Oral correction

In one way, oral correction is more difficult than written correction because decisions usually have to be made quickly about **what** to correct, **when** to correct, **how** to correct and **how much** to correct. Without experience, you may not even recognize the error, particularly if you're not relaxed and not really listening to the students!

One way of helping yourself cope with errors that come up in the classroom is to try to *anticipate* any errors that *might* come up by:

1 Familiarizing yourself with all aspects of an item of language you are presenting or practising (e.g. likely pronunciation problems can often be worked out by writing out the item in phonemic transcription in your lesson plan beforehand: so *should have* in a taped model might be transcribed /ʃʊdəv/, revealing a contraction, a weak vowel for *have* and an absent /h/!)

2 Familiarizing yourself with the typical grammatical and pronunciation problems associated with the nationality of the students in your group (this is obviously easier in monolingual classes than multilingual classes).

If you know what *might* come up you are likely to be more alert to the errors that *do* come up.

A useful exercise to develop your awareness is to play a tape of your students speaking time and time again and to try and make a list of their errors, under such headings as:

FORM Grammar/Pronunciation/Word choice/Word order and MEANING

Although it's easier said than done, in the classroom, try and get so involved with your students that you relax and worry less about yourself. However, don't spend too long thinking about what they're saying. You need to process it and respond very quickly.

When do you correct?

In general, the principle is: if the language is controlled by you and the student is practising forms you have presented, then errors should be corrected. The tighter the control, the tighter the correction. If, however, your aim is to get students to produce a lot of language quickly and fluently, rather than a small amount accurately, then correction will be less because the students' main aim will be to communicate meaning and correction of form by you will be an unwelcome intrusion. So, looking at the stages of Presentation and Practice:

Presentation

When you give the students an example of a new item of language and you want them to repeat it so as to practise the pronunciation and memorize the form, correction is absolutely essential. Students must be given the maximum opportunity to get it right, although you will of course have to balance the amount of correction any individual in the group needs with what the group needs as a whole. If, however, you are eliciting ideas for a context through which you will present the item, then correction need only be of very typical and persistent errors unless a useful word comes up and you want to practise the pronunciation.

Practice

In a drill, if the students have choices about which language to use, and they are not merely repeating a given form, then other types of errors can creep in such as tense endings (*he go*) or word order (*he speaks very well English*) although you will need to make sure that the students are not making errors because your prompts are not clear. In activities where the language is semi-controlled by you (e.g. when you ask the students to reconstruct a story) the amount of correction will depend on the aim of the activity, the time you've got, its relevance to the other students etc. You might wish to work on a typical problem briefly (e.g. the way a Japanese student misuses the /l/ /r/ sounds) without necessarily expecting to clear it up in one go.

Communication activities

During communication activities you will probably be allowing the students to use any language they like in order to communicate, in which case the students will usually need to learn how to do it for themselves and experiment with any language they've learnt.

Many students are contradictory about correction at this stage. If they've got something to say (i.e. some meaning to communicate) they can't usually take in a correction of form unless you completely disrupt the activity. On the other hand they often feel they wish people would correct them when they are speaking freely. (It is after all, a marvellous opportunity for you to note what their errors are.)

Guidance and correction, however, can't be given during the act of communication, only afterwards. It might consist of:

1 Going over a tape or a video of the interaction (though this can be dull and discouraging if done too meticulously and too often).

2 Asking them to repeat what they said, with the focus this time being on how correct the language is (not a very convenient approach for role-plays or discussions!).

3 Giving individual students notes of errors they have made with instructions on how to correct them.

4 Providing the class with remedial sessions on errors common to the majority (particularly fruitful for monolingual groups).

How much do you correct?

Errors are usually made only by individual students, so correction usually has to be on an individual basis too. Even more problematically, in multilingual classes, the types of errors vary according to the students' different mother tongues. The problem for you is how to spend enough time on any one error with any one student without alienating the rest of the group. To reduce that likelihood:

1 Involve the whole class as much as possible in the correction process.

2 Spend less time correcting what is only a problem for one student and more time on problems common to the whole group.

There is such a thing as over-correction. That is, the more you try to correct something, the worse the student gets. So, often, it is worth spending a short time correcting some items and not trying to get everything perfect at one go, and coming back to them the next day. Correction of major errors is perhaps best considered as something that should be done as quickly as possible but is likely to be a long-term process over a series of lessons.

How do you correct?

The basic principle is that students learn more effectively if they are guided in such a way that they eventually correct themselves rather than if they are given the correct version of something straight away. The struggle to get it right also helps them understand *why* they are wrong. The main stages in the process are as follows:

1 *The student must know something is not accurate*
But first let him finish the utterance. Students find it disconcerting to be interrupted mid-stream, even if you can stop them from shooting on regardless. Then make some gesture, like a wave of the finger, or give some not too discouraging word, like *nearly*. You must be gentle. Errors and mistakes are an important part of our learning; we have to make them in order to learn. So, 'black looks' or shouts of *No, you idiot*! will only serve to reduce the students' desire to try out the language!

2 *The student must know where the error is*
So you need to isolate for the student the part of the utterance that's wrong. If the student says *I see John yesterday* and he meant *I saw John yesterday* then telling the student to try again might be of no use. He's put the word *yesterday* in to indicate past time so he may think he's made a correct utterance. What he needs to know is that the word *see* is incorrect. You can say *the second word* or *not 'see' but . . .?*. More effectively, you can use your fingers or a row of students to represent each word. When you get to the word that's wrong, indicate that that is where the problem is and see if they can get it right.

3 *The student must know what kind of error it is*
He'll need to know whether the problem is grammatical (e.g. wrong tense), syntactic (e.g. a missing word) or phonological (e.g. a wrongly-stressed word). Common gestures used to indicate the type of error can be found on pp 11–12. Another might be:
A word is missing: with fingers representing each word and the students speaking slowly, the finger for the missing word is tucked behind the palm of hand and then produced at the end.

You can no doubt think of other useful gestures. However, it is important that the students understand them and that you use the same gestures each time to represent the same thing.

Until you get confident in using gestures to help you correct students, you might find it easier to use the board. So if a student says *She buy some apples*, you can write the word *buy* on the board, cross it out and write up the word *Past*. See then if the student can tell you what the correct form should be.

The basic steps then probably go something like this:

(a) Indicate that an error has been made.

(b) Show the student *where* the error is.

(c) Indicate *what sort* of error it is.

(d) Get him to try again and see if he can get it right (it might have been a simple slip). Possibly give him some clues. (If it's not a very serious problem or you're in a hurry, then simply give the correct version and get the student to repeat it. However, he hasn't had to work for the correct version and may not have fully absorbed what he has got wrong).

(e) If the student still can't get it right, it's probably because he doesn't know how to. So, with a hand gesture, hold his attention and get another student to help out. This has the advantage of:

 (i) involving all the students in the correction process

 (ii) making the learning more co-operative generally

 (iii) reducing the students' dependence on your models

 (iv) increasing the amount the students listen to each other

 (v) giving the better students something to do.

However, such student-to-student correction, as it is known, needs to be done carefully. Not *Oh, no! Wrong again, Juan. Go on, Sami. Tell him.*; but *Not quite, Juan. Do you know, Sami?* Alternatively, do the whole thing by gesture. Indicate 'not quite' with your face or hands and gesture another student to help.

(f) If that step fails, you must assume that either the student hasn't understood what you're getting at or he doesn't know what the correct version should be. If it's an important point and the others don't know it either, you may have to teach it from scratch (i.e. present and practise it). If not, and the meaning of the item is clear, your simply saying it and getting the students to say it should be enough.   ·

(g) No matter how you have done the correction get the student to say the correct version, if possible in its original context. This is a vital part of any correction process. You can do this by gesture or saying something like *OK. Again. The whole thing*.

(h) If the student makes the same error later in the lesson, a quick reminder, perhaps by making an appropriate facial expression, should be enough.

Further suggestions

1 *Don't let any student think he's being picked on*
 Maintain a co-operative working atmosphere. Correction can seem threatening if done badly.

2 *Try not to 'echo' the errors, even in a mocking, astonished way*
Some teachers find this an easy way of indicating an error but although the humour can be beneficial it tends to reinforce the teacher's superior relationship and inhibit the student's ability to work things out for himself.

Written correction

The principles behind correcting written work are basically the same as those behind correcting oral production.

When?
Controlled writing (e.g. copying) : correct tightly

Cued writing : correct less

Free writing : either react to it as communication (e.g. *Oh, really. I didn't know you thought that.*) or evaluate it as communication (e.g. *Well argued*) rather than quibble over grammar or points of syntax and spelling. The aim is fluency and comprehensibility rather than strict accuracy, unless (e.g. for exam purposes) that is the reason the writing has been set.

How much?
Smothering a piece of written work with corrections can be defeating. Even if students look at them they probably won't learn much. 'Free' writing at the low levels will inevitably be full of inaccuracy and as such should only be set for communicative purposes (i.e. how well the meaning has been got across) and not be marked and corrected on the basis of correct form.

When correcting cued writing, it is often worth focusing on a particular area (e.g. punctuation or spelling) and ignoring the rest. You can then work remedially on that area with the students.

How?
With some modifications in procedure, the principles again are the same as for oral correction.
1 Make sure students write on every other line and leave a margin.

2 Depending on the aim of the exercise, underline the errors you wish to focus on so that students know *where* they occur.

3 To show them what type of errors they are, put symbols in the appropriate place in the margin (e.g. *P* might represent punctuation, *S*: spelling, *WO*: word order, etc.) If the students don't understand the symbols, teach them.

4 Give the piece of writing back to the students to see how much they can correct for themselves.

5 Sometimes written work may be exchanged with other students or discussed in groups so that they all correct each other's.

6 Correct their corrections (or the corrections of their colleagues).

7 Mark, or comment, according to the aim of the written work. If communication is the aim, don't mark according to spelling. Always decide whether marks are to be quantitative (e.g. a mark for punctuation might be arrived at by deducting the number of errors from 100) or based on a general impression. Sometimes it's worth giving different marks for different things within the

same piece of written work as well as an overall mark based on its communicative worth.

8 Get the student to write up a neat copy and hand it in.

9 Set follow-up exercises for bad errors, perhaps giving appropriate page number references in exercise books.

10 Note down errors that are common to the group and prepare a remedial lesson for them.

This procedure may seem heavy and slow as it is thought of as forming part of a series of lessons (obviously it will be adapted to the class and the occasion) but one piece of written work, properly done, will achieve far more and give a far greater sense of achievement than a hundred badly-done 'free' essays covered with red ink! In such cases the teacher sweats and frequently it's all for nothing!

Exercises

Ex. 1

AIM
To establish the difference between mistakes and errors.

PROCEDURE
1 Ask a couple of students to record three or four minutes of them talking to each other or to write a small composition, on a single page if possible.

2 Note down which inaccuracies of form you think are merely slips and which are ingrained errors.

3 Go back to the students and see which inaccuracies they can correct for themselves.

4 Compare what they can and can't do with your original list and discuss some of the individual language problems with the students.

Ex. 2

AIM
To practise breaking up an utterance so as to aid correction.

PROCEDURE
A: 1 Give the following utterances to a partner:
   I see him yesterday.
   He likes tennis table.
   He's gone to the work.
   I must see dentist.
   I see you tomorrow.
   He is the student who makes these mistakes.

2 Correct them by slowing him down when he says each utterance, showing him that each finger on your hand represents a word. By gesture alone, indicate what the correct form should be in the problem area.

3 By gesture alone get him to say the correct form at normal speed.

B: 1 Distribute the above utterances to the whole group.

2 Try and correct each one, as in 2 and 3 above, by making a row of students

represent the utterance (e.g. S1 = I, S2 = see, S3 = him, S4 = yesterday), making the appropriate gestures and moving the students.

COMMENT
Both exercises are great fun and although the above errors are structural, a similar exercise can be devised for pronunciation problems.

Ex. 3

AIM
To establish a realistic code for written correction.

PROCEDURE
1 With a partner, select a student and make a list of the kinds of errors you think he might make in his written work (refer to the list on p 149).

2 Work out an abbreviation or a code for each one.

3 Work out how you would explain them to the whole class.

4 Collect a piece of written work from your student that needs close correction and make a copy of it.

5 Each partner marks the student's work using the code.

6 Compare corrected versions.

Ex. 4

AIM
To help with the anticipation of error when teaching new structures.

PROCEDURE
1 As a group draw up a list of ten structural areas (e.g. REGULAR PAST TENSES, THE PRESENT PERFECT, THE THIRD CONDITIONAL).

2 In pairs, list as many potential problems as you can under the headings of the following grid:

Errors of			
FORM	MEANING	PRONUNCIATION	REASONS?

3 Compare your list with another pair.

4 Think of other structures where similar problems might occur.

Ex. 5

AIM
To illustrate how common errors can be used as the basis for future work with a class.

PROCEDURE
1 Ask a class of students to do a piece of written work (e.g. based on a picture composition), remembering to give them adequate guidance.

2 Collect it in and divide the work among your colleagues.

3 Each member of the group should make a list of what they consider the most serious errors in their piece of written work.

4 The lists should then be compared and the common errors listed.

5 Prepare a remedial lesson on one or more of the areas of error.

COMMENT
This exercise can also be done using a stretch of recorded oral work but it takes longer to do. Also, the most suitable place to do the recording is probably the language laboratory but, because of the tracking, the tapes often cannot be played on ordinary tape players.

5.3 Promoting interaction between students

It is one of the teacher's tasks to manage the learning situation so that students interact. In general terms, a group which is co-operating, sharing ideas, providing help and evaluating the success of activities is likely to be taking more overall responsibility for what it learns and how it learns it than a group that is used to filtering everything through the teacher. Such responsibility usually aids the success with which students learn a language.

Students also need to interact in the classroom because it is one way they can learn to communicate through the language. Many of the activities that involve the teacher 'receiving' (i.e. listening to) language from students (e.g. drilling) are activities where the students are, in one sense, displaying the language for the teacher to comment on or correct. Very often in a language classroom, particularly at the lower levels, there is little real communication with the teacher unless the student wants to do something like borrow a pen or ask what something means. Activities which encourage the students to communicate fully with others, then, are vital in developing the skills we employ when we talk to each other.

Even at the level of practising language items, interaction is essential if all the students in the group are to have adequate practice. Make sure that:

1 You give everyone a chance to get things right

2 You don't make everyone wait while you listen to everyone in turn.

Pair work and group work, then, where the teacher's role is one of organizer, manager, adviser and, sometimes, evaluator, are essential. Encouraging the students to by-pass you certainly does not mean that you have abdicated responsibility for what is going on.

How can you encourage interdependence between students?

1 By redirecting students' enquiries to other students and only answering them yourself as a last resort. If it's done regularly, a simple gesture should be enough to encourage it. In time, the students should by-pass you all together.

2 By not supplying everything yourself. Get them to lend each *other* pens, to share books, to open windows and so on.

3 By getting students to help each other. If a student doesn't know an answer to something or know how to do something like pronounce a word or complete a written exercise, get another student to help. In oral work, a simple gesture may be enough to indicate that you expect this to happen.

4 If a student can't correct himself, by getting another student to correct him, don't jump in yourself unless you have to (see pp 146–154).

5 By getting students to evaluate each other's work. So if a student offers you some language for approval, turn to the others and say *Is that all right?* or *Do you agree?* Equally, get the students to look over each other's written work. Even at the low levels, where, say, they have just copied something from the board, this can be a useful exercise. If, at higher levels, they have individually jotted down a few ideas on a topic, ask them to look at their neighbour's and talk about them while they are waiting for the rest to finish.

6 When checking comprehension, (rather than asking all the questions yourself) by getting the students to prepare and ask questions. Before they ask them, go round quickly to make sure the questions are more or less understandable and answerable (though sometimes when they are not it can cause useful interaction!) Questions can be prepared individually, in pairs or in groups.

7 By allowing students to take over the teacher's role. This may be at the level of operating OHPs or tape recorders. Also, for example, if a new student arrives and he is unknown to the others, it might mean getting someone to introduce the other students to him and getting someone else to ask him friendly questions! Also, if a student is late, you might get the other students to find out why. It sometimes works wonders! At very advanced levels, you might ask students to prepare lessons which will teach the others something specific (like a grammar point some of them are shaky on). At intermediate levels, you might ask students to prepare short talks on some aspect of where they come from or, where all the students are of the same nationality, their specialist skills (e.g. photography).

8 If the students' English is good enough, by getting them to help you prepare their timetable for the coming series of lessons. Such negotiation encourages the students to be much more involved in their learning and helps you to realize what they think they need. Be careful, though. Most classes will want to be sure that you have a clear idea of what you think they need and will expect you to direct the programme to a certain extent.

9 By encouraging students to talk about the classes. Regular discussion among students, in pairs or groups with no interference from you, about what they found difficult, what they found easy, what they found good, what they found confusing is useful, not only because it promotes genuine interaction in itself but because it develops a much greater awareness among students of what is actually happening in the classroom and helps you understand better how they react to what you do. Sometimes, it is worthwhile analysing the value of a particular technique. If the students' English is too poor for this kind of discussion, in monolingual classes it is sometimes still worth having it in the students' mother-tongue.

Communication activities

These have already been written about in 4.8, but here are three general points:

1 During a communication activity, encourage students to circulate and not just stick with one partner. You should try and encourage an atmosphere where students are keen to move on to other partners and get more practice.

2 Make use of the 'pyramid' or 'snowballing' technique to encourage discussion. For example, each student might list the five most important things a language school must have (e.g. a tape recorder). The students then form pairs and

agree on a list of five things. Then pairs form groups of four and have to agree on their five things. Then groups of four move into groups of eight, and so on until the whole class is discussing the topic together. The pattern looks like this:

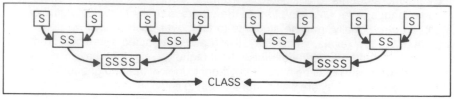

Figure 17

3 Exploit the information gap, where one student, or a group of students, knows something another student or group of students doesn't know but needs or wants to know. Some activities like *Describe and Draw* (see p 140) are done in pairs. Others, like the following, are done by the students getting up and mingling:

   Each student has to choose, from the following, a month, a hotel and a town they most want for their holidays:

JUNE	AUGUST	OCTOBER
RITZ HOTEL	PARK HOTEL	ROYAL HOTEL
BRIGHTON	BOURNEMOUTH	SOUTHEND

N.B. each town, Brighton, Bournemouth and Southend, has a Ritz, a Park and a Royal hotel.

Students then have to stand up and talk to each other to find other people in the group who have made the same choice.

Exercises

Many useful exercises can be devised observing the way your group interacts during input sessions. What you learn from different communication structures can provide a good basis for discussion. Such exercises, however, are best set by the course tutor.

Ex. 1

AIM

To help evaluate how far discussing one's work with colleagues can help one's own learning.

PROCEDURE

1 Ask each member of your group to submit a lesson plan.

2 Redistribute them among the group.

3 Mark each other's work according to agreed criteria (e.g. practicability, originality, variety, logical staging, etc.) on a scale of 1–5.

4 Mark your own on the same scale.

5 Discuss the marks and whether the criteria were appropriate.

COMMENT

This exercise may be worth doing several times on various pieces of written work. This will help reduce self-consciousness and embarrassment as well as the possibility of succumbing to group pressure!

Ex. 2

AIM
To develop understanding of the value of interaction between colleagues and mutual evaluation.

PROCEDURE
1 Write a report on one aspect of several of your colleagues' contributions to the course (e.g. TP, the social atmosphere, discussion groups etc.) The report should be framed positively, noting good points first, and making criticism in the manner of *It would be better if he . . .* rather than *He doesn't. . . .*

2 Make sure your colleagues do the same for you!

3 Discuss the results.

COMMENT
Seriously conducted, this exercise can vastly improve the working relationship of a group and develop the habit of being able to comment critically without being destructive or making everyone feel threatened. For this reason it is essential that no teacher trainer should approve or disapprove of the content of the reports.

Ex. 3

AIM
To discover the value of interaction activities.

PROCEDURE
1 In pairs or as a whole group, do a selection of interaction activities. Ideally they are best done in a foreign language. (e.g. Find someone in your group with whom you have three things in common.)

2 Discuss how you felt doing the activities, discuss language areas that arose and, if done in a foreign language, discuss language problems you had.

5.4 Showing visuals

Before taking any kind of visual into the classroom make sure:
1 It is big enough to be seen. A minimum size of 10″ × 8″ is a rough guide for most classrooms.

2 It is unambiguous (i.e. as simple as it can be for the purpose it has to fulfill) unless the ambiguity is deliberate and productive

3 It is presentable, preferably mounted. Pictures simply ripped out of magazines look scrappy and unprofessional.
Among other things, visuals are used to:
– create a need for new language which the teacher then satisfies

– elicit already known language

– supply a context for an activity, like a role-play

– stimulate discussion.

It is usually essential that every student sees the picture, so:
1 Before the class, make sure that the appropriate details can be seen from the back of the classroom, by propping it up on a table where you would normally stand and looking at it from the most distant part of the room.

2 When you first show the picture, hold it up so that everyone can see it. Don't stand so that there are two students on either side who can't see it properly. Stand back, hold it vertically at the top and the bottom and don't let it flap about. Pause to allow the students time to take in what they see. Perhaps ask them if they can all see. If they're screwing up their eyes, craning their necks or reaching for their glasses, then move in and show the visual close up.

3 Ask one or two quick questions not related to your main aim to make sure the students are interpreting the picture in the way you intend. They may be focusing on a part that you are not interested in, or they may see a man crying out in pain where you see a man who's very angry. One student saying what his reaction to a visual is helps to focus the class's attention as a whole.

4 Show the visual round the class. If necessary, walk around slowly, showing the picture to each student in turn, making sure he has enough time to take it in properly.

5 Display the picture by sticking it on the board, on the wall or on the notice-board (Blu-tack, Sellotape or drawing pins can be of use). This makes it easier to refer to later in the lesson, particularly when you are summarizing what has been done. It also leaves your hands free to control any oral work you are doing with the class and also enables you to write relevant language next to it later.

Work out a system for storing your visuals and classifying them so that they become a resource you can keep re-using and adding to. It is also useful to put a note on the back of each visual after you have used it to show what you have used it for. For further advice on this topic refer to *The Magazine Picture Library* PLT3 by Janet McAlpin (Heinemann).

Exercises

Ex. 1

AIM
To discover the ideal viewing distance for visuals.

PROCEDURE
1 Select a picture about 10″ × 8″ with some bold figure in the foreground but a considerable amount of detail in the background.

2 Write a list of five or six graded questions which first elicit the image as a whole and then elicit some of the detail.

3 Stand a number of your colleagues at distances of 2′, 4′, 6′, 8′ and 10′ from you and hold up the picture.

4 Ask the questions and notice the cut-off point in terms of the detail they can perceive.

Ex. 2

AIM
To practise showing visuals to a group.

PROCEDURE

1 Select one large (10″ × 10″), one medium-sized (8″ × 8″) and one small (5″ × 3″) picture.

2 Stand in front of your group and display each in turn, asking them to look carefully. Then put them on the board.

3 Discuss which would be suitable for what activity.

COMMENT

1 It should be noticed how differently one can treat the pictures.

2 You may be able to stand back and all the group will see the large picture but you will have to go round and show the small one individually before any oral work can be done. It might be felt that the small one is more suitable for pair and group work only.

3 This exercise can be tied in with any exercise on how to conduct substitution drills, using the visuals both to establish the context and provide the prompts.

5.5 Using the board

It is unusual to find classrooms without a board of some kind, whether it is white, black or green. It is essential, then, to organize your use of it in order to obtain the maximum effect.

Three basic prerequisites:

1 Start with a clean board or with a board that only has on it what you have just put on (i.e. don't start your lesson with the remnants of someone else's still up).

2 Write legibly. If necessary, get some practice outside class time. (This includes writing in a straight line!) It is particularly important if you are teaching learners who are accustomed to a different script.

3 Use the right implement. This doesn't apply so much to chalk boards (although some chalk is better than others) as it does to white boards. Find out if the board is dry or wet wipe and which pens have to be used on it.

What sort of things will be put on the board?

What you will want to put on your board will probably fall into one of the following categories:

1 Permanent or reference material
This may not go on the board at the beginning of the lesson but once it's up it will probably stay until the end. Things that might come into this category are new vocabulary items, model sentences and reminders of items that students persistently get wrong.

2 Material for the development of the lesson
This will be the material that relates to the stage of the lesson that you are at at any one moment. It could be a dialogue the students are rehearsing, a substitution table you want the students to copy down, a model sentence, a picture, an outline of a grammar rule or even the score for a team game you are playing. Some of it may be transferred to the permanent section of the board.

3 Impromptu work
This is the work you use to illustrate or exemplify the answer to an unpredicted

question or to back up an alternative explanation when the planned one doesn't work. It may be a drawing or it may be the written word. Space must always be left on the board for such work.

4 Notes and reminders

In low-level classes it is worth writing the full date (Thursday 25th December 1982) in a top corner at the beginning of a lesson; it is a good way of helping the students learn the days of the week and the dates, particularly those not used to the Gregorian calendar. Also, questions that are answered with *Ask me later* and things that you don't want to or can't answer on the spot are well worth noting in a corner. It shows that you are not just fobbing off the student and when you clean the board at the end of a lesson it will act as a reminder to you to prepare something for the next lesson.

It is essential that you plan the board in your lesson plan and decide which part you are going to allocate to which use. The development area is likely to be the largest so that will probably command the most central part. The 'permanent' area is the most predictable area and should be easy to plan for. You might start by dividing off one side for that purpose. The remaining two areas need separation from the rest of the board so give them the other side. Therefore:

– separate the different parts of the board by drawing lines: it reduces confusion

– decide beforehand what is going to go into each section and how much space to leave.

The development of a board through a lesson, then, might look like this:

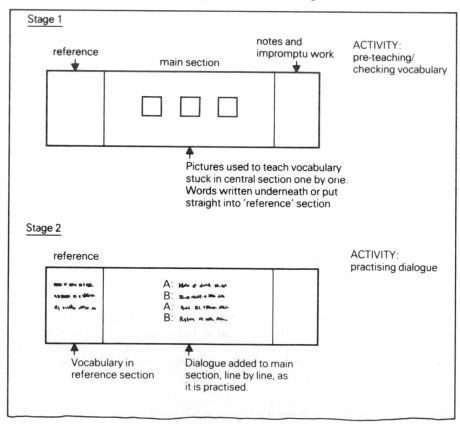

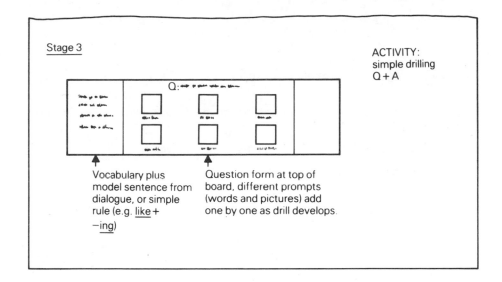

Stage 3

ACTIVITY:
simple drilling
Q + A

Vocabulary plus
model sentence from
dialogue, or simple
rule (e.g. like +
−ing)

Question form at top of
board, different prompts
(words and pictures) add
one by one as drill develops.

Further points

1 Don't get so dependent on the board that you fail to give adequate oral practice. It's easy to think that writing things up is teaching. As a general rule, the writing stage is best thought of as consolidation unless you are specifically developing the writing skill. It is best done when the oral work is over. If students are impatient for you to write things down (particularly new words) and you can't get them to wait, it is sometimes better to write the word on the board, get them to copy it, rub the board clean and get them to close their books before returning to the oral practice. If the spelling seems to indicate different sounds, it is then worth comparing the two later. Having said that, exactly when the writing up is done is a controversial point and needs constant thinking about in relation to your students' normal styles of learning.

2 If you think it is important for the students to write something down, allow yourself time to do the job properly: write it up neatly, give the students time to read it (perhaps aloud) and then copy it down. You may wish to check they've copied it correctly, particularly at the lower levels.

3 Try and build up board-work bit by bit after each activity rather than put it up in one go.

4 Involve the students in the writing process by eliciting what you're going to put up, the spelling of difficult words and so on. In general, though, it is unwise to get students to write things up themselves unless you can trust their handwriting and spelling!

5 Transferring work from the main part of the board to the permanent part provides students with a useful summary of the main stages of the lesson.

6 Adjust the size of your writing to the size of the room and the size of the board.

7 Finally, clean the board at the end of the lesson!
For further advice on this topic, refer to *Planning and Using the Blackboard* PLT1 by Patricia Mugglestone (Heinemann).

Exercises

Ex. 1

AIM
To highlight stages in the use of the board as a lesson progresses.

PROCEDURE
1 Look at the lesson plan and transcription of a lesson on pp 76–78 (*You could. . . .*)

2 Decide what you would need to put on the board and when.

3 Draw a diagram of each stage of the board.

4 Compare it with a colleague's diagram.

Ex. 2

AIM
To help with the skills of writing and drawing on the board.

PROCEDURE
1 Project an OHP transparency of a drawing or a piece of writing on to the board.

2 Write directly over the projected image.

3 Clean the board, turn off the OHP and try again without it.

COMMENT
This exercise can be modified on some boards by making the first copy in pencil (but do check you can first) and then without the OHP, going over it in ink or chalk.

5.6 Using audio and video tape recorders

The amount we use mechanical aids in the classroom and the need there is to be efficient in operating them mean that we need to be more familar with them than is necessary in a domestic environment. Preparation and practice are essential. So:
1 Before you prepare your lesson check the quality of the recording you intend to use, preferably on the machine you will be using.

2 If you intend to record your own tape, do so before preparing the lesson (there's no point in preparing a lesson around a tape which turns out to be unusable).

3 Make sure you actually *use* the controls of the machine a number of times beforehand, so you can manipulate them without having to look. (Check the following: Does the machine go straight from 'play' to 'fast forward'? Does the 'pause' remain in operation after the machine has stopped? When the 'pause' is released, does the tape start exactly where it was stopped or does it creep forward a fraction? Does the machine have 'cue' and 'review' buttons? Will the counter accurately find the place after two or three goes? Do you know if you have to use a separate speaker? What effect do 'volume' and 'tone' controls have on playback? How does the machine load? For open-reel, does it have to be set in a 'free' position? For cassette, which way does the tape go in and which way does it travel? On open-reel, how do you change tracking and speed? For recording, what are the optimum 'volume' and 'tone' settings? etc.)

4 *Before the lesson*, put the tape on, wind it forward to the beginning of the piece you want to use and 'zero' the counter. If you wait until the class starts you'll keep the students waiting.

5 If necessary, check the volume and tone from different parts of the room during the class (if the volume's too high it'll distort the sound).

6 Make sure you rewind to the right place (a moment's silence while you concentrate is better than losing your place and fumbling).

Recording your own tapes

If professionally-produced materials do not suit your needs or are not available when you want them, you may have to make your own. To get the best quality:
– find a quiet room (drawing the curtains will help) although some background noise can add authenticity

– use a separate microphone (built-in microphones tend to pick up a lot of noise from the machine)

– stand the machine on a soft surface to reduce the amount of noise it makes

– rehearse your piece before recording it (first recordings sound fresher than third or fourth attempts).
Two other hints:
1 If you put your recording at the beginning of a tape, it makes it easier to find (with cassettes, make sure you wind past the leader tape).

2 If you know you are going to play something several times, it is sometimes useful to record it that number of times to save you having to rewind (remembering when to stop is often a problem during the class). Dialogues can also be 'exploded', i.e. leaving a pause after each line to allow the students time to repeat.

Using video

A video set-up is basically the same as an audio system, with a recorder and TV monitor for playback and a camera and microphone for recording. The controls are also basically the same. However:
– the leads connecting the parts of a video system are slightly more complex so it is essential that these are checked beforehand

– unlike audio systems, there are several types of video system which take different tape formats, so make sure the tape you want to use is compatible with the available machine.
Video is infinitely superior to audio when it comes to helping the students understand what is being said, because gestures, the physical context and behavioural clues are all present. However, students sometimes judge the quality of home-made productions against the highly-polished professional standards of TV companies. One is therefore sometimes more dependent on published video materials. For further advice on this topic, see PLT7 *Video in the Language Classroom* edited by Marion Geddes and Gill Sturtridge (Heinemann).

General reminders about the use of tapes

(These points are covered more fully in 4.6)
1 Don't play any sort of tape without anticipating what language or skills work you hope to get out of it.

2 Nearly always give the students something to listen or watch *for* while the tape is playing (this may get increasingly difficult or detailed with each play).

3 Don't play a tape without giving an introduction to the topic or setting the context (unless there is a good reason for not doing so).

4 Let the tape do the work. Don't 'bridge' it by saying yourself what the tape says. Play it as many times as necessary.

5 Don't play a tape for too long without stopping, especially when the students are obviously finding it difficult to understand.

6 Be sensitive as to how far you are expecting the students to memorize what they hear and see. Be realistic and try not to overload their memories.

Exercises

Ex. 1

AIM
To develop familiarity with the controls of a recorder.

PROCEDURE
1 Select a short dialogue (about six lines) spoken at fairly normal speed.

2 Find the beginning and 'zero' the counter.

3 Play the dialogue through several times, each time using the counter to return to the beginning.

4 Play the dialogue again, stopping after one line.

5 With one finger on the 'rewind' and one on the 'stop', rewind the tape by one line of the dialogue only.

6 When you can do this successfully, move on to the next line.

7 After two or three lines, look at the furthest corner of the room and repeat steps 5 and 6!

Ex. 2

AIM
To become familiar with the problems of recording the voice.

PROCEDURE
1 Make a recording of a dialogue in an ordinary room, without shutting out background noise or making any special arrangements and without rehearsing it.

2 Record the same dialogue, taking note of the precautions on p 163 and getting suggestions from any experienced person you can find.

3 Compare the results for clarity and realism.

5.7 Indicating sounds, stress and intonation

Individual sounds, sounds in connected speech, stress within words, stress within whole utterances and intonation patterns are all difficult for students to perceive in isolation since, naturally, the main interest of someone engaged in the act of communication is in trying to understand the meaning of what is being said. However, some sort of instinctive perception is essential for a full understanding of what is being said, and some sort of analytic perception is useful for correct production, so it is helpful to give an indication of these features in order to highlight them even when the students are examining other aspects of form or listening for meaning.

Contrasting how things are said

Obviously, clear modelling is important and frequently needs to be done so as to *contrast* certain features of sounds, stress and intonation. A student can more readily perceive that a sound is 'voiced' by placing it along side a sound that is 'unvoiced'. A rising question tag becomes easier to recognize when it is heard immediately before or after a falling one. Attention can be drawn to stress on a particular syllable by saying it correctly and then repeating the word with the stress on a different syllable. And so on.

This can be taken a step further and students can be asked to identify which of a pair of words has a particular sound in it, which utterance has the rising intonation, which question starts with a stressed word and so on.

Indicating individual sounds

1 Stressing the syllable containing the sound

This has the advantage of bringing it clearly to the students' attention but the disadvantage of distorting the stress pattern of the utterance, as well as running the risk of changing the production of the sound as it would occur in connected speech. This is a particular disadvantage in the case of sounds in unstressed syllables (e.g. the 'schwa' /ə/ is often heard as the weak form of another sound).

It is best, then, to follow the simple rule that if you stress sound unnaturally for any reason, it sould immediately be repeated normally. In this way the final thing which stays in the students' mind is the sound produced as it would be in the context from which it has been taken.

2 Mouthing the word

This involves exaggerated movements of the lips, teeth and tongue so that the students can see clearly what is happening. It can only really be applied to the sounds produced at the front of the mouth, except in the case of those vowels where the shape of the lips is important.

Once students have learned about one aspect of pronunciation (e.g. 'voicing') then you can indicate that feature of the sound by making a gesture to remind them of it (e.g. with 'voicing', you might place your hand on your throat or ask them to put their hands over their ears).

3 Finger indication

A word or an utterance can be broken down into syllables, sounds or words and each segment associated with one of your fingers. You then point to the appropriate finger and say the sound:

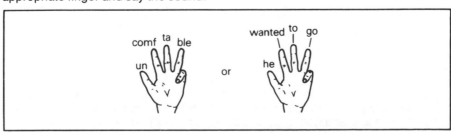

The sound can be isolated by going through the word or utterance slowly, finger by finger, then going back to the finger representing the important sound (or syllable) and getting the students to repeat it in isolation. At the end you should always put the sound back in its context in the utterance by either giving a sweeping gesture across all the fingers or closing the fingers and giving a clear, normal model.

4 Visuals

A diagram of the mouth showing how a particular sound is made can be drawn on the board or displayed on the walls and indicated whenever a problem occurs with that sound. This is obviously more useful in classes where pronunciation problems are common to the group.

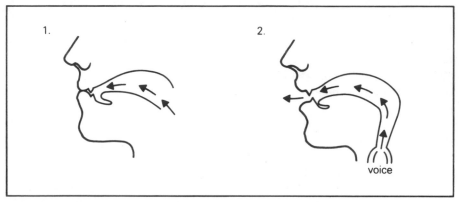

Taken from *Ship or Sheep?* Ann Baker (CUP).

A picture representing a problem sound (e.g. a picture of a man called Bill to represent the /ɪ/ sound) can be referred to when the need arises. Pictures representing other words containing that sound can be added below it as they occur (e.g. *fish, gin, lips).*

A chart can act as a useful reminder of sounds and their spellings:

Sheep /iː/			
ee	ea	ie	ey
fee	read	achieve	key

The key word is at the top and each column represents a different spelling. As new words are presented to the class, students can suggest which column they should be added to and write them in.

5 Hands
For consonant sounds such as /ө/ one hand can represent the top teeth and the other hand the tip of the tongue to show the light contact the tongue has with the teeth.

6 Phonetic symbols
Students and teachers alike are often put off by the apparent difficulty of using a phonetic, or more correctly, a phonemic transcription. It is worth remembering that it was developed as a kind of short cut, a way of representing sounds without having to give an explanation each time. It is also in common use in dictionaries.

Having said that, it is probably not worth trying to teach the whole of it to a class. However, the symbols for common or difficult sounds (e.g. /ə/ /ө/ /ð/ /ŋ/) can be introduced to help the class note down problems more easily.

Indicating stress

1 By overstressing
This technique makes stress in utterances more readily perceived by students and experience suggests that there is little danger of them repeating the exaggeration outside the classroom. There is also little danger of distortion unlike when a particular sound is stressed.

2 By gesture
This is done by any of the following ways:
(a) Beating time like a conductor, perhaps using a clenched fist.

(b) Quietly clapping on the stressed syllable.

(c) Clicking the fingers.

(d) Tapping the desk.

3 By making marks on the board
There are a number of possible ways. For example, take the sentence *He wanted to go* with the stress on *want* and *go* (although of course it might go on the *he* in the right context). These are some of the options:
(a) *Capitalization*:   He WANTed to GO.
    This shouldn't be used with a class having difficulty with the Roman script!

(b) *Underlining*:   He wanted to go.
    Simple though not very graphic. Underlining is also often used in written correction.

(c) *Stress marks*:   He 'wanted to 'go.
    Used by most dictionaries for word stress, with marks at the top indicating primary stress and those at the bottom indicating secondary stress. However, these can easily be confused with apostrophes and speech marks in sentences.

(d) *Boxes*:   □ ☐ □ □ ☐   He wanted to go.
    Useful because the whole pattern can be shown without the words.

    ☐   ☐
    Or: He wanted to go. *Or:* He wanted to go.
    Both of which show just the stressed syllables.

(e) *Musical notation*:   He wanted to go.
    ♩ ○ ♩♩ ○

Comprehensible only to those with knowledge of music, but used in some books.

Whichever you choose, your system should be clear and immediately understandable to students. It is advisable to keep it consistent within any one teaching institution to reduce the possibility of confusion.

Indicating intonation

1 By exaggeration
When you exaggerate the main features (e.g. a falling tone in some questions) the pattern is more noticeable and more memorable for students. When they try and imitate it, however, it is important that they don't make it too silly or they won't think of transferring it to their normal speech behaviour.

2 By gesture
It is possible to 'draw' an approximation of the whole intonation pattern in the air with your hand but this is usually unnecessarily complicated. It is far easier, and perhaps more useful, to give a clear sweep of the hand either up or down in order to indicate the general direction the voice should take on a particular syllable. Some teachers use a balloon or a large, soft ball to indicate a falling or a rise-fall pattern. Hands can also be used to show whether the voice starts on a high or low pitch.

3 By making marks on the board
Again, there are a number of possible ways. For example, take the sentence *It's a lovely day, isn't it?* with a fall on each part.

a) *Curved writing*:   It's a lovely da_y isn't it?

Difficult to do neatly, but clear. However, it can interfere with students' writing development!

b) *Arrows*: It's a lovely day, isn't it?

Clear and simple and can be used by students. Can be tied in with stress, e.g.

It's a lovely day, isn't it?

c) *Lines and arrows*: It's a lovely day, isn't it?

Very clear and the whole pattern can be shown without using words. The definiteness and straightness of some of the contours, however, can be misleading. On the other hand, if it were more accurate it would probably contain more information than the students need.

d) *Musical notation*: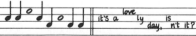

Again clear to those who have some musical knowledge and indicates both stress and intonation as well as pitch level.

This can be simplified to: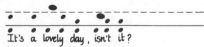

Again, select one system according to the sophistication, the level and the needs of your students and *stick* to it.

6 For the Trainer

6.1 Organizing TP

A: Different structures

TP has to be organized according to local constraints and the aims of a course. Tabulated overleaf are some of the ones we have come across. This is obviously not an exhaustive list but does cover most of the major possibilities, others being possible through a recombination of the different elements.

These schemes have different names, e.g. apprenticeship, peer teaching, micro-teaching and whole-class teaching. Of these, perhaps the one that most requires definition is micro-teaching since it is used to cover the widest range of different activities in different centres. There will be exceptions but in most cases it includes one or more of the following elements:
- teaching a small group of students, either a part of a class or a class formed especially for the purpose

- not teaching what is normally regarded as a whole lesson, either in terms of time or in terms of content

- teaching in a situation where the observers focus on specific elements in the micro-lesson.

It might be thought from the table that there is some progression from peer teaching to the teaching of whole lessons. This should not be seen as the ideal to work towards, nor should it be seen as the kind of progression that should necessarily take place throughout a course, although of course in some circumstances it might provide a convenient structure. Peer teaching for the improvement of technique is usually useful at any stage in a course and the teaching of whole lessons, provided it is not actually going to disadvantage unwilling students, is useful from the earliest stages.

B: Aims

It is worth discussing the overall aims of TP with trainees, what it is they should be trying to do, how they will be assessed, the kind of comments that will be made and so on.

It is also worth trying to present some kind of progression to trainees, even if your course is non-linear in approach. The progression might be represented in the form of milestones they can tick off along the way, under such headings as *technique* and *stages of lesson* (e.g. under *technique* the list to tick off might include: *using a tape recorder; using the OHP; eliciting dialogue.* Under *stages of lesson* it might include: *introduction; setting the scene; presentation.*)

In courses that are non-linear in approach if you don't have a ticking-off process of some sort the whole thing might appear to be organized rather randomly.

It is the trainer's job to structure TP in such a way that it is clear who is going to get what out of it. You may want your trainees to try out a narrative building exercise to give them practice in eliciting language, the trainees may want to try out a 'situationalized drill' that they have just seen demonstrated and the students may want to develop their reading skills. On top of that, the trainees may see their bits of teaching as just a series of isolated techniques whereas the students may be looking for a whole lesson. With such a potential clash of interests there have to be compromises and it is your job to ensure that the balance is maintained and the purpose of TP is clear to everyone. Section D considers this in more detail.

C: Who teaches with whom

This means forming effective groups of trainees for TP or, in some cases, making sure the trainees are 'apprenticed' to the most appropriate teacher and the most appropriate class.

TRAINEES: ACTIVITIES AND GROUPING	SOURCE OF STUDENTS	OBSERVERS
1. Trainees, as whole group or in small groups, teach specific points for short periods (e.g. five to ten minutes).	Other trainees sometimes assuming predetermined roles (e.g. a quiet student, slow to participate).	Course tutors; peers.
2. Three to eight trainees per group. Each teaches a separate point for a short period (between five to ten minutes, depending on whole time available and stage in course).	Groups of volunteer students.	
3. As above but each trainee takes part of a lesson; the students receive a whole lesson.		
4. Individual trainees or pairs of trainees take part of a whole lesson.	Real class taking place at usual time.	Normal class teacher; peer(s); possibly course tutors.
5. Individuals teach whole lesson.	Real class or volunteers.	

The formation of TP groups

Obviously you can't decide on the composition of a group without meeting the people concerned but the following factors should be borne in mind:

1 *Age*

Are all the trainees from roughly the same age group or is there a significantly older, or younger, person who is likely to be particularly aggressive or defensive? Since they stand out from the rest of the group by the obvious age difference this should not be allowed to develop into a barrier which hinders the learning process. Care should be taken not to put them in a group where they are likely to do damage by criticizing too heavily. Similarly they should not be 'apprenticed' to a teacher where the age difference is likely to be resented for any reason. Age difference need not always be a problem and an older trainee can often represent a very supportive element in a weaker group.

FEEDBACK	COMMENTS
Usually immediately after someone has 'taught'; possibly leading to the same trainee trying to teach the point again.	Allows everyone to concentrate closely on physical techniques (e.g. gesture) but really a false situation; trainees cannot focus on achieving language teaching aims. Nevertheless, valuable for certain tasks.
From course tutor and peers, either immediately after each teacher has taught or after the whole 'lesson'. Re-teaching is sometimes possible with the same group but it is more realistic with a different group.	As above but with real learners. Allows for real teaching tasks and enables one to judge the effectiveness of the teaching. Close observation possible but tends to encourage lack of development and relatedness in the series of 'lessons'.
Usually in discussion after whole session. Re-teaching not normally possible unless two groups of students available.	'Real' teaching points with the students' needs in mind give trainees a greater sense of a whole lesson and how learners respond and develop. A more systematic use of course books is also possible.
Usually after lesson but interruption, demonstration and re-teaching possible provided it is acceptable to any students paying for their classes and to the institution.	Observation of experienced teacher combined with practice and help can encourage the teaching to be more meaningful. Difficulty of trainee fitting in and problems of planning and co-ordination with class teacher. Feedback by class teacher more individual but trainees can miss the support of colleagues.
Afterwards; no re-teaching possible.	Very close to real situation but can discourage experimentation and not be very helpful in developing specific teaching techniques.

2 *Sex*
A balance of the sexes is worth going for if it is at all possible. However, there may be an overall imbalance on the course which prevents this or one of the student groups which is being used for practice may have a cultural background which prevents them from being taught by men or women.

3 *Teaching Style*
It is impossible to predict accurately how any one individual's style will develop, so matching or complementing different potential styles within a group is very difficult. This may of course be easier if the trainees are re-grouped after the course has started. However, it is worth trying as far as possible to get a mix of personalities so that they can compare how different people approach the same classroom problems.

4 *Experience*
Even though in this book we are more concerned with training courses where the participants have little or no experience, there are often those who have had some classroom experience, even if in a different subject. Should these people be spread about or grouped together? If they are spread about it is possible that any bad teaching habits they have will become an unconscious model for the others and prove a hindrance to the general progress of the course. If they are grouped together they might become entrenched in their own preconceptions.
Other factors: If the group is to be asked to work closely together is it physically possible for them to do so? Do they live close to one another? Do they have telephones? Is there a room in the school or college they can use? Is travel likely to be involved and if so can they share a car? Simple considerations like these may easily be overlooked and yet they can in the end outweigh all the other factors. A well thought-out application form or a questionnaire at the beginning of the course is often the answer.

Given that there is frequently very little time to answer these questions, grouping is often done on an intuitive basis. However, there are ways of finding out how people react to each other. An informal party early on in the course will often reveal how people group themselves naturally and whether there is anyone who is likely to be out on a limb. A classroom 'icebreaking' activity can show how they react to each other in a more formal atmosphere.

Apprenticeship: The same kind of factors affect the pairing of trainees with full-time teachers, although it is sometimes better for the trainees to meet the apprentice masters before decisions are made. The advantage here may be that those teachers are your colleagues and this makes it much easier for you to arrange a meeting to discuss any problems.

D: Teaching points

Who are they for?
Teaching points can either be set so that the trainees are gradually introduced to different techniques and different teaching points or they can be set to follow the students' progress. The progression is either appropriate for the trainees or the students.

The question you need to ask yourself before setting teaching points is whether the TP is for the trainees or for the students being practised on. Should the teaching point be chosen to allow the trainee to develop a particular skill or technique or should the aim be to teach the students something?

The simple answer would seem to be that since TP, except in strict micro-teaching situations, is in many ways an attempt to simulate the real situation then it is always the students, needs that should be satisfied and it is any change from this that needs to be justified and not vice versa. So, to put it simply, 'teaching points set for TP should always be aimed at the students in the class unless there is good reason for it to be otherwise'.

In the face of such a seemingly dogmatic statement it is worth adding that there is often likely to be good reason but an element of real teaching must always remain. Let us consider the example of the TP situation where trainees are teaching a group of volunteers whose presence is guaranteed somehow – so their goodwill is not important, except in human terms – and the trainees' aim is to develop a particular teaching skill. It would seem that the teaching point itself is almost irrelevant and that the technique that the trainees are going to practise is the only consideration. However, if the teaching point is not pitched at the right level then true practice of the technique becomes impossible; if it is too easy it becomes the same as peer teaching; if it is too difficult it blocks the practice of the technique. So even in this situation it needs to be a teaching point which is appropriate for the needs and level of the students in question. Besides, any teaching must involve selecting and staging teaching points appropriately and success or failure in the selection will be an important discussion point.

Another important factor is that the way you present your points will to a certain extent indicate the way you expect your trainees to teach. So if you don't devise teaching points for the students, you are denying them the opportunity to see the principles of any student-centred teaching you may have talked about being applied in practice. You will be showing them lessons prepared in a vacuum. An unfortunate side-effect of this approach is often to encourage trainees to become over-preoccupied with themselves as teachers which, in TP, has the effect of making them self-conscious and nervous!

Should teaching points relate to skills or structures?

Any experienced teacher will realize that no teaching point is discrete and that the links with other parts of the language must be brought to the students' attention by the teacher at some stage (the word *point* suggests discrete items and perhaps ought to be replaced by something like *directives*). In an attempt to preserve the 'watertightness' of TP, trainers have sometimes resorted to the idea of using more infrequent idioms as a way of guaranteeing something which will be new to students, teachable, and relatively free from problems of dependence on other areas of language. This may be a useful approach in some circumstances, particularly in the area of micro-teaching, but it can easily give trainees and students a false impression of what is important to teach.

At the other end of the scale is the approach which seems to ignore the systematic presentation of new language and treats teaching practice as skills practice for the students. This too can be problematic, since the trainees may not be given the chance to see true skills practice as part of a developing programme for the students and they may be denied the opportunity to learn how to identify a language aim in a text.

The answers seem to be to:

1 Fit the language points to the students' needs as far as possible (and to include the trainees in the process of discovering those needs).

2 Relate the points to each other as far as possible, i.e. have a programme of points.

3 Lead from discrete language points into skills development or, if the level makes it impossible, start with skills development and deal with discrete language items later. So with language points you might consider skills development aims, and with skills points you might identify a language focus, but at no point will you forget either.

4 Take the trainees' needs into account only when the other criteria have been satisfied.

As a general rule, however, at the lower level one is likely to spend more time on individual language items, whereas at the higher levels one is likely to see how the items relate to each other and distinguish between often-confused concepts (e.g. the PRESENT PERFECT and the PAST SIMPLE) and work on developing the students' ability in listening, reading, writing and speaking.

What should you identify when setting points?

Either an item like a structure or a function and/or a skills aim, depending on the level of the class and how much time the trainee is given for teaching. One can list the aims under the following headings:

1 Language aims as discrete items (e.g. The PRESENT PERFECT in *He's broken his arm.*)

2 Language aims as communicative behaviour (e.g. being able to ask for directions)

3 Skills aims (e.g. improving listening abilities).

Is there anything else one must identify?

There are many things one *may* identify but again it will depend on the level of the students, the stage of the course the trainees are at and your aims in setting the points. At the beginning of their training you might identify quite a few things, whereas later in the course the trainees might prepare their own points based on what they have learnt about the students.

Always, though, it's worth encouraging the trainees to distinguish between learning and teaching aims, even though both aims will, in the experienced teacher's mind, be one and the same thing. So a 'learning aim' might be 'By the end of the lesson the students should be able to . . .' whereas a teaching aim might be 'Present and give controlled practice to . . .'.

Other things you might want to identify, depending on the amount of control you want over the trainees' lesson, are, for example:

– the steps required to achieve an aim (e.g. 1. show pictures and elicit context. 2. present dialogue from tape, etc.)

– the stages and timing of lessons together with mini-aims for each stage (i.e. the shape of the whole lesson)

– the materials and aids to be used and any reference to resource material, course books, reference books, etc.

– the activity (a role-play; a situationalized drill).

How far should trainees be allowed to experiment on students?

One aspect of the above approach to the setting of TP points is that it will often require trainees to do things in the classroom that they have not talked about, tried or seen demonstrated on other parts of the course. This should not be seen as a disadvantage since it resembles the real situation where we try out new material and new ideas all the time. On a training course it also reduces the risk of too much emphasis being given to imitating the trainer's techniques instead of ways of achieving students' particular learning aims. Consequently they don't feel they have failed if they don't do something 'right'. Trainees are encouraged to come up with their own solutions to particular problems and develop their own safety devices for ensuring not only success but, to be realistic, in some cases their own survival. For this reason, TP points should often not be too prescriptive.

However, trainees should not be left in a stage of permanent insecurity, so opportunities should also be given for them to try out what they have been shown how to do (i.e. balance your points between tightly directed points, if the appropriate techniques have been demonstrated, and loosely directed points if they haven't. This might seem the opposite to what common sense would dictate but in our experience it's a sounder principle.)

Who tells the trainees what to teach?

For micro-teaching the options are:
1 The overall teacher-training course tutor. This has the advantage that techniques, approaches, ideas etc. can more easily tie in with what trainees are learning on other parts of the course and it gives the trainer greater overall control. Unless it is done in close liaison with the actual TP supervisors and unless the points are made specific to a group of students, it has the disadvantage of making the students' needs secondary.

2 The trainees' supervisors, when they know the group of language students being taught on TP. This has the advantage that teaching points can be tailored to the students on a day-to-day basis and so reflect the real teaching situation more closely. It also has the advantage that particular teaching skills can receive the amount of practice appropriate to the individual trainees in a group. Such an approach, however, demands supervisors with a great deal of experience and knowledge, as well as close liaison with the group tutor to ensure that what is being asked is not too much out of phase with what is happening on other parts of the course.

3 A 'floating' course tutor, who is not tied up supervising another group. It's often not a very economic scheme but it combines the advantages of both the above schemes and does away with the disadvantages. However, it might be thought a serious disadvantage if the group tutor does not get involved more intimately with the trainee's development.

4 The institution. Although this scheme takes the pressure off trainees to plan points well and so ensure a certain standard in the setting of points, it tends to be very rigid and encourages non-student-centred approaches.

How should what to teach be staged throughout a course?

It has been remarked that trainees are frequently asked to do the most difficult things first with little or no practice, such as 'up front' teaching with expectations of, say, tight drilling and sensitive correction.

Consequently, after the first session, which should probably be concerned with finding out about the students (interviewing them, getting them to fill out questionnaires, testing them informally, perhaps recording them for later analysis – one or two trainees per small group of students), early tasks might be:

– monitoring some easy-to-set-up group work

– going over grammar exercises, the informal test, the tape-recorded interview with just one or two students

– going through, say, a newspaper article (again in ones and twos)

– getting the students to talk about pictures.

All of these give trainees greater sensitivity to the students in the group and take the pressure off them to 'perform' skilfully with techniques that are as yet unpractised. They also give rudimentary practice in classroom management skills and the basis for a diagnostic analysis of the students' abilities which might help both you and the trainee to construct a 'syllabus' for future lessons. Of course, if the training group is very inexperienced you will have to be fairly directive.

As many courses try and give TP at different levels, it might happen that the early days of TP are with a beginners' group and there is a greater need for whole-class, 'up-front' teaching. If that is the case, to prevent the classes from being a shambles it is a good idea some time before TP to have supervisors available and make each supervisor responsible for one area (e.g. Supervisor 1 – **Presentation**, Supervisor 2 – **Controlled Practice**, Supervisor 3 – **Communication Activities**). The supervisors then take a trainee from each TP group and help them prepare the lesson, perhaps giving peer practice of specific techniques. When the trainees come back together in their TP groups, between them they have a complete lesson. Another advantage of this approach is that all trainees see a selection of basic techniques very early on.

As stated previously, at the beginning TP points will probably be given in some detail. Probably a lot of help will have to be given with a supervisor or the group tutor going over lesson plans prepared by the trainees before they are executed. (Sometimes, though, it is worth giving just the aim and a few suggestions as to how to achieve it, rather than a complicated procedure to follow.) You might also supply materials, since preparation and selection of materials is a complex and onerous task that needs experience. If such tight monitoring isn't done then both trainees and students very often suffer unless the expectations of language students and trainers are specific and limited.

As the course progresses, less information and help will need to be given with the trainees assuming more responsibility and the supervisor or group tutor relaxing control. As they get to know their students better and learn what is expected in teaching terms so they should take more responsibility in the setting of TP points and in the selection and preparation of materials.

Near the end of a course, trainees, in co-operation with a supervisor or group tutor, may wish to work out a timetable for the final TP sessions and then flesh it out in lesson plan terms entirely by themselves, although under your tight direction such an approach can often succeed earlier in a course.

The trainers and supervisors become more like advisors and resources who are only used when there are real problems. The difficulties of weaning from dependency, however, should not be underestimated.

How should teaching points be presented to trainees?

Telling the trainees what they are to teach orally without having anything written down has severe disadvantages:
– It encourages misunderstandings.

– Trainees can easily forget what they've been told, especially the subtleties.

– Without anything to refer to, trainees can panic if they're not clear.

Writing things out and going through them orally with trainees forces trainers to elucidate clearly. It also give trainees something memorable to refer to. There is a danger that trainer's shorthand explanations and jargon will not be understood unless challenged.

It is always worth bearing in mind that a well-presented point is a vital part of any trainee's awareness of:

1 The language

2 How he is expected to approach teaching (so it might reflect how *you* would teach the group yourself if you had them over a period of time).

If you use course books as a source for TP points it can also show how the trainees might identify what can be taken from published materials and also how to exploit it.

In the early days, if in the micro-teaching situation, a form such as the following is useful and forces the trainer to think of many of the aspects that the trainee will have to think about and, in the case of grammar points, research in a grammar book:

TEACHING PRACTICE POINTS

TRAINEE: Anne   LEVEL: Intermediate

STAGE OF COURSE: 25 hours   LENGTH OF LESSON: 20 minutes

SUPERVISOR: Peter

Language item(s) to be focused on:
'have — done'. Main aim: Presentation and Controlled Practice as in 'They've had the door repainted'.

Notes on Grammatical Rules, Meaning and Pronunciation:
Research concept and form on P.106 of Practical English Grammar. Make sure you check the following aspect with the students: Did the owners make the changes themselves or did someone else? Beware contracted 'have' in 'they've had ...'

Skills Aim(s):
No separate skills focus. Make sure you write up a short substitution drill on the board and that the students copy it correctly into their books.

Materials Suggested:

Use the picture of the house in bad condition that Richard used yesterday plus another showing it in a good state now (so before and after)

Techniques/Methods/Stages:

Stages: 1. Quickly revive yesterday's vocab. (redecorate, whitewash etc) (3-4 minutes approx.)

2. Establish context. Lead to mini-dialogues and model (7-8 minutes approx.)

3. Substitution drill (4 minutes approx.)

4. Write up.

Further Comments (e.g. Revision/Homework etc.):

Make sure you liaise with Debbie so that her further practice of the item through a listening comprehensive exercise can relate to the same context.

Later in a course the instructions may be as skeletal as this:

TRAINEE: Rob

DATE: 2 August

SUPERVISOR: Roger

LEVEL: Intermediate

LENGTH OF LESSON: 35 minutes

NUMBER OF MAIN STAGES: 3

Exchanges Unit 5. Lesson 21

Following on from Susan's lesson, exploit the extensive listening on P.57 to develop listening skills. Work out attainable learning aims. Extend into a role-play and set homework prepared by Susan.

Generally, it is better if:

1 All TP lessons on real students interrelate so that for the students they are integrated fragments of a course and the trainees can see the whole picture (both students and trainees benefit from a timetable so that they all know where they are going). For this reason, you might use a section of a course book as a basis. This is normally essential at intermediate levels if the students are to receive a coherent programme.

2 Points are given well in advance so there is plenty of time for preparation. Considering the six main stages on TP:

(a) The setting of points

(b) Trainees prepare lesson plans

(c) Lesson plans presented to trainers for comment

(d) Trainees re-prepare

(e) Trainees teach

(f) Feedback

If stage (d) is to be worthwhile then stage (c) must happen in sufficient time. At the beginning it is advisable to give over 'class' time to preparation so that it can be done in conjunction with trainers. Whatever, trainers must be careful not to suggest changes to lesson plans at such short notice that trainees are thrown. Such going over, though, is very rewarding in the early days and irons out radical problems inherent in the *preparation* of lessons as opposed to the *execution*.

3 Trainees are given copies of each other's lesson points.

4 You work out a system to ensure that the trainees are given the opportunity to cover a wide range of teaching skills (to avoid, for example, one trainee giving three presentations but no communication activities).

6.2 The role of a supervisor

The role of a supervisor varies according to how TP is organized. In many situations the supervisor may be the training Group Tutor or the usual classroom teacher but in others he may be someone whose job on a course is primarily to supervise TP. On some courses supervisors not only set teaching points but may also give considerable help and support to trainees at the planning stage. On others the supervisor's function may be limited to the practice sessions themselves. In all situations where observation is possible, feedback is essential. (Of course it may sometimes be necessary or desirable that trainees will teach unobserved.) With an apprenticeship scheme, the class teacher will obviously dominate the relationship but there must be clear-cut guidelines on his or her role in TP at different stages, whether interruption or comment are acceptable and so on.

How should a supervisor behave during TP?

Supervisors should normally keep a low profile while their trainees are teaching and not interrupt, regardless of the difficulties a trainee might be in. Trainees need to learn what it is to be responsible for a class and build up their confidence in their ability to conduct it. It is the supervisor's duty beforehand to reduce the risk of things going wrong, although it is an inevitable part of an experimental situation like TP that things do go wrong. This shouldn't matter provided that the students don't feel they're being cheated (some institutions in fact rely on non-fee paying volunteers or children coming during school holidays). It also won't matter if the atmosphere is friendly and workmanlike and the supervisor provides the sort of feedback that encourages the trainees to learn from their experience. Of course, at the same time, the trainees have to realize that techniques only go wrong in so far as they do not aid the students' learning objectives, which is just as true of perfect techniques inappropriately used as imperfect techniques appropriately used (in fact, the latter is probably preferable). A lot of misconceptions about the most suitable way of achieving aims can be sorted out at the planning stage with a supervisor's help, so things should never go *disastrously* wrong.

If trainees are practising on their colleagues, on the other hand, interruption would be justified and quite normal, for here the focus is on the techniques rather than the learning situation. Class teachers to whom trainees are apprenticed might also find it necessary to interrupt if they feel their trainee is doing damage to the class. Clearly, such intervention should be carried out gently and trainees should be encouraged to teach again as soon as possible after any disasters.

Other forms of interruption, such as 'scream cards' (where a supervisor, or another trainee, sitting at the back of the class, holds up cards with instructions or urgent reminders on) or 'five-minute warning signals' (e.g. *You've got five minutes left.*) should only be used with prior agreement of trainees and quickly phased out, since they can be very disturbing. Besides, to be always told when you've only five minutes left is not good training for developing a sense of timing!

Supervisors should also be careful not to be too obvious a presence in other ways. If you are too friendly and chatty with the students, you organize the classroom too conspicuously and give impressive demonstrations on the class, then the students will forever regard you as the real teacher and never feel 100% confident when the trainees are teaching. The aim really should be to get the language students to turn naturally to the trainees for help. Also:

– Be gently supportive. It can be a traumatic experience being watched when you have little experience!

– Be silent during TP. Don't talk to other trainees.

– Regard yourself as a developer of the trainee's teaching skills rather than a critic and an evaluator of lessons.

– Blame yourself first if things go wrong – not the trainee.

– Don't undermine or demolish a trainee's confidence.

– Don't be sarcastic.

– Don't show off your knowledge. Simplify what you have to say in direct relation to how experienced the trainees are.

– Give advice and ideas, but be careful not to overload trainees with too much going in too many directions!

6.3 Co-operation among the trainees

In many TP situations trainees are expected to work together in the preparation of classes and in the sharing of views after the classes. In such cases, the success of TP depends to a great extent on how well the group works together. An institution in this situation therefore needs to:

1 Preselect trainees with a view to mutual compatibility.

2 Explain to them the degree of co-operation necessary.

3 Group trainees with a view to the dynamics of the group.

4 Make it clear that the trainees are directly responsible for their students' learning.

5 Make sure that supervisors do not take away responsibility by being too noticeable in a class.

6 Provide facilities for preparation and feedback.

Co-operation can then be encouraged by:

1 Getting trainees to offer constructive help to each other in preparation and to check each other's plans (when setting points, making sure lessons interrelate can sometimes help).

2 Getting trainees to comment on each other's lessons.

3 Appointing trainees to act as chairmen in group discussions, timekeepers, etc.

4 Making sure trainees work on problem areas in groups.

5 Allocating criticized areas (e.g. poor use of visuals) to individual trainees so that they are responsible for commenting on them and organizing improvement exercises.

If TP is failing because of poor co-operation it is well worth setting up a group co-operation exercise or 'having it out' with the group before trying to shuffle people around. The problem may be cured by making everyone aware of it. Recording feedback sometimes and discussing what makes *good* feedback, focusing on the way the group talk about each other, can also be useful.

6.4 What do other observers do during TP?

Any other observers in a class, e.g. trainees not teaching, and, possibly, a trainee supervisor, should sit apart from the students, to allow the trainee who is teaching to concentrate on the students. In a micro-teaching situation it is probably as well, also, to tell trainees early on to be as silent and inconspicuous as possible while another trainee is teaching and try not to make eye contact. There are obviously exceptions to this, when, for example, a trainee wants help with monitoring pair work (though it is better if this is organized by the trainee teaching, not the supervisor, and then only at the early stages of a course) or when supportive laughter might be helpful.

It is also well worth directing trainees to focus on particular areas when observing their peers and committing them to comment afterwards. It can provide a clear framework in which to operate, particularly at the beginning of a course when they may not really know what they are looking at! You can set a whole general area – perhaps related to topics currently being dealt with on their course if it is running concurrently, e.g.: Classroom management; Aims; Shape of lesson; Awareness of students; Correction; Interaction between students.

Or it might be a bit more specific – perhaps relating to a problem that observing trainee has, e.g.: Instruction-giving; Eye contact; Concept checking.

Alternatively, observers may concentrate on problems that the trainee teaching has – provided it doesn't seem too much like persecution!, e.g.: '*All trainees. After watching John I want you to comment on his position in the classroom. When watching Cathy make notes on the appropriateness of her language to the "level of the class!"* '

If more detail needs to be considered you might like to draw up a specific observation checklist around the type of lesson being given (e.g. Communication activities).

Of course, all observers should make notes as discreetly as possible when trainees are trying to concentrate on the lesson they are giving. Otherwise this can create unwelcome pressure!

6.5 Giving feedback on lessons observed

In general, the supervisor should:

1 Be constructive and encouraging, concentrating on the good things first. Also remember to include them in any final summary.

2 Focus on the aims of a lesson and whether they were achieved or not, rather than individual techniques and how well they were done.

3 Look at *why* things have succeeded or failed.

4 Concentrate on the central issues rather than the detail.

5 Focus on a few things rather than try and cover everything.

6 Consider how the trainee had understood and used the language taught as much as the way in which it was taught.

7 Give the trainees a clear idea as to their overall development after each observation.

It's worth remembering that for trainees TP is at the best of times a nightmarish experience, so when they have very few teaching skills and minimum experience, lack of confidence is likely to be a major cause of inadequacy.

Overall, a supervisor should remember that his duty is not to judge a trainee but to make him self-critical and aware of how far he can affect what goes on in the classroom, so that on future occasions he is able to improve by himself even if a supervisor is not around.

Types of oral feedback by a supervisor

1 You tell the trainees about the lesson

ADVANTAGES:
(a) It is economical in terms of time and focuses only on what you wish.

(b) Your views have authority and are listened to.

(c) It is more useful where there is only one trainee.

DISADVANTAGES:
(a) Trainees tend to be overconcerned with whether you think they did a good or a bad lesson and not listen to anything else.

(b) Trainees are encouraged to discover less for themselves and so are less well trained in being critical for themselves.

(c) There is a reduced sense of responsibility towards the students.

2 You elicit comments from the trainees

ADVANTAGES:
(a) Eliciting from the trainee who has taught and any colleagues who may have observed, you can direct the trainees' attention towards an understanding of the strengths and weaknesses of a lesson without having to tell them (thus trainees are guided to be critical for themselves).

(b) Key areas can be focused on.

(c) Trainees can contribute to each other's development (they will often take criticism better from peers).

(d) It aids motivation.

(e) You can assess the degree of awareness that trainees have.

(f) It is less time-consuming where there is only one trainee.

DISADVANTAGES:
(a) It demands great skill and sensitivity on your part.

(b) If points don't get elicited you end up telling anyway.

3 You chair, you invite each trainee to comment on his lesson, then any other trainees to comment. Finally, you sum up

ADVANTAGES:
(a) Most of the advantages of 2, provided that observers are given something to look for during TP.

(b) Trainees express a variety of opinions.

(c) A greater sense of responsibility is felt by the trainee.

(d) There is less concern for the supervisor's view.

DISADVANTAGES:
(a) It can take far longer.

(b) Far more misleading comments fly around unless the trainees are given direction.

(c) The main issues tend to get obscured by the detail unless the summing-up is good.

(d) It can only be done where a group of trainees have observed the same lesson.

4 A trainee chairs

ADVANTAGES:
(a) As in 2 and 3.

(b) An even greater sense of responsibility is felt by the trainee and there is a decreased reliance on the supervisor.

DISADVANTAGES:

(a) Poor chairing can ruin the feedback.

(b) Uncertainty as to your role can cause the trainees to feel insecure.

(c) It is unlikely to be successful in the early stages of a course.

5 Structured discussion

Each trainee lists the three best and three worst points about a lesson, then pairs off with another trainee to compare lists to thrash out the three best and three worst points from both their lists. The pair then groups with another pair and performs the same task. This can be repeated until all the trainees agree.

You ask each observing trainee to note the strongest and weakest points in the lesson. As a group, without your intervention, they come to some agreement.

ADVANTAGES:

(a) It is good for the dynamics of the training group.

(b) A lot of important issues get discussed.

(c) It is more trainee-centred.

DISADVANTAGES:

(a) It takes a long time.

(b) It's possible for all trainees to miss the point.

(c) What does the trainee who has taught do?

(d) It can only be used occasionally.

(e) It is only suitable when more than one trainee has observed the same lesson.

6 Free-wheeling discussion

ADVANTAGE:

The informality can reduce the pressure and discourage talk about a teacher's 'performance'

DISADVANTAGE:

Lack of guidance can create insecurity.

Further points

1 Beware the trainee who accepts everything and changes nothing.

2 Beware the trainee who is always producing a defence and accepting nothing.

3 Give step-by-step guidance in how to evaluate teaching to trainees who accept nothing or who change nothing. Make them feel confident that criticism is not a personal attack on them.

4 Leave yourself enough time. A rushed feedback session can be a waste of time.

5 Don't go on too long. Be sensitive to just how much can be absorbed, particularly by trainees who have just finished teaching.

6 Don't delay feedback until the next day. Too much will have been forgotten.

7 Conduct feedback in privacy and comfort. You can't talk freely about others' lessons or listen happily about your own if other people are in the room.

8 Ask for occasional criticism if you can from the language students, possibly given straight to the trainees in your absence.

9 Make sure feedback is ongoing, that there is a logical development and that it is seen as contributing to improving the trainee's skills.

10 Vary the style and types of oral feedback although you may need to be fairly directive at the beginning.

Finally, be sensitive. Disastrous lessons are often self-evident and don't need lengthy and demoralizing post-mortems. Sometimes it is worth talking things over with trainees in private.

Written feedback

With peer-teaching, where the focus is on techniques, feedback is usually immediate and leads to the trainee having another go. Oral feedback is all that's necessary.

Where there's no possibility of re-teaching, some sort of written record is useful for trainees.

One common practice is to use a book which gives carbon copies so that both the supervisor and the trainees have a record of comments and both can look back over a series of lessons. A book can be kept by a supervisor (though this might make it difficult for other supervisors to see his comments about a trainee) or a group of trainees (the advantage being that the comments about one trainee are in one book). In the latter case, the book stays with the group regardless of who they teach or who observes them.

Layout of notes

Method 1

Take notes as soon as the trainee begins teaching, writing down comments as the lesson goes on. This requires considerable alertness and an ability to watch, listen and write at the same time but it has the advantage of giving both you and the trainees a fairly accurate reminder of what went on from minute to minute. You can also stage the comments according to the stages of the lesson, perhaps with the help of a copy of the trainee's lesson-plan handed in beforehand.

However, this approach, where comments are undistilled, sometimes prevents trainees from getting an overall balanced picture of the general strengths and weaknesses of a lesson and can lead to a lot of crossing out and apologies. Because of this, you may wish to wait a while and convert rough notes into considered comments as the lesson draws to a close.

Method 2

Tell trainees that the session is only going to concentrate on certain areas. This helps to remedy problems and saves trainees from seeing reams of comments on every aspect of the lesson.

Method 3

Divide the page into two columns, one saying what was good, the other making suggestions for improvement, then at the bottom an overall comment. Usually, you can't start writing immediately as you end up with too many comments. It's better to wait a few minutes for a few examples of a problem to occur before you commit it to writing. You can of course keep rough notes on a separate sheet.

Method 4
Some institutions prefer to have a printed form which, when completed, they give a copy of to trainees. The headings might be as follows:

1 *Lesson plan and intended aims*
  (including shape, development, staging etc.)

2 *Achievement of aims*
  (i – language, ii – skills)

3 *Timing*

4 *Aspects of language*
  (attention to meaning, grammatical rules, pronunciation, errors, fluency)

5 *Classroom manner and management*
  (including metalanguage, instruction giving, student interaction)

6 *Techniques*
  (including use of aids and materials)

7 *Suggestions and ideas*

8 *General comments*
  (including overall progress on the course)

If necessary, some headings may have subdivisions (Stage 1, Stage 2 etc.) to indicate which stage of the lesson the comment refers to.

Further suggestions

1 It is often better to concentrate on matters of group interest in the oral feedback and leave individual comments to the written notes.

2 Keep the form and style of feedback consistent within the same institution if trainees see different supervisors (trainees learn what to expect and can follow the notes of new supervisors).

3 If separate supervisors have been observing lessons they should keep in close touch with the training course Group Tutor, not only to provide consistency of approach and attitudes – fairly important in the early days of teaching – but so as to know what areas have been covered and tell the Group Tutor what areas need to be covered in input sessions.

4 It is sometimes better not to write your overall comments until you have discussed the lesson with the trainee as points may seem to be more or less important as a result of the discussion.

Index

acting out lines of a dialogue, 124
announcements
  making (information), 55
  making (of intentions), 53
apprenticeship schemes, 169, 172, 179
attention
  gaining, 23, 24, 84
  maintaining, 7, 8, 23
  spreading, 9, 20, 46, 57, 86
authentic materials, 87, 92, 125, 127, 128, 129

board
  using the, 16, 79, 159–162,167, 168
  students copying from the, 161

chain drills, 94
checking
  on how well students produce language, 97
  that students understand: the meaning of language, 73,
    80, 85, 98; what is happening, 101, 116, 129, 131,
    155; what they have to do, 46, 90
classroom management, 11–12, 31–59
'closed' pair work, 32
communication, 42, 89, 91, 133, 155
communicative activities, see interaction activities
comprehension checking, see checking that students
  understand what is happening
'concept' questions, see checking that students
  understand the meaning of language
contexts, see language practice, contexts for
conveying meaning, 11, 13, 14
co-operation
  with other teachers, 3
  with other trainees, 4, 181
correction
  oral, 16, 26, 46, 48, 86, 89, 97, 146
  written, 151, 153
course books, 40, 66, 124

diagnostic assessment, see testing
dialogues
  building, 110, 113
  standardising lines of, 113
  using, 72, 79, 121–6
dictations, 8, 107, 108
dictionaries, 67, 68
discussions, 98, 137, 141, 155
discipline, 20, 52, 56, 59
drilling, see language practice, controlled

'echoing' the students, 26, 151
eliciting from students, 72, 89, 110, 143
error-correction, 16, 48, 147
evaluating an activity, 2, 54, 134, 155
extension activities, 132
eye contact, 7–10, 20, 31, 85, 89, 97

facial expression, 10–15, 26
feedback on lessons, 6, 29, 54, 182, 185
floating course tutor, 175
'free stage', see getting students to communicate

games, 13, 138
generative contexts, 86; language, 89
gesture, 10–15, 17, 83, 85, 97, 149

getting students to
  communicate, 30, 133–4, 148
  help to correct each other, 8, 16, 20, 85
  listen to language models, 11, 14, 84
  repeat in chorus, 11, 14, 20, 21, 84, 96, 112
  repeat individually, 11, 14, 85, 112
grammar books, 67, 68
grammatical rules, 68; structures, 26, 65, 67, 68;
  terminology, 26
group
  dynamics, 55–9
  needs (v. individual needs), 54, 55–9
  work, 8, 17, 20, 21, 30, 33, 35, 41, 42, 43, 44, 45, 49,
    58, 154

help and encouragement, 46, 113
homework, 49, 53, 54

icebreaking activities, 30
individual help, 16, 20, 23, 33; needs, 56, 57, 59, 65, 86;
  work, 47, 54, 57
information
  gaps, 90, 141, 156
  transfer, 105
instructions, giving, 15, 25, 36–41, 50
interaction activities, 90, 93, 94, 98, 107, 133ff., 140–1,
  150, 154–7
intonation, 14, 69, 75, 84, 95, 164–8

jigsaw texts, 131

language
  acquisition, 66
  concepts, 65, 73
  contexts, 70, 72, 73, 79, 80, 81
  forms of, 11, 65, 68, 69, 73, 81, 83
  grading of, 25, 27
  functions of, 65, 68, 72, 99
  meaning, 69, 70, 71, 73, 81
  models, 72, 73, 75, 78, 79, 86
  prompts, 87
  register of, 121
  use of, 65, 70, 81
language laboratory, 33
language practice
  contexts for, 84ff.
  controlled, 8, 9, 15, 37, 41, 88ff., 106
  cued, 42, 66, 91, 92, 93
language production, accuracy of, 97; fluency of, 98
large classes, 20, 23, 32, 85, 86
late arrivals to class, 52, 155
less-controlled practice, see language practice, cued
lesson
  aims of a, 42, 60, 64, 65, 67, 86, 174
  finishing a, 44, 53, 54
  pace of a, 8, 58
  planning, 5, 57, 60, 71, 74, 76, 79, 80, 82, 101, 118
  plans, see lesson, planning
  preparation, see lesson, planning
  staging a (lesson shape), 23, 58
  starting a, 44, 51, 53
  timing of a, 43, 54
listening skill, 14, 17, 61, 128, 129
listening to students, 26
lower-level classes, 39, 42, 56, 67, 72, 128, 134, 138,
  160

metalanguage, 25, 37
micro-teaching, 5, 169, 175
mime, 14, 15, 72
mistakes v. errors, *see* error correction
monitoring what students are doing, 45
motivation, 28, 30, 54, 129, 131, 143
multiple-choice statements, 106

naming students, *see* students' names
narrative building, 110
new arrivals in class, 52
noise levels, controlling, 21

'open' pair work, 32
overhead projector (OHP), 16

pair work, 8, 11, 17, 20, 21, 31, 41, 43, 47, 49, 87, 89, 90, 93, 114, 135, 140, 154
peer teaching, *see* micro-teaching
personalizing topics with students, 131, 146
phonetic symbols, using, 167
prediction exercises, 131
presenting new language, 7–8, 15, 58, 65, 83, 106, 121, 126, 134, 148
presentation stage, *see* presenting new language
'problem' students, 58

questions
   asking, 50
   comprehension, *see* checking that students
      understand what is happening
   concept, *see* checking that students understand the
      meaning of language
questionnaires, 119

rapport with a class, 6, 7, 28, 53
reacting to what students say, 29
'real thing', the, *see* authentic materials
register, *see* language, register of
register, keeping a, 49
remedial lessons, 134
revision, 124
role-play, 39, 58, 119, 134, 142

'scream' cards, 180
seating arrangements, 31–6, 37, 43, 140
sequencing activities, 51–5, 58, 60–2
skills development, 5, 128
slips of the tongue, 48
songs, 72
sound sequences, 72
sounds of English, indicating, 164–8

spelling, 108, 150–2
stress, 14, 69, 75, 84, 95, 164–8
students
   higher level, 42, 55, 56, 57, 65, 67, 84, 128, 134–5, 143, 155
   lower level, 39, 42, 56, 67, 72, 84, 128, 134, 138, 143, 160
   motivation of, 28, 52
   promoting interaction between, 8, 16, 20, 30, 85, 150, 154
students'
   mother tongue, 26, 44, 67
   names, remembering 30, 50; using, 7, 8, 9, 48, 50, 85
   progress, 29
   pronunciation, 16, 50, 52, 64, 69, 71, 83
   talking time (STT), 25, 78, 143
substitution tables, 86
syllabus, a, 57, 66

tape recorders
   using, audio, 24, 79, 80, 124, 162–4; video, 24, 162–4
tapes, listening to, 17, 79, 124
teacher's
   attitude, 5, 7, 26, 29, 52, 55–6, 131
   personal appearance, 4
   position and movement in the class, 15–19
   role, 7, 85, 90, 133, 154
   talking time (TTT), 25, 78, 97
testing, 107
texts, using, 72, 125, 126–133
TP
   diaries, 6
   different structures, 169
   files, 6
   objectives, 1, 169
   supervisors, 4, 175, 176, 179–181, 182
   teaching points, 172–4
'transfer' activities, 119
translation, 67
true/false statements, 106, 131

understanding
   extensive, 61
   intensive, 75, 78
   'up-front' teaching, 7, 15, 23, 31, 42, 62

visual aids, 72, 87, 157–9, 166
vocabulary, 52, 65, 68, 71, 72, 75, 100, 116, 128, 146
voice, using the, 23, 24, 25

'whole-class' teaching, 169
writing skill, 38, 47, 161